D0093466

ALSO BY ELLIOTT CURRIE

Whitewashing Race: The Myth of a Color-Blind Society
(with Michael K. Brown, Martin Carnoy,
Troy Duster, David Oppenheimer,
Marjorie Shultz, and David Wellman)

Crime and Punishment in America

Reckoning: Drugs, the Cities, and the American Future

Dope and Trouble: Portraits of Delinquent Youth

Confronting Crime: An American Challenge

America's Problems (with Jerome Skolnick)

Crisis in American Institutions (with Jerome Skolnick)

THE ROAD TO WHATEVER

THE ROAD TO
WHATEVER

Middle-Class Culture and the Crisis of Adolescence

ELLIOTT CURRIE

METROPOLITAN BOOKS
Henry Holt and Company | New York

Metropolitan Books
Henry Holt and Company, LLC
Publishers since 1866
115 West 18th Street
New York, New York 10011

Metropolitan Books™ is a registered
trademark of Henry Holt and Company, LLC.

Copyright © 2004 by Elliott Currie
All rights reserved.
Distributed in Canada by H. B. Fenn and Company Ltd.

Library of Congress Cataloging-in-Publication data

Currie, Elliott.
    Road to whatever : middle-class culture and the crisis of adolescence / Elliott Currie.
        p. cm.
    Includes bibliographical references and index.
    ISBN-13:978-0-8050-6763-7
    ISBN-10:0-8050-6763-9
    1. Youth—United States.   2. Middle class—United States.   3. Youth and violence.
    4. Narcotics and youth.   5. Despair.   I. Title.
    HQ796.C896 2005
    305.235'086'920973—dc22   2004059600

Henry Holt books are available for special promotions
and premiums. For details contact:
Director, Special Markets.

First Edition 2005
Printed in the United States of America
10 9 8 7 6 5 4 3 2 1

CONTENTS

THE ROAD TO WHATEVER

INTRODUCTION: "A WHITE KIND OF MESSING UP"

I

During the past few years, we have discovered, not for the first time, that all is not well with the youth of America's mainstream.

For many people, it was the horrific images from the Columbine school massacre that brought home the recognition that, in a time of prosperity in America, something was seriously amiss—not among those who were left *out* of that prosperity but among those who, at least on the surface, were its beneficiaries. The school shootings, of course, were rare events and might have been dismissed as aberrations, but they were only the most visible expressions of much deeper trouble.

Across the country there were stories of suburban teenagers overdosing on heroin, or dying after episodes of binge drinking, or being killed, maimed, or disabled in reckless car accidents. Many middle-class parents resonated to the imagery in Steven Soderbergh's film *Traffic* of a judge's bright, attractive daughter going off the deep end on drugs and winding up trapped, addicted, and sexually exploited, in an inner-city drug dealer's hovel. It wasn't that so many of us had faced that kind of nightmarish experience ourselves, but we probably knew people who *had*: parents whose children had inexplicably descended into addiction, or become suicidally depressed, or been killed or injured in accidents or apparently meaningless incidents of violence.

And the statistics back up those impressions. It is increasingly clear that being middle class and white does not provide reliable protection against even the worst perils of adolescence. By some measures, indeed, white youth are now the group at *highest* risk of some of the most troublesome and deadly of adolescent ills. They are more likely to kill themselves or die in traffic accidents than blacks or Hispanics; they use most illegal drugs at a higher rate than any racial or ethnic group except Native Americans; and their rates of binge drinking, smoking, and prescription-drug abuse are the highest of all.

It is possible to debate the finer points of these statistics, and it is difficult to pinpoint how much these problems have increased in recent years, but it is no longer possible to deny that there is widespread alienation, desperation, and violence among the youth of what we have sometimes persuaded ourselves is a tranquil and unproblematic middle class. Yet for the most part, that crisis has been either ignored or, when it explodes into public view, misunderstood. And that is a tragedy, because there are lives at stake. There is much real suffering among middle-class adolescents. Most of it is far less spectacular and far more routine than the handful of incidents that reach the news. But it takes lives, cripples spirits, and destroys futures every day in the United States. The absence of adequate explanations leaves us unprepared to help where help is urgently needed; worse, it leads us to adopt strategies that, if anything, may make life more difficult for adolescents who are adrift and in pain.

Part of the reason for the lack of credible explanations is that, when it comes to drugs, delinquency, and violence, our focus has usually been on a different part of the social landscape. We are accustomed to deploying the image of a stable and successful middle class as a measuring stick against which the less fortunate and less successful parts of our society, especially the stuck and threatening "underclass," can be judged. In much of our routine discussion of social ills, the middle class is presumed to be that to which everyone else should aspire: it is the solution, not the problem. It is the embodiment of those values that we have collectively held out as our best and most fundamental, the values held by the people who, in former president Bill Clinton's phrase, work hard and play by the rules. The people we worry about are those who cannot or will not make it into that idealized middle.

So when several teenagers in an upscale suburb commit suicide or die of drug overdoses within months or weeks of one another or when a troubled boy from the heartland brings his rifle to school and shoots several of his classmates, the initial response has typically been shock and disbelief and often bewildered incomprehension. We understand that these things happen in America, but they don't happen to *our* kids, they happen to—well, *their* kids.

One response has been to deny that these troubles really tell us much about ourselves as a society or a culture. Some observers, for example, rushed to assure us that the spate of suburban high school shootings indicated nothing of significance about the lives of the people who lived in the communities where they took place: sociopathic children, after all, could be found anywhere. More disturbing was a tendency, especially in the mass media, to demonize the teenagers involved. Since we couldn't fathom what could have caused such horrific behavior by young people whom we thought were "our" adolescents, we concluded that not only must there be something very wrong with them but they must be fundamentally different creatures from the rest of us. After the Columbine massacre, a major newsmagazine plastered the faces of the two perpetrators on its cover under a banner headline that read "The Monsters Next Door." The phrase was striking not only for its explicit dehumanization of the boys but for how clearly it revealed our inability to absorb the reality that middle-class American youth could do something remotely like what they did. We knew, the headline suggested, that such awful things could happen in other countries or in the scarier parts of our own urban wastelands. But we could not understand how they could happen next door, in our own communities. Categorizing the boys as something other than human revealed an inability or unwillingness to connect what they did with anything comprehensible about the rest of their lives. They could not really be what they seemed. They had to be, in effect, aliens who had mysteriously landed among us.

At the other extreme was a wistful denial that there was a problem at all. Some argued that the worry over adolescent violence and drug abuse was an example of what sociologists call a "moral panic," an expression of our media-driven culture's penchant for sensation and of our reflexive tendency to blame the young for many of our social problems. But while it is true that the media sometimes presented an exaggerated picture of an entire generation gone over the edge, there was too much real suffering and tragedy among the children of the American middle to justify the claim that there was no deeper problem. The paradox was a real one: in a time of widespread prosperity, large numbers of the children of that prosperity were turning up drug addled, locked in juvenile institutions, adolescent mental health wards, and drug treatment facilities; all too many were losing their lives in accidents and violence, and far more, although less drastically impaired, were adrift, at risk, and emotionally lost.

Even when we did not go to the extremes of demonization or denial, we still lacked the conceptual tools to explain what appeared to be an endemic problem among an important segment of middle-class youth. In academic social science, as in the public mind, the angle of vision toward the problems of adolescence has mainly been downward rather than upward or sideways. And there is, of course, reason for that emphasis. A teenager from the Chicago projects or an impoverished Los Angeles barrio is still more likely to be the victim—or the perpetrator—of life-threatening violence, for example, than his or her counterpart in a leafy suburb. And in the 1980s and early 1990s, when inner-city youth were killing one another in unprecedented numbers, a focus on the troubles of middle-class teenagers might have seemed misplaced.

But well before the troubling incidents of the past decade, we knew that the contrast between poor adolescents and those from the middle was frequently overdrawn. Those of us who had grown up in middle-class communities were often aware from our own experience that much more went on among kids in those places than their parents or the authorities ever knew about. And a long tradition of research on juvenile delinquency had shown us again and again that the problems of drugs and violence among middle-class youth were both widespread and surprisingly severe, though mostly absent from our official statistics on youth crime. But despite the substantial evidence that there was a great deal of hidden "deviance" among relatively affluent youth, most of the explanations of why adolescents hurt one another, shot up dope, or stole cars still focused on why these things happened so often among the poor—and especially the dark-skinned poor. As a recent textbook on juvenile delinquency puts it, "the state of knowledge concerning middle-class delinquency is relatively weak" and "the investigation of middle-class delinquency presents one of the most significant challenges facing students in this field, one which has yet to be accepted."

A comment by one of the young women who appear in this book makes clear how readily we identify "real" delinquency as a problem of the minority poor. She had heard that I was interested in the problems of teenagers, and she wanted to talk with me about her own harrowing suburban history, which included heavy drinking and drug use, self-mutilation and attempted suicide. But she wasn't sure that her experience would be useful to me—that it would be sufficiently serious to be of interest—because it was "more of a *white* kind of messing up."

II

To the extent that there has been an articulate explanation of the problems of mainstream youth, it is one that points the finger of blame at a familiar list of suspects: the erosion of discipline, a growing spirit of leniency and indulgence, an emphasis on children's rights over their responsibilities, the weakened authority of parents and schools, a timid juvenile justice system. These ideas have been prominent in the American discussion of youth problems for generations, but the new concern over suburban school violence, rising drug and alcohol abuse, and reckless sex among middle-class youth brought them back with a vengeance, as conservative commentators seized on these problems as evidence that the spread of "liberal" values was corrupting children and hindering the ability of adults to discipline and control them. A popular book on parenting, taking its text from the biblical declaration that "foolishness is bound in the heart of a child, but the rod of correction shall drive it far from him," blamed the rise in youth problems on the decline in corporal punishment and urged readers, in the words of Proverbs 23:13–14, to "withhold not correction from the child" but to "beat him with the rod . . . and deliver his soul from hell."

Other critics inveighed against the spread of an ethos of self-esteem and youth "empowerment," which—in this view—had bred a generation of young people who were resistant or indifferent to authority and were now more than a match for beleaguered parents, teachers, and principals. Adult authorities had been hobbled by liberal court decisions granting unprecedented rights to schoolchildren and by a cadre of self-described experts who preached the importance of self-esteem and self-expression over the traditional norms of discipline and conformity. As the authority of parents has increasingly been replaced by "the empty heart of child empowerment" and "the empty formula of self-esteem," one observer wrote in the late 1990s, we have created "the vanguard of a new, de-cultured generation" of youth who, in the new culture of empowerment, "find support for—or at least indifference toward—their worst impulses." Weak schools were equally to blame. An article asking "Who killed school discipline?" pointed to "the courts and the federal government," along with "psycho-babble spouting 'experts,'" who had caused a "collapse of adult authority": "Quaking before the threat of lawsuits and without support from their superiors, educators hesitate to assert the most basic civic and moral values that might pose a challenge to the crude and status-crazed [adolescent] peer culture."

From this perspective, in short, the problems of middle-class adolescents were not incomprehensible at all: they were indeed all too comprehensible, a clear consequence of the corrosive spread of misguided and indulgent liberal values. But though this view became extremely popular in the 1990s, it seemed, on even a moment's reflection, to be strangely at odds with the reality of how teenagers were actually being treated in the United States. This was, after all, an era in which many institutions were publicly and visibly taking a much harder stance toward adolescents than at any time in our recent history. We were, for example, increasingly sending juvenile offenders to adult courts in the name of cracking down on youth crime. We had launched a host of so-called zero-tolerance policies toward juvenile misbehavior in schools, which made it easier to suspend and expel students for even minor infractions. We had passed a spate of draconian drug laws that were putting large numbers of young people—including many from the middle class—behind bars, often for lengthy sentences. In a nation where it was increasingly possible for a boy to be sentenced to prison for writing graffiti on a wall or a girl to be suspended from school for carrying Advil in her purse, blaming adolescent problems on the corrupting effects of leniency seemed far-fetched.

More generally, the United States had long been a country distinctive in the advanced industrial world for the harshness of its policies toward children and youth, and especially toward adolescent deviance. Where many other nations had formally abolished the use of corporal punishment of children in homes and schools, we had formally upheld it in the courts—and practiced it widely. We were the only industrial nation that executed people for crimes committed while they were juveniles, putting us in the sparse company of countries like Iran and Nigeria. We were also the industrial nation with the weakest and least reliable social supports for the young: we had no system of family allowances, no universal health care system, no paid parental leaves from work to care for children, no national apprenticeship system to link school with stable and rewarding work. And all of these long-standing historical differences had widened in the conservative social policy climate of the 1980s and 1990s. We had increasingly become, as two British observers put it, the land of the "nonhelping hand."

III

If we wish to understand the current troubles of middle-class youth in America, we need to locate them within that distinctly Darwinian context: and that is the connection I will explore in this book. It is based on interviews with young men and women who have in common the fact that they are white, that they come from somewhere in that broad American "middle," and that, at the time I talked with them, they were either suffering through a desperate period of their adolescence or looking back at that period from the vantage point of a few months or a few years later. They represent the human face of the disturbing statistics on the problems of drugs, violence, and self-destruction among middle-class youth. They are children of the American "mainstream" who shot heroin and speed, drank themselves into emergency rooms, tried to kill themselves with prescription drugs, flirted with death on the highway or in gang fights on the street. I came to know them in a variety of ways.

Some were former students in my university classes. For many years I've taught courses on crime and juvenile delinquency at several large public universities. Early on, I noticed that each semester a steady trickle of students would come to talk to me, privately, about their personal experience with the issues I was discussing in class. One of the first was a young man in his early twenties who fidgeted uncomfortably for some time in my office, hemmed and hawed, and finally said, "I just wanted to tell you that I *know* about this stuff." At first I thought he meant that my lectures were too predictable or old hat, but that's not what he wanted to say: he wanted to say that he had "been there," that he knew firsthand about some of the problems of the criminal justice system I'd been lecturing about, and also something about the social pressures that might drive young people to do things that ran them afoul of that system. To illustrate the point, he pulled up his pants leg to show me the electronic bracelet that his parole officer had attached to his ankle so his movements could be monitored, and so we talked at length about how he'd come to have that bracelet in the first place.

It became clear that there were a surprising number of similar students in my classes, even if I counted only those who came of their own accord to tell me about their experiences—there were surely plenty of others. Though they had mainly (though not always) grown up in middle-class America, the stories they told about their teenage years were often startling and sometimes frightening. Yet they were now at top-level colleges and doing well, presumably on the road to productive and engaged lives. Some were, in fact, terrific students, among the very best in their classes, who were going on to graduate or professional schools. They had come a long way, sometimes in a very short time, from what had often been extreme states of personal crisis. I became intrigued by the question of how they had managed to get through what may have been truly horrific adolescent experiences and make it, intact, to a first-class university. Over the past few years I've engaged many of them in extended conversation about their adolescent and postadolescent lives, and especially about how and why they had gotten into trouble when they did and how they had succeeded in turning their lives around.

Although these were thriving university students when I spoke with them and had stabilized their lives to an impressive extent, they had with few exceptions gone through a very hard time at some point in their teenage years. Some of them had led lives that were traumatic and dangerous in the extreme. One had served time in prison after threatening to blow up his high school and kill the principal; several had spent most of their teen years deeply addicted to hard drugs; another had almost killed another youth in a brawl and lost a good part of his adolescence to youth prison. Some had tried to kill themselves; others had routinely engaged in the kind of reckless driving that could easily have gotten them (and others) killed, and a few had nearly died of overdoses of alcohol or illegal drugs. Several of the women had gotten into violent or degrading relationships with men, often much older men. Most of them, despite their later academic success, had had serious difficulty with school, and many had either quit high school or been pushed out. Almost without exception, they had at some point been deeply estranged from their families: a startling number had been thrown out of their homes or had run away to face the perils of life on the street. Moreover, all of these young people had experienced *several* of these problems during their high school or middle school years. None of them had *just* a drinking problem when they were teenagers: they had a drinking problem *and* had been kicked out of school, or had gotten deeply depressed and tried to kill themselves *and* been kicked out of their parents' house and forced to sleep behind a Dumpster at the mall, and so on. Often one problem predominated, but I cannot think of an instance in which there was only one kind of trouble in the lives of any of these students.

Another group of adolescents who appear in this book came from a different source. For about two and a half years—from 2000 to 2002—I conducted a study, funded by the U.S. Department of Health and Human Services, designed to explore the lives of adolescents who were in treatment for substance abuse. I cannot reveal exactly where I studied those teenagers or where they came from. But like my university students, they formed a broad and diverse group. Their parents ranged from retail salespeople to corporate executives, from police officers to college professors. They had grown up in a variety of settings—upscale gated communities, leafy suburbs, down-at-the-heels blue-collar neighborhoods, small semirural towns. I interviewed them intensively, often several times, from early in their period of crisis, through the difficult time when they left treatment and returned to their communities, and, in a few fortunate cases, up through the time when their lives began, at least haltingly, to change for the better. I got to know some of them very well, and sometimes their parents too, and I had many chances to observe, up close, the way in which they were treated at home and by the various agencies of help and control that they encountered as they tried to get their lives back on track.

Though I initially sought out this group because they were enrolled in drug treatment, drugs were invariably only one of their troubles, and not necessarily the most important one—certainly not the most important one in their eyes. Like my college students, these adolescents didn't *just* have a problem with alcohol or heroin or methamphetamine. Some had histories of serious violence. Many had spent time living on the street. Nearly all had been in trouble at school and some, despite being still of school age, had no current connection with any educational system at all. Many had suffered from depression, and some were in the depths of it as we spoke. A few had tried suicide, several had cut themselves routinely, and more than one had been in treatment for an eating disorder.

With both groups, I've altered certain details in the interests of confidentiality—even though many of those I interviewed said they were more than willing to have me use their real identities. The names I've given them here are not their real ones, and I have altered many other things about them as well: the places where they grew up, the schools they attended, the kind of work their parents did, and much else. As a result, the teenagers who appear here do not exactly match anyone in the real world. But their words are altogether real, and I've made extensive use of them in what follows because I do not think we can begin to understand the sources of behavior that troubles us until we begin to pay closer attention to what the people who engage in it have to say about why they do what they do and what it means to them. One of the reasons for the inadequacy of our conventional explanations is that we have rarely made much effort to learn what adolescents themselves feel about these issues. In the public discussion of youth problems, the least-heard voices have been those of the people most deeply affected. Nearly fifty years ago, one of the most respected American scholars of juvenile delinquency, Albert K. Cohen, wrote in his classic book *Delinquent Boys* that future research on the roots of delinquency needed to focus more than it had on what he called the "spirit, the quality, the emotional tone" of the "delinquent act": that is an important part of what I have tried to accomplish in this book.

I do not claim that the young people in this book are a systematic sample of all troubled middle-class youth in America. But they represent a set of compelling examples of the kinds of adolescents whose behavior worries us the most. And wherever they come from and whatever their current situation, certain themes recur in their stories. Though each story is unique, there are striking commonalities in the way they felt during their periods of worst crisis, the way their families stimulated their troubles and responded to them, and the way they were treated by schools and other institutions. That there are so many common experiences suggests that the current crisis among many middle-class adolescents is more than just an aggregation of individual problems: in the words of the American sociologist C. Wright Mills, their private troubles reflect larger public issues. Looming behind the individual stories are powerful social and cultural forces that have created a world in which it is very difficult for many mainstream teenagers to grow up.

The middle-class world these young people describe is not the stereotyped one of indulgence, overconcern with children's rights, and erosion of "personal responsibility." On the contrary, it is a world that is remarkably hard on its young—a world shaped by a careless, self-serving individualism in which real support from parents, teachers, or other adults is rare and punishment and self-righteous exclusion are routine. It is a world that places high expectations for performance on adolescents but does remarkably little to help them do well, a world in which teenagers' emotional problems are too often met with rejection—or medication—rather than attentive and respectful engagement.

Our society makes adolescence unduly difficult, then, not because it is too soft on teenagers but because it is too hard on them. The peculiarly harsh version of middle-class culture that the teenagers in this book describe is not the only version; twenty-first-century America can be a supportive and hospitable place for many mainstream adolescents. For some of them, in fact, this is a fine time to be growing up: on the whole, they enjoy a much wider range of social and personal opportunities than their counterparts did in earlier generations. But for others—especially those who have trouble fitting in to an increasingly competitive and unsupportive social order—these are hard times indeed.

Fitting in, to be sure, is a problem for adolescents in most cultures. But it has always been particularly difficult in the Darwinian culture of parts of mainstream America and has arguably become more so in the social climate of the last twenty years, the period in which the young people in this book grew up. One way in which we misread the condition of adolescents today is by assuming that their troubles are simply the expression of universal stresses that afflict everyone at this tumultuous stage of life. There is obviously some truth to this: no one would deny that adolescence has its unique developmental stresses, and no one has ever argued that being a teenager is easy. But those *general* pressures exist for adolescents everywhere, while only some of them wind up in desperate straits. Many of them—most of them—go through difficult patches, make worrisome mistakes, perhaps skirt the edges of real trouble. But this book isn't about that kind of "normal" deviance: it is about *serious* trouble. And the forces that breed that kind of trouble among mainstream adolescents are more specific. Understanding that those forces are neither universal nor inevitable not only gives us a better grasp of the problems teenagers face today but allows us to begin thinking of ways in which we might take action to solve them.

In exploring some of those forces, I will start by examining the state of mind that many adolescents experience at the point when they get into serious trouble. I have titled this book *The Road to Whatever*—as in "whatever, dude"—because so many teenagers use that word to describe how they felt just before they did something dangerous or self-destructive—an emotional place in which they no longer cared very much about what happened to them and that made trouble not only possible but likely. The road to that place typically begins in their families, which often embody the "sink or swim" ethos of the larger culture—a neglectful and punitive individualism that sets adolescents up for feelings of failure, worthlessness, and heedlessness that can erode their capacity to care about themselves or others. To be sure, not all teenagers in trouble grow up in families like those I'll describe. But I will show that a particular syndrome of cultural attitudes—about the role of nurturance and of punishment, the provision of help and support, the responsibilities of parents and communities to children—appears repeatedly in the lives of troubled middle-class adolescents.

The road to "whatever" continues through the schools and the various agencies of intervention that, in theory, are supposed to help. Again, one version of the conventional wisdom about adolescent problems is that teenagers are led astray by timid schools and well-meaning but misguided experts who bend over backwards to coddle them in the name of self-esteem and youth empowerment. But, as we will see, serious help from schools or mental health professionals was relatively rare for the young people in this book and was often given grudgingly when it was given at all. Worse, "intervention," when they did receive it, often became part of the problem for them: it became one more mile marker on the road to "whatever" and an obstacle to getting their lives back together. There are plenty of examples here of genuinely helpful encounters with counselors, teachers, or therapists. But for many adolescents, the schools and "helping" agencies mainly recapitulated, in a different setting, the "sink or swim" individualism that characterized their families, and compounded the problems that had begun at home.

As I've said, one of my initial interests was in learning how young people who were able to emerge successfully from periods of self-destructiveness and desperation had managed to do so, and I will explore what it was about their backgrounds, their values, or their encounters with the institutions around them that enabled them to transform their lives and to triumph over circumstances that sank others. Again, there were striking commonalities in how these transformations were achieved, and those life-changing experiences point to things that adolescents need more of—and less of—in order to grow up healthy and unimpaired. Accordingly, I will say something, in the last chapter, about steps we might take as a society to help make the transition to adulthood less painful and less risky. I will not outline a detailed agenda for public policy, but I will suggest ways in which the experience of these adolescents shows us how we may begin to offer a better deal for all of our children.

"WHATEVER, DUDE": THE ELEMENTS
OF CARE-LESSNESS

One clue to the sources of trouble among adolescents is that if you ask them why they did something dangerous or self-destructive—something that put them or others at risk—they rarely have a clear or specific answer. They will say that they just "did something stupid" but will have a hard time saying why, exactly, they did it. If you ask what pushed them to start shooting heroin, or to pull a knife or a gun on someone, or to race a car at ninety miles an hour with the headlights off on a narrow road, they often describe a state of mind that allowed them to do these things, rather than a particular reason that pushed them into doing them. And the core of that state of mind is often a general feeling of simply not caring very much *what* happens—to them or to anyone else.

When I met Terry he was only fifteen, but he was regularly drinking a fifth of gin a day, "plus beer and stuff"—and he liked to drive cars, preferably stolen ones, at high speeds while he was drinking. He liked it best of all if he could get chased by the police in the process. He was also a frequent user of methamphetamine, along with several other drugs, and he had experimented with heroin, which would soon become his drug of choice. At one point he had fallen in with a group of militantly racist kids in the sprawling suburban town where he lived, who were into "white power" as well as hard drugs. He didn't stick with them for long, but this is how he describes his state of mind at the time: "I don't know what their trip is. But I know what my trip was, which is that I really didn't give a fuck about anything, not even myself, so why should I give a fuck about anyone else?"

At twelve, he was arrested for assault and battery. A kid had thrown something at him in school; in response, Terry "gave him the boot." He was sent to juvenile hall for what was to be the first of many stints behind bars. "I didn't even care," he says. "I was like, whatever. Take me to jail. I don't give a shit."

When he was in seventh grade, a friend got hold of some pain medication left over from his mother's surgery:

> And he'd come to school, he'd get like a fifth of whisky, and I'd put it in a two-liter bottle, and then you'd put like half a bottle of Vicodins and stuff, or codeines in there, all smashed up, and then you'd put a little bit of Kool-Aid in there. . . . And we'd just drink that stuff like it was water.

During that year, Terry would sometimes smoke dope, and even sell it, while sitting on a small tree-shaded patio that happened to be just outside the principal's office. "I used to sit there and sell pot all *day*," he says, "and I didn't give a shit." He hadn't ever gotten caught and therefore didn't think he would be, but he "didn't really care" if he was, in any case. One day, when he was fourteen, he had forgotten to bring his own stash of pot to school, so he bought some from another boy "that was like laced with PCP or something":

> It was like really orange and stuff, not just like orange hairs, the whole thing was kinda like tinted red. And so I was like, you know, whatever, dude, I don't care . . . and I tried a little bit of it. I took a hit or so, and it tasted good and, you know, it got me pretty high and stuff. So I smoked the rest.

Thoroughly stoned on the mysterious orange pot, Terry and a friend decided to borrow his girlfriend's pickup truck and go for a drive. "And I just started going *nuts* with the truck. Like I was a good driver—you know, I always had control over it? But I'd still do just crazy, off-the-wall stuff." He drove the truck up into some nearby hills, where a narrow, winding creek bed had been turned into a treacherous road. "And I'd just *haul ass* around it. And if I would of slid off, I could have like . . . and I'd slide around all the time. Every turn I *took* I'd slide, you know? I could control it, but still, but still . . ."

Laurie was a sixteen-year-old ex-cheerleader and honor student when I met her, shortly after she had been released from a closed psychiatric ward after overdosing on such a bewildering variety of drugs that she "couldn't even remember" everything she had taken. It wasn't the first time she'd overdosed: there had been several other occasions when she had gotten so sick on drugs that she thought she should have gone to the emergency room. When I asked her if she had been afraid at those times, if she'd been worried about what she was doing to herself, she said that she hadn't:

> I don't know. I just didn't care. I didn't care about anything or any*body*. I didn't care about my life. I didn't care if I—if I died. I didn't care if I woke up dead the next morning. Sometimes I *wanted* it. I was just like— you know how you can be alive but not really living? I was like a zombie.

Even after her massive overdose and emergency hospitalization, when she was hallucinating for days and thought she saw blood dripping from the ceiling, she told me that she "just laughed" at how "miserable and messed up" she was. "Physically I always felt so shitty. And I'd just laugh. I didn't care."

This attitude emerged over and over in my conversations with adolescents who had put themselves or others at great risk. However their crisis was expressed—as a suicide attempt, a descent into uncontrolled drinking or drug abuse, an episode of violence or recklessness—they almost invariably described the underlying state of mind as a feeling of simply not caring what happened: "I was like, whatever, dude, let's go." "I really just didn't give a shit." "I didn't care about myself at all." Their response to questions like "Why did you get in the car when you knew your friends were planning to break into a house or rob a store?" or "Why did you wind up doing heroin after all when you swore you'd never do it because you knew that getting hooked on it could ruin your life?" or "Why did you continue to put yourself in dangerous situations when you knew that you were risking your future, your reputation, and perhaps your life?" was some version of "Because I didn't care enough *not* to."

Sometimes adolescents do talk about specific issues that led up to the moment when something "crazy" happened: "I went out and partied and did every drug I could think of because my boyfriend . . ." or "I got in a fight because this dude was . . ." But there is usually a history of choices—or of failures to choose—that have put them in situations where such things are more likely to happen. And making those choices means they have had to abandon many of the concerns that would otherwise inhibit them from getting involved with troublesome people or hanging out in risky places in the first place.

For some of the young people I spoke with, that feeling of not caring began when they were small children; for others, it was more sudden—starting around the time they hit junior high school and worsening over a period of months or years. But it always involved a progressive erosion of the ability to care about most of the things that keep us, at whatever age, from acting "crazy" or "stupid" in ways that could hurt us or someone else and bring disapproval from people who matter to us. Adolescents on this downward path stop caring about what parents, friends, teachers, the community as a whole think about them; they stop caring about the physical consequences, for their bodies and minds, of what they are doing; and perhaps most importantly, they stop caring about how they will feel about themselves—about how doing something stupid or destructive will affect their sense of who they are, their claim to be regarded as competent and worthy, as people to be taken seriously.

They stop caring, too, about official consequences—what social scientists call "formal sanctions": getting thrown out of school, having to go to court, being locked up in juvenile hall, acquiring a criminal record. A seventeen-year-old I'll call Josh, who when I first met him had recently made a nearly successful suicide attempt after dropping out of school and becoming badly strung out on hard drugs, expressed that state of mind succinctly. "I didn't really care about anything," he told me: "Kids would stress over school or whatever, and I just didn't even care at all. I'm not sure why, but I just never did the homework, never did *anything*." Josh was living in an upscale suburb at the time; his parents, divorced, were both financial executives. He was bright and creative and had often done well in school as a child. On the face of things, he had everything to gain by being careful. But all he was interested in was getting high. When he was sixteen he was put on probation for dealing drugs, and he knew his probation officer would send him to juvenile hall if he was caught using them again. But, as with most other things, he didn't care:

> Like it wouldn't matter what was in my way or whatever. . . . I remember one night I had to go see my P.O. the next day and go take a drug test, and I just didn't even care, I was using all night. And my friends were like, "Don't you have to see your P.O. tomorrow?" I'm like, "No, it's okay, don't worry about it." And they're like, "OK, dude, whatever."

Danny, an engaging but combative sixteen-year-old whom I interviewed in juvenile hall after he and a friend had beaten up and robbed another boy over a trivial slight, described a similar state of mind. His friend, he said,

> was just like, you know, "Let's beat that kid's ass." He was hella mad, and he was like, "Let's just go *do* that shit right now, we're gonna jack him," and all that shit. So I was like, "All right, you know, whatever. Get on it."

So I used to be, like I don't care about nothing. Whatever, you know? You want to do it, let's go. I mean you want to rob the store, let's go. I was just like that.

What makes such indifference so dangerous is that there are an extraordinary number of opportunities for American adolescents to do something seriously risky—and, at least for the "mainstream," far more than there used to be. When I was a teenager there were, to be sure, plenty of ways to get hurt or get in trouble. But they were not as pervasive or as accessible as they are for middle-class adolescents today. That is particularly true when it comes to drugs. When I was Josh's age alcohol was by far the most common drug among middle-class adolescents, and plenty of us abused it. But even alcohol was not always easy to get. And as for other drugs, the choices paled beside what is routinely available to middle-class teenagers today.

I grew up in an economically and racially diverse neighborhood in a very large and turbulent city, but the only drugs, other than alcohol and tobacco, that were readily obtainable where I lived were minor stimulants like Benzedrine and Dexedrine. I had a broad group of friends from every stratum of the local community, including some who wound up getting in serious trouble of one kind or another. But I never met a drug dealer when I was in high school, and to the best of my knowledge none of my close friends did, either. In my neighborhood, there were a few men who were rumored to be heroin addicts. But I never saw any heroin during my entire adolescence, nor, as far as I know, did any of my friends. We had never heard of crystal methamphetamine; there was no such thing as Ecstasy.

Today for adolescents in virtually every community in the United States the drug scene has changed so dramatically that it is as if we were talking about another planet. In the past few years I have spoken with teenagers from big-city neighborhoods, affluent and not so affluent suburbs, middle-sized "heartland" towns, and the rural and semirural countryside, and all of them have said that on any given day nearly every drug you can think of is available to them with disturbing ease. Drugs are "everywhere," they say; whatever they want, they "can get it in fifteen minutes." Many frazzled and frightened parents have discovered this to their alarm as they've moved away from what they imagined to be the peculiarly dangerous influences of a big city or a tough blue-collar town to a leafy and pretty suburb or the bucolic countryside—only to find that crystal meth, Ecstasy, and even heroin were, if anything, easier for their children to find than before. "There's heroin up the ass everywhere," Terry says about his suburban town; heroin is "like how pot is in other places, 'cause everyone does it." Jessica, a fifteen-year-old from an affluent suburb twenty miles from the nearest big city, says that in her days of using methamphetamine, "I could get mine like *that*. I would page him, I would tell him what I want, and he'd be there within half an hour." Wanting to be reassuring, she quickly adds that "I only had sex for it *once*."

But though the social environment of middle-class America offers abundant opportunities for danger, most adolescents—out of guilt, lack of interest, or fear of the consequences—do not succumb to them, at least not seriously or repeatedly. Those who do sometimes say that they do risky things because it's fun, and there's surely truth to that, up to a point. Many of the things that can get an adolescent hurt or killed are intrinsically pleasurable, at least at first, and we won't understand why teenagers do them without acknowledging that. Terry, for example, explains his stunningly reckless driving in those terms: speeding on narrow mountain roads while he was stoned was "a blast," he says. "Having fun was more important than taking care of myself, basically." But that explanation doesn't, by itself, tell us why some adolescents are willing to go so far in pursuit of these kinds of "fun" that they risk everything or why they keep on even after it has become clear that bad things are happening to them as a result. When we probe more deeply into their state of mind, we discover that something else is involved.

I first spoke with Dale just after he had been released from an adolescent psychiatric ward, where he'd been sent following a violent incident in which he'd "gone off" on a teacher at his school. At fifteen, Dale was tall, lanky, and bespectacled and was often, he said, mistaken for a nerd, but he was widely feared among his peers because of his temper and volatility. He had drunk himself into the hospital emergency room more than once and sometimes cut himself deliberately. He'd also become addicted to crystal methamphetamine, which he'd begun using when he was thirteen. By the time I met him, he was not only smoking crystal meth regularly but had "slammed" (injected) it on several occasions. He was fully aware that any of these practices could kill him and, short of that, could affect his health in a variety of frightening ways—including some that I'd never heard of. Describing the arcane technology of methamphetamine use, for example, he told me that

> you've got to cut it in a certain way, and if it cracks the wrong way, it's fucked up. And if you cut it the wrong way, if you smoke it you can get these little green bubbles on you. . . . It still gets you spun, but if you smoke the whole thing, in a couple of days you get these little green bubbles like right here [his arm] and on your hands. That's why you gotta have somebody that knows how to cut it, cut it.

But, he said, he had never worried much about that problem or about what his heavy meth smoking was doing to his health generally. "I didn't really care," he told me. "I didn't care if I was dying slowly, because you gotta die *sometime*. And I was having a fun life. So I liked it." I pointed out that while it was certainly true that everyone had to die sometime, fourteen or fifteen was awfully young to do so. Dale agreed but said that he probably wouldn't die in the *very* near future from his habit because he could handle the drug well enough to avoid overdosing: "You know how much it takes to OD off of coke? For someone that does it a lot? Two and a half eight-balls [an eighth of an ounce] for me. 'Cause I've done it a lot.

For crystal, if I smoked *two* eight-balls by myself, I'd probably OD and die. But I can smoke an eight-ball by myself and not die."

Dale did recognize that the longer he continued using, the more likely he was to overdose and that, in any case, smoking meth at this level would probably shorten his life considerably. "I understand what it was doing to me. Crystallizing my lungs. And crystals never get *out* of your lungs. So if you smoke a lot of it, that's why the crystals build up on top of each other, and you can't breathe. That's when you OD." He'd in fact seen people overdose, including one of his best friends, but that experience only confirmed his lack of concern because his friend had, after all, survived. "He's OD'd like *nine times*," Dale assured me, "and never died." I remarked that nine overdoses seemed to indicate something about his friend's general state of mind. "Yeah," Dale said. "He doesn't care about *anything*."

When I asked Dale why neither he nor his friends particularly cared whether they OD'd or not, he said at first that it was because they were having so much fun. "It's like you're having such a good time you don't really think about it. See, if you don't think about it, you don't care." I told him it seemed like it worked both ways: if you don't care to begin with, you don't think about it. He agreed.

He described himself as having gotten, by about thirteen, to a place in his mind where he was, as he put it in an interesting turn of phrase, "care-less"—meaning not just "careless" in the conventional sense of neglectful or inattentive but truly without care: he "cared less" about long-term consequences. At one point he had gotten stoned at a party with some friends and they had ended up stealing the host's credit card, taking several hundred dollars out of ATM machines with it, and then deciding that they might as well take the family's Jeep Grand Cherokee too. So they drove the stolen Cherokee up and down the suburban streets at high speed with the lights off, "cut doughnuts" in parking lots and fields, and generally had a fine time—all while stoned out of their minds. When I asked Dale if he had been afraid that he'd be stopped by the police while driving the stolen Cherokee—stoned, and with no driver's license—he said no, it was all the same to him whether he got busted or not. He told me that if the flashing lights and the "woo woo woo" of a police siren had appeared behind him, he would have just pulled over, jumped out of the car, put his hands behind his head, and said, "OK, here I am, arrest me." It's not that he particularly wanted to be arrested: he said that he wouldn't have cared if it happened, and he wouldn't have cared if it didn't happen.

This "care-less" feeling—even on Dale's level—rarely represents a complete inability to care about anything at all, though at times it can come disturbingly close. It is not that adolescents in this state care about absolutely nothing but that what we ordinarily think of as more fundamental concerns fall by the wayside and are replaced, to the extent that they *are* replaced, by more immediate, and often perversely practical, ones. Dale's attitude toward injecting drugs illustrates this shift in perspective. He was well aware that though smoking crank was dangerous enough, shooting it intravenously, or "slamming," was even more so. He knew that you could "tear your veins" injecting drugs, and in fact he did during a three-day binge, because when it came to slamming, he admitted, he was just a beginner. But he had gone ahead and shot up again anyway. When I asked why, he told me that he "didn't want to waste" the drugs that were already in his syringe. "You know, I packed it in the syringe, it was there, I couldn't get it out really, and if I just left it in there, I'd be wasting all that money." What mattered most to him at that point, in short, was the thirty dollars' worth of dope. The erosion of his capacity to care about his health, his family, or his future had led to a fundamental reordering of the hierarchy of his concerns, so that the short-term desire to conserve his supply of drugs became, by default, the top priority.

Laurie, similarly, says that all that mattered to her in the months before she overdosed and ended up in the psychiatric ward was the pragmatics of getting high:

That was pretty much what was on my mind all the time—drugs, how am I gonna get high, how am I gonna get the money to get high, how am I gonna get my drugs, or what drugs am I gonna do, or what do I feel like this weekend. . . . But at the same time, I didn't want to deal with anything. I didn't want to care about anybody. Just because I felt that was so much energy, to have to care about people. I know that sounds really lame, but it's true. It's so much easier not to.

Terry says that when he was drinking and doing drugs heavily, living on the street, and regularly stealing cars, he was never completely unaware of his needs and that he tried, most of the time, to look after himself in small ways. But, as he puts it tellingly, he couldn't think in terms of an "ending":

I made sure I had showers and some food and everything. But I mean— I never had an *ending*. You know? When I was on the run, I never had an ending, like oh, OK, one of these days I'm gonna get arrested and go back to jail and blah blah blah blah blah. It was like, OK, I gotta steal another car . . . and that was my thinking.

He "didn't really care" about the possibility of cracking up a car and killing himself, but he gave some thought to "the practical stuff": "You know, if I get hurt, how am I gonna—what the hell am I gonna do to get help without being arrested? That was my thinking." Since he wouldn't have dreamed of seeking formal medical attention under the circumstances, he'd considered his alternatives: if he was really seriously hurt, maybe he could "go to a friend's house and drink a bottle of whiskey and hit some codeines or something." But he didn't think about what all of this meant for the rest of his life.

This narrowing of care to the immediate is often exacerbated by heavy drug use, in a truly vicious cycle. Not caring about consequences allows adolescents to use drugs indiscriminately; after a while, the drugs begin to dominate their lives, and the more this happens, the less they care about anything else. The less they care about anything else, the easier it is to slide even more deeply into drugs, and so on. As Laurie puts it:

I got depressed and didn't really care about that many things. But I *really* stopped caring when I was deep into my drug use. Stopped caring about everything. . . . For me it was just—or for a lot of people, their addiction takes over, and the thing they care most about is their addiction. Over their family, over their job, over their friends, over whatever.

In the folk song "Sometimes I Feel Like a Motherless Child," there is a verse that goes: "Sometimes I feel like a feather in the air/A long way from home/A long way from home." The image captures a central aspect of what many adolescents experience at their deepest point of personal crisis. Loosened from the normal concerns that could otherwise moor them, and increasingly unable to care very much about what happens to them, they are vulnerable to being pushed by whatever currents come along, able to drift into doing attractive but dangerous things that in a different frame of mind they would have avoided. We may understand this outlook more clearly if we contrast it with that of adolescents who, surrounded by similar dangers, do not give in to those dangers so totally. When I interviewed Lacey, for example, she was a successful university student, happy with herself, and on her way to a promising career. But she had had a tough time in adolescence, beginning in junior high school. She'd flirted with drugs and serious drinking, hung out with a troubled crowd—some of whom had "gone down the tubes" in high school—and ultimately spent time in a series of adolescent psychiatric facilities. Like so many others, she felt, during this period, "like I didn't care about myself." She speaks of frequently falling into what she describes as a "sort of abandonment," in which she let herself be pushed and pulled in one direction or another, rather than setting a direction of her own:

Abandoning myself to the situation and not knowing how to care. That may be a better way to put it. Because I think we all do care about ourselves on some weird kind of level. But just to let myself be moved around by these situations that would happen . . . and that would sort of lead me around in some ways.

In high school, Lacey often found herself drifting, without much thought, into situations "where no parents were around" but there were "a lot of drugs":

I had a friend who was addicted to coke. And she was very much into rich men and coke. So we would end up in these big parties with these very wealthy men. You know, there'd be a pack of girls. We were all girls. Fifteen, sixteen. *Children.* And we'd be going around with guys in their forties. And I remember one time being at this guy's house. . . . And they had rocks of cocaine all over the table, you know . . . and I went upstairs to do something, and I pulled open a drawer, and I saw a ton of cash. And I went, "Uh oh."

But unlike many of her friends, Lacey retained the capacity to stand outside the situation and to pull back when things got too "crazy":

We'd be doing drugs or something, and I'd realize that I was starting to feel really sick. And my body was telling me, "That's enough! That's enough! What are you doing? Stop!" And so I *would.* I listened. Right, I listened to myself, and then I said, "OK, if I survive tonight, I promise I won't do this again." And then I *didn't.* Yeah, I made deals with myself. And I kept the deal.

Many of her friends were also sleeping around indiscriminately: "There was a lot of sex sort of *around* us. A lot of STDs were being passed around. But I was resistant to it." As with drugs, she didn't abandon herself completely; there was always, she remembers, "something held back":

A friend I'm still very good friends with from that time period . . . said to me the other day, "Do you remember that night when we were all hanging out in that abandoned house, and there was like three guys and four girls or something, and somebody said, 'Let's have an orgy. Let's all have sex.' And you got up and said, 'Well, I'm leaving now.' " And I got up and I left. And he goes, "And we all had the orgy." . . . They all went and drank and had sex and did drugs. He goes, "Yeah, you just said, 'No, I think I'm leaving now.' And you got up and you left."

Lacey continued for a while to hang out with her friends who were strung out on drugs and recklessly courting STDs, but at seventeen, she said, "I can't do this with you anymore. I can't go with you, with these guys. I can't, you know." And that was that.

Jessica, the fifteen-year-old who "only had sex for it once," also managed to extricate herself from hard drug use before it over-whelmed her. She'd gotten involved with a group of kids who were into methamphetamine and often stayed out "tweaking" for nights on end. She knew her mother was "petrified," but "I didn't care about anything. I told myself, I said, 'Hey, I don't care, so I'm just gonna go out, and as long as I don't care, I'm just gonna go out and do whatever the hell I want, because I don't care what happens.'" Although she was using very heavily at one point, at first she didn't think about the consequences: "It just never came to my head, like I never thought, Oh, I could die from this. I never thought about that at all." But she caught herself after only a few weeks, switched from harder drugs to softer ones, and began hanging out with different people. While some of her friends had "dug themselves such a big hole that they can't even climb out anymore," Jessica hadn't: instead of "a huge, like, gigantic canyon," she had only "dug myself a little *divot*, so I can still come out of it."

The feeling of "abandonment"—of being "moved around by situations," in Lacey's phrase—has echoes in an idea that has sur-faced from time to time in the scholarly study of juvenile delin-quency. In the 1960s, the sociologist David Matza, in an insightful book, *Delinquency and Drift*, criticized many of the most influential explanations of the causes of delinquency because they assumed that delinquents were driven, almost inexorably, to break the law by overwhelming forces outside themselves. Matza argued that while this sort of compulsion might fit in some cases, what was more common was for youth to "drift" into delinquency. By drift, Matza wrote, he meant "motion guided gently by underlying influences." What *started* the process of drift was often difficult to pinpoint: drift "may be initiated or deflected by events so numerous as to defy codification." It was a "gradual process of movement unperceived by the actor, in which the first stage may be accidental or unpredictable." By the same token, "deflection" from the path into delinquency— going straight—"may be similarly accidental or unpredictable."

Matza went on to say that by "drift" he did not mean a condition of freedom but rather a state of mind suspended "midway between freedom and control." The youth who were most likely to become delinquent were those who, for whatever reason, had been loosened from normal social controls but who also lacked "the position, capacity, or inclination to become agents on their own behalf." And that state of mind closely resembles the feeling of "whatever" that so many of my informants describe. They speak of themselves not so much as subjects making a variety of choices in the world but as people to whom things just *happen*. They show very little of the quality that Erik Erikson called "initiative." And their path *out* of trouble, as we will see, often does involve developing a new capacity to "become agents on their own behalf."

The significance of that general state of not caring about consequences is driven home when we recognize that most adolescents who fall into serious trouble fall not just into one kind of trouble but into several—sometimes all at once. By the time he was fifteen, Terry had done hard drugs, been homeless, drunk himself into unconsciousness, broken into stores, engaged in unprotected sex, stolen cars, driven while drunk and stoned, gotten in countless fights, and been repeatedly suspended from school. Danny had been addicted to methamphetamine and alcohol, robbed other kids on the street, sold drugs, joined a white street gang and taken a baseball bat to another boy in a fight, and seen two close friends die in car accidents. Dale, in addition to his heavy drug use, had a history of "going off" on both other kids and adults, had left school at four-teen, and was once admitted to the hospital with a blood alcohol level five times that qualifying for driving under the influence. So it is with most teenagers in serious trouble: the boy with a drug prob-lem is also likely to be "at risk" of being the perpetrator or the vic-tim of violence, to have problems with school, to drive dangerously; the girl with a bad drinking problem is also likely to carve her arms, starve herself, engage in unsafe sex with inappropriate or dangerous men. There may be exceptions to this pattern, but I haven't met them. Among the adolescents who appear in this book, I cannot think of any who "presented" just one of these issues to the exclu-sion of others. Every one would be described as what is sometimes blandly called a "multiproblem" adolescent, but that term is both inadequate and misleading because it suggests that they are afflicted by an assemblage of separate ills that may or may not be related to one another. What I have in mind is something different: that there is a pervasive state of mind that often underlies all of those prob-lems and links them. And at the core of that deeper state of mind is the loss of "care" about the consequences of one's actions.

The question of why so many American teenagers do not care enough to avoid hurting themselves or others is especially puzzling when it comes to the children of the middle class, because they have, at least presumptively, so much to lose. Most of our tradi-tional theories of juvenile delinquency have been designed to ex-plain the behavior of lower-class youth and in one way or another have argued that they get into trouble precisely because they have relatively little to lose. If all you have to look forward to is a life of dead-end work and rock-bottom status in a society that is over-whelmingly devoted to the celebration of material success, one argu-ment runs, there is little to pull you away from the intrinsic lures of crime or drugs. In a variant of this argument, the lower-class adoles-cent, unable to "make it" according to the values of the dominant middle class, reacts by challenging, expropriating, or destroying the symbols of middle-class life. In another version, poor youth are more likely to be drawn into delinquency because the cultural support for conforming to the law is understandably weaker in their families and communities. All of these explanations assume that the reason lower-class adolescents get in more trouble than others is that they have less of a stake in playing by the rules.

But for the child of the middle class, the benefits of staying "straight" are much more tangible. Most of the adolescents I spoke with were well aware of what they were potentially throwing away by their behavior, but they engaged in it anyway. Most understood that they were putting their minds and bodies at risk on a regular basis, and many had enough friends and acquaintances who had essentially destroyed themselves in one way or another to know what the consequences could be. But if they thought about those consequences at all they generally dismissed them; at the extreme, they embraced them.

A young woman I'll call Tracy illustrates this paradox so starkly that it is worth considering her story in some detail. Tracy was sixteen when I met her. She had grown up in a comfortable gated community in a large southern city, one of three children in an intact family that seemed to embody most of the conventional aspirations of middle-class America. But she hadn't lived in her parents' house (which she described as a "beautiful home, really a beautiful home") for almost two years. During that time she'd been badly hooked on methamphetamine and had crashed in a series of drug houses with a succession of problematic boyfriends—most of them older, many of them men who had been in and out of prison. She had participated in sprees of robbery and burglary that could have put her in prison as well.

The change from one way of life to the other had happened, she said, "just in a flash. Like *boom*. All of a sudden, I was into it deep." She started doing drugs when she was thirteen. At fourteen, she ran away from her parents' house for the first time: "And I was on drugs really bad. . . . I mean I couldn't even *think*. I had no feelings. I would steal anything from anybody. *Anything*. . . . I was a very, very bad person. I hated who I was. I *hated* who I was. But like most of the time I didn't care." While she was living precariously in the drug houses, she says, "a lot of people, guys, took advantage of me, or whatever." But at the time she didn't care much about that, either. She went home periodically, moving back and forth from her parents' home to the drug houses to the street. She also began stealing from her family to pay for drugs:

> I'd go and get my sister's bank account. I'd basically rob our *house*. You know what I'm saying? It got really hard. I've stolen hundreds and hundreds of dollars from them, and probably in the thousands. So it just got to the point where my dad was like, "You can't stay here no more, Tracy, if you're gonna be like this." And I said, "Well, I don't care. I *want* to leave. I'm gone," and I'd pack all my stuff up and I'm out. Like out the door.

She moved in for a while with an older cousin but spent most of her time on the street, using speed and hanging out with her drug-using friends: "I'd come in, take a shower, and I'd leave. So I was basically on the streets. I was on my own." I asked Tracy what a typical day was like during this time: what did she do after she got up in the morning? "*If* I slept," she said, laughing.

> A normal day would just be trying to find a place to smoke crank, . . . going out in the middle of the fields, smoking crank. If we were low on money, . . . trying to come up with money by stealing. Just basically plotting on people. . . . Just going from crack house to crack house to crack house, smoking crank. People who needed crank, giving them crank or selling them crank, ripping people off, selling them bunk drugs, just basically trying to get money.

At first this life had been enjoyable:

> To be honest, I would have fun. It was fun. I'm not gonna lie. 'Cause I wouldn't be doing it if it wasn't. When I was on drugs, the robbing

houses and stuff, it was such a rush. I mean at the *time* it wasn't fun, it was very, very scary. But afterwards you get that adrenaline rush, and something overcomes you, and it gets addicting just like the drug. It became a habit. It became an everyday thing, you know, to steal. . . . It was like, "Yeah, let's go do it. Yeah!" And we'd laugh about it, like it was a joke or something.

But soon she began to feel, as she put it, that she had become a different person: she no longer recognized herself. She couldn't figure out how to get her old life back, or even clearly remember what her old life had been: "I forgot who I was before. And I forgot that I had goals. I forgot that I had a family. I forgot that I could be so much happier. . . . It felt like just that was the only way there was to be. That was who I *was*, I could never be anybody else."

As she progressively "forgot" who she had been before, she became more reckless and oblivious to consequences. At one point she and her boyfriend broke into the home of the local police chief: "And that's like, shit, you know? That's *real* smart of us." The possibility of getting caught didn't faze her: "It's like charges and stuff don't scare me. The *first* time, like my first time going to court, I was like shittin' my pants. But after that, it's just like, 'OK, let's go, let's go.' I was paranoid, sure. I was *very* paranoid. But it's just like . . . if it happened, it happened." When she went along with her boyfriend to rob houses she usually didn't go in herself but would sit in the car, thoroughly stoned on methamphetamine, and act as a lookout:

And I'd sit there paranoid, hallucinating that he was getting caught, and almost taking off in the car. . . . I could see other people walking around the house chasing him! And then twenty minutes later he'd walk out of the house with all this shit and, "Let's go." I was like, "What happened? What happened? Oh, my gosh, are they after us?" And he's like, "What are you talking about? No one's even *home* in the house." So I mean it messes with your mind. . . . I used to hallucinate that people were on my roof, trying to break in my house. Nobody was ever there. I thought my *dog* was on crank one time!

The deeper she got into the drugs, the less she cared about what she was doing to herself: "I totally disrespected myself 'cause I was on drugs. It makes you a low person, very low. You don't care about yourself. You don't respect yourself at all." She had always been athletic and, as she put it, something of a "health nut"; now she stopped taking care of herself, in small ways and big ones. When she was on a "run" of speed, she would neglect to eat and would stay up for days at a time:

> I would go like eight nights without sleeping, and then sleep for one or two days straight. . . . My nails are like—they're getting better now, but I'd chew them till they bled. . . . My ear got infected and I—see how it's ripped? I'd pick it until it was just a scab, and it was swollen, and it'd bleed and bleed. . . . Just like the worst things, worst things.

Most alarmingly, she stopped caring whom she had sex with or under what conditions. "It grosses me out," she told me, to remember how "dirty" some of her partners were. "And it wasn't like I had sex with them for drugs. It was just like I was fucked up, and I could have cared less. Basically."

Tracy spent more than a year ricocheting between home, various drug houses, and the street. At sixteen she spent several weeks in a drug rehabilitation center after her parents threw her out of the house and refused to let her come back unless she got clean. When I talked with her during that time, she seemed almost giddily optimistic about her plans to get off drugs, but once she left the program, she managed to stay clean for less than three months. The drugs, she told me, "took me down really fast this time." She couldn't explain why. Getting back into crank just seemed to happen: "I didn't run into nobody or nothing, just one night picked up the phone, said, 'I'm coming over,' I don't even know why." She ran away from her parents again and went to live in another drug house, one even worse than the others:

> Everything was there, crank, crack, heroin. It was pretty bad. I mean people were *shooting* in there. I never shot when I was in there, but I was smoking it a lot. Every day. I didn't go home on Christmas. I didn't care about anything.

Eventually the house was raided by the police. The boyfriend she had been living with there was arrested, and the situation began to feel too dangerous, even for her. Forbidden to go back to her parents' house and having burned most of her other bridges, she lived for a while in a friend's car on the street, stashing most of her possessions in the backseat and surviving mainly by stealing. Desperate now, she decided to try drug treatment again and was accepted at a facility in a different state but ran away after a couple of weeks with a friend she'd made in the program:

> And we were running around like stupid little girls, and we met these guys, . . . these gangsters or whatever, and we go to their house and there's like fifteen gangsters and we're just having a good old time. I relapsed. I was drinking. I was on coke. And Ecstasy, too. And they were trying to rape us. And it was bad. . . . That was a crazy night, one of the craziest nights that I ever had. That was scary. . . . This one guy was threatening to kill me with a screwdriver in my face if I didn't have sex with him, a whole *bunch* of stuff.

Though she ultimately returned to the treatment program and formally finished it, she went back to the old life within days after she got home: "I went back to crank and I was just using and using." She started doing "speedballs"—smoking heroin and crank together. "And that was real hard to come down off of, like my body ached and everything. Really, really bad." She moved in briefly with a new boyfriend, who lived with his parents, but she was still thoroughly out of control: "I was still using. I drank all their alcohol out of their house. I mean I was just—I was a horrible person. I was mean, and I was ugly, and still throwing up my food."

She later said that she had never imagined she could ever reach such a low point. She'd lost all respect for herself and all concern for what her family or anyone else thought of her. Looking back, she worried that her out-of-control drug use might have damaged her permanently: "At night when I go to bed, I twitch and stuff, like really bad. *Really* bad. And I can feel what it's done to my body and, like, my brain. It's like I wonder where I'd be right now physically and mentally if I didn't use all that crap." But at the time, "that was the least thing—didn't even cross my mind." She knew plenty of people who manufactured and sold methamphetamine, and in fact she had dealt it herself, so she had no illusions about its safety. It was dangerous enough in its unadulterated state, let alone with everything it got cut with: "People are putting so much different shit in it and just so much chemicals that just mess with your head, you don't even know *what's* in it." She'd been in meth labs while the drug was being cooked, and the experience was "horrible": "I felt like I was going insane in there. I mean I felt like I was burning. I had goggles on—I had to run out." She was intimately aware, then, that she was regularly ingesting chemicals that not only could burn her lungs but might also be mixed with rat poison and antifreeze. But,

> I never cared. Never cared. I saw people OD and stuff. Which is sad and stuff. But what went through my head was they can't handle their drugs, you know? . . . A lotta stuff tripped me out. A lotta stuff, you know, 'cause different shit's in everything, but I never cared about it. Nuh-uh. I didn't care at all. Shows how much I care about myself, huh?

I am not sure what happened to Tracy. When we last talked she had been clean again for a few months but felt as if she were poised precariously over an abyss. She marveled again at how far and how fast she had come:

I look at my life before I was using . . . and how much more innocent it was, and it was just a different *life*. It was like I was a normal person living a normal life. And then I look at my life when I was using, and it was like I was in a whole different world. . . . Before, I could have never seen anything like that, what kind of world that was.

Tracy's movement between these worlds was especially dramatic, but something like this journey takes place among mainstream adolescents every day in the United States. Like Tracy, they arrive at a place in their lives where they care so little about themselves that they "forget" who they were and don't think about what they might become, a place where they routinely put themselves at risk of injury, illness, or death. Some of them move on. Some do not.

As we will see, there is more than one path to that destructive place—more than one road to "whatever." But there are common themes in the stories of adolescents who take that road. They tend to have remarkably similar experiences across a variety of settings—in the family, in the schools, and in the mental health, juvenile justice, and drug treatment systems. And this suggests that the reasons these teenagers end up at grave risk are neither random nor simply expressions of individual temperament or experience.

If we want to understand why kids like Tracy or Dale or Terry seem to throw everything to the winds, we need to explore what it is about life in the American middle that undermines adolescents' capacity to care about themselves. In the next chapter, I will argue that there have long been strains in mainstream American culture that make it unusually difficult for many adolescents to develop a sense of their own worth that is strong enough to enable them to sustain that level of concern for self and others without which risky behavior becomes likely. We live today in a culture that makes it all too easy for adolescents to define themselves as failures, losers, fundamentally flawed, especially those who do not "fit" well in their families, schools, and communities—who are out of synch with our dominant conceptions of what adolescents *should* be. And the problem has become even more serious in recent years as a result of shifts in the values that guide our ways of rearing children, as well as much else in our social life.

In many respects, I'll argue, life has long been tougher, less supportive, and more precarious for middle-class youth than we have been willing to acknowledge, and those conditions worsened in the social climate that prevailed in America during the lives of the young people in this book. Just as life has become rougher for the poor, the jobless, or the criminal, it has simultaneously become rougher for many of the children of the middle. We have increasingly become a culture that is itself disturbingly heedless of consequences, and it is not at all accidental that many of the young who grow up within that culture become heedless themselves.

THE SINK-OR-SWIM FAMILY

I had known Dale, the fifteen-year-old I introduced in the last chapter, for about two years when I went to interview him, for what turned out to be the last time, at his home—a modest but sparkling ranch house in what had once been a traditional working-class suburb but was now rapidly gentrifying, with oversized modern houses springing up alongside older blue-collar bungalows. The family's new SUV stood freshly washed and gleaming in the driveway.

Dale's stint in a locked psychiatric ward after jumping a teacher who had "mouthed off" at him was not the first time he'd been institutionalized, nor was that attack his first incident of violence. When we'd first talked, Dale had spoken with some pride of having regularly robbed other kids, including much bigger kids, beginning in sixth grade. He and his friends would sneak into amusement parks without paying, find kids who looked like they had money or drugs, threaten them and take whatever they had, then head back out the gate before anyone noticed, or they would hang around the public bathrooms and wait for kids to leave their backpacks lying around, then take everything worth stealing out of them and run.

He'd started smoking weed and drinking in fifth grade, and by eighth grade he was heavily into hard drugs, mainly cocaine and crystal methamphetamine. By his fifteenth birthday Dale was specializing in crystal meth, and when I last interviewed him he candidly admitted that the drug had gotten the better of him. He told me that as he lay in bed at night trying to sleep, he would have hallucinations in which his bowls of meth called out to him from the kitchen table: "Dale . . . Dale . . . I'm not empty . . . come and smoke me. . . ." He said that it had become impossible for him to resist that call because the drugs helped fill an "empty spot" inside him. But this only worked for a while, Over time, he needed more and more meth to fill that spot, and after a certain point it didn't really work at all anymore. And by then, the drugs had become too powerful to quit.

When I asked about the empty spot—what was missing that should have been there—Dale didn't hesitate: what should have been there, he said, was his family. But so much "negative stuff" had happened that the place inside him that should have held good feelings about those closest to him held nothing. The empty spot was also, he told me, about feeling terribly alone: he wanted desperately to talk with his parents about his problems but was afraid to. The pain of the empty spot was intolerable—so much so that the need to fill it took precedence over everything else, including his health and his future.

At fifteen, Dale knew an astonishing amount about the chemistry of speed and what it could do to you: he'd seen kids overdose on it, as well as other drugs, and he knew some who had died. But he didn't spend much time worrying about the consequences of his own use. Early on, Dale's explanation for that absence of concern was the rather insouciant one I've described: all of us were going to die sometime anyway, and the chance that he'd kill himself or wreck his brain or his lungs by smoking crystal meth daily wasn't going to keep him from enjoying the pleasure it gave him. But later, after the drug had truly overcome him and he knew he couldn't get off it without help even if he wanted to, his bravado fell away and he acknowledged that it was the need to fill the empty spot where his family should have been that continued to drive his heavy use, despite his growing awareness that it was now the drug that was in the driver's seat.

Dale's family seemed reasonably "together" on the surface, but I'd always been troubled by the way they related to one another when I'd seen them at home. The family was intact and relatively prosperous: both his parents had steady work. Dale had two younger brothers, and on one occasion when I visited him at home there was a scene that went like this: one of the little brothers was making noise and running around the house, and Dale's mother began comparing him unfavorably with the other child, informing me that he didn't listen and refused to pay attention and was constantly up to something; in that respect, she said, he was just like Dale—not like the other little brother, who was terrific. Dale, who was beginning to get his feet on the ground after spending some time in drug rehab and enrolling in an alternative program for troubled students at his local high school, visibly crumpled at this and became more and more sullen and tight-lipped as his mother, without skipping a beat, continued to rank her children for my edification. He'd been doing well, was off drugs and sticking with school for the first time in years, but you wouldn't have known any of that from his mother's very public diatribe.

Dale's mother went on to tell me that she was a great believer in what she called "the tough-love thing": to be sure, "your kids were your kids" and you needed, as a parent, to provide them with opportunities to succeed to the extent that you could. But there was a limit, she thought, to how much parents could do for their children. Indeed, Dale had been provided with too many opportunities, she felt, too much coddling of one kind or another; he was a privileged child, very fortunate in what he'd been given. But children also had to learn to take the consequences of their mistakes, and this was not something anyone could really help them with, least of all their parents: they had, as she put it, to "hit their face" before they could straighten themselves out. I think she was awkwardly mixing up two phrases—hitting bottom and falling on your face—but in any case she believed that Dale had yet to "hit his face" hard enough, or often enough, to really understand his own situation or to make a serious effort to change.

That was the last time I saw Dale. I talked to him briefly on the telephone a few months later, but he was clipped and uncommunicative, hard to pin down for another meeting. We finally did schedule a time to talk, although his mother warned me that he had "been really irresponsible lately and I don't guarantee that he'll show up." When I arrived at the house on a parched suburban summer afternoon, sure enough, Dale was nowhere to be found. There was a large cardboard box on the front porch, piled high with Dale's clothes and other belongings, including some of the craft projects that he'd become interested in since he'd gotten clean and gone back to school.

His mother explained that Dale had been increasingly hard to live with and had gotten in trouble at school again; there had been some kind of violent incident. He was not taking responsibility for being home when he was supposed to be and was hanging out with "some other bad kids." She and her husband had gotten sick and tired of Dale's behavior and of the whole scene he was involved in—so much so that they were planning to sell their home and move farther out into the country. Dale wouldn't be going with them. I asked what he *would* be doing; in response, his mother jerked her head toward the cardboard box, smiled, and said, "Technically, we're not supposed to say we're kicking him out, since he isn't even seventeen yet, his birthday isn't for another two weeks, but I think when he sees that box he'll probably get the general idea." Had things gotten that bad, I wondered? What had gone wrong? Well, his mother said, he was still doing OK with the drug problem—"He hasn't gotten back into his drug of choice, at least as far as I know." The problem was more basic: Dale, she told me, "hasn't been dealing well with his mental illness."

And that was the end of the discussion. Dale's mother asked if

I could please leave because she had injured herself at work and really wasn't feeling very well. If and when Dale returned to pick up his belongings, she would let him know I'd come by.

Several things seemed clear, in her mind, about the situation. The first was that though Dale did indeed have a serious mental health problem, it was his responsibility to "deal with" it. The corollary was that neither she nor her husband had much responsibility of their own for dealing with it, or, at least, that the principal burden lay with their sixteen-year-old and not with them. And it followed that beyond a certain point, which in her view Dale had long since passed, their responsibility for his welfare could and should come to an end—even though in the eyes of the law he was still, as she knew, officially their charge. The formal responsibility that the law placed on them, in other words, was not, in her eyes, matched by a moral one; and Dale's mother clearly assumed that I shared that assumption or could at least understand it. She was not saying that putting a mentally troubled sixteen-year-old boy out on the street to fend for himself would in the end be for his own good. Her point was that it would be for *her* good and her husband's, and she saw that justification as more than sufficient. What now happened to the boy was out of their hands; it would have to be mainly up to him.

Some version of the themes that emerge in Dale's story—the abdication of parental responsibility in the face of trouble or transgression, the assumption that children themselves bear the primary responsibility for their own well-being and for steering their own path in life, the readiness to sever ties with them when things get tough—recurred again and again in my conversations with troubled middle-class adolescents, and these themes reflect an underlying vision of the problems of families and children that is widely prevalent in America.

The belief that teenagers are adrift because something has gone wrong with the traditional family has been prominent in the popular discussion of youth problems for generations. But in recent years the lament about the "breakdown" of the family has increasingly centered on the idea that parents have lost the upper hand—that we have become a society that is too lenient and indulgent with children. We are far too tolerant when they break the rules, far too forgiving of their "bad choices." As a recent bestselling book on raising children in "an indulgent age" puts it, "Parents give their children too much and expect too little." To drive home its point that parents are besieged today by "an overall sense of entitlement" among their children, the book's cover features a picture of a bratty child making a face at the reader. The idea that youthful entitlement and a lack of discipline are at the root of the problems of American families has stimulated a host of self-consciously "tough" social policies in recent years, from "zero tolerance" of student misbehavior in the public schools to the growing use of adult courts to sentence juvenile offenders, and it has become the mantra of a nationwide movement for "parents' rights." Dale's mother's enthusiastic support of "the tough-love thing," for example, is widely shared: the International Tough Love organization, which claims more than five hundred "support groups" in the United States (as well as Canada, Britain, New Zealand, and South Africa), is based on the "core belief" that "parents have rights too"—among them the right to "stop helping your child and start taking care of yourself."

But the idea that teenagers get into trouble because they feel too entitled and their families too solicitous fits badly, as Dale's story suggests, with the real-world experience of many American teenagers, including those in this book. Far from being lenient or indulgent, their parents were often simultaneously punitive and heedless. The inner culture of their families embodied a harsh and neglectful individualism that worked in multiple ways to breed the problems that ultimately overwhelmed them. Their homes were not places where they could feel progressively more competent and self-assured but arenas where they came to feel progressively worse about themselves and less certain that they were, at bottom, worth very much.

Typically, my interviewees grew up in families in which it was easy to fail and difficult to find either sustained attention or consistent approval. To an unusual degree, moreover, they were left on their own to deal with life's uncertainties and attend to their emotional (and sometimes even practical) needs. Many grew up within what we could call a high-demand, low-support environment. At worst, their parents' approval was contingent on their meeting rigid standards of competitive performance that were hard, if not impossible, to meet—all the more so because these parents often did little to help their children develop the emotional or intellectual tools that would have enabled them to perform on the level expected of them.

In these families, too, children's behavior was often viewed in stark black and white: children were quickly defined as either "in" or "out"—either basically OK or, in some fundamental sense, damaged goods. These families, in other words, tended to be remarkably intolerant of deviance on the part of their children—even if the parents themselves struggled with serious problems of their own, such as heavy drinking or drug abuse. They were also highly punitive families, in which the rules of acceptable behavior were narrowly drawn and the reaction to breaking them unusually severe or rejecting. In most of these families, it was easy for children to "mess up" but hard for them to get help when they did. And when, as often happened, they began to get into more serious trouble as a result, the family's response frequently set in motion a downward spiral. Further evidence of failure or bad character was met with still more punishment and rejection, which, in turn, plunged adolescents deeper into a sense of failure and alienation and confirmed their sense of themselves as flawed and unworthy people. As the cycle progressed, they were pushed farther away, emotionally and sometimes physically, from the family, and they slid or stumbled more and more definitively into a world mainly populated by others in the same boat—kids who had begun to be defined, and to define themselves, as outsiders or "screwups."

In these families, adolescents were not reliably contained, cared for, and guided through the trials of growing up: they were forced to sink or swim on their own and punished or abandoned if they sank. Many of them swam—and their resilience is both impressive and encouraging. But many sank, and they sank in ways that put them in grave danger. Their families, in short, reflected a broader culture of neglectful and punitive individualism—a modern social Darwinism in which those who are able to do well on their own, meet expectations, play by the rules, and play successfully are generally able to get along and even to prosper, while those who cannot do so face what is often an escalating process of abandonment, punishment, and exclusion. It is that culture—not "indulgence" or entitlement—that helped to propel these teenagers into the perilous state of not caring very much about what happened to them.

Four themes are especially important in understanding the character of this culture and its fateful impact on children and adolescents in America. I call them the inversion of responsibility, the problem of contingent worth, the intolerance of transgression, and the rejection of nurturance. In the real world, these themes are rarely found in isolation. I've teased them apart here, somewhat artificially, to show how each contributes to an environment that makes growing up unduly difficult for teenagers in the American mainstream. They represent a kind of mosaic, a pattern that, in one combination or another, turns up repeatedly in the lives of troubled adolescents.

On Their Own: The Inversion of Responsibility

One of the most common laments among troubled middle-class youth is that they were saddled with too much responsibility for managing their lives as they were growing up. They experienced childhood and adolescence not as a time when they were "brought up" in any meaningful sense by competent and admirable adults but as one when they had to figure out how to navigate life on their own. Often, they will say that, even when they were small children, they "had to be the adult" because no one else was. This is a problem with many shades: the degree of parental abdication ranges from the subtle to the glaring. Some describe their parents as having been basically AWOL—as having, for all practical purposes, abandoned (or never taken on) anything resembling an authoritative and nurturing role in their lives. They speak of parents almost wholly absorbed in their own "issues" or, at the extreme, in a state of something like serial collapse. In these circumstances, some teenagers wind up having, literally, to take care of their parents; at the very least, they are forced to conclude, early on, that if they do not learn to take care of themselves, it is not certain that anyone will take care of them at all. At worst, they may be essentially discarded by their parents—something we once assumed happened only in lower-class families.

Sometimes, their parents seem simply overwhelmed and unable to cope—and, as I'll suggest later, the social and economic situation of the middle class today has made this a disturbingly common condition. But there is often more involved. For many of these parents, this inversion of responsibility is not simply a reaction forced on them by external pressures: it is what they believe is right. It reflects their broader views about responsibility and mutuality, and they justify it in a variety of ways. On the simplest level, parents may explain their willingness to abandon the parental role on the ground that the child is just too much trouble for them to handle—even the cause of the family's problems. The parents may complain that they are too fragile to deal with a child who is so burdensome. More frequently, the justifications draw on deeper cultural themes—ideologies about the proper role of parents and, beyond that, the proper place of "help" and support in general. The withdrawal from commitment to their children is rooted in a thin and ultimately self-serving individualism: they believe that children need to learn to "make good choices," and making good choices is not something that anyone *else* can do for them. They believe that it is bad for children (as for adults) to be given too much help in dealing with life, and they often complain that their own children make demands for nurturance and tolerance at a level that, in their view, parents should not have to provide.

The inversion of responsibility is linked to adolescents' descent into serious trouble in several overlapping ways. Part of the problem is practical: the parents' abdication exposes children to the multiple perils of an increasingly risky world, without the reliable supervision or assistance that could help them navigate it safely. Since they are not provided with clear norms or expectations to guide them or with strong models of adults who themselves navigate their worlds honorably and competently, teenagers must construct working guidelines on their own, which necessarily involves a good deal of trial and error. But relying on trial and error in a dangerous world can get you in trouble very quickly. The problem with having to take care of yourself as a child, in other words, is that you probably *can't*, at least not without running some very serious risks and enduring some very hard landings.

Often, children in these AWOL families are physically on their own at some point because their parents have put them somewhere else to live—anywhere from grandparents to neighbors to the street. They wind up living all over the place, partly because their families tend to move a lot and partly because their parents tend to shunt them off if they become problematic—which can be often, given how easily these parents define their children as too much to handle. This can sometimes be mistaken for leniency but is better understood as a kind of neglect.

The parental abdication may also be combined with the message that the child, not the parent, is the problem; the child is responsible not only for his or her own troubles but for the family's as a whole. It is all too easy, in that situation, for children to internalize that message, to come to think of themselves as unworthy, even fundamentally bad, and to feel guilty over the damage they have done.

And if that is how you think of yourself, at least some of the time, you will be less inclined to shrink from doing things that the world defines as bad: you are already bad, and so you have little to lose.

There is another side to this. For some adolescents, the experience of being attended—or largely *un*attended—by self-absorbed or dysfunctional parents leaves them with a certain strength that, though unsolicited, turns out to be of great help later on, as they try to forge a more centered and productive life on their own. Some of them say that this kind of upbringing either kills you or makes you stronger; if you survive it, you come out having learned much that is of value in coping with life. We will come back to this phenomenon in looking at how some troubled adolescents manage to turn their lives around after a period of crisis. Suffice it for now to note that the experience of parental fragility or withdrawal often has a dual effect: it loads adolescents with a great deal of troublesome baggage that can help to precipitate serious problems, but it can also give them a capacity to handle themselves in difficult situations, to find inner resources when they are most needed, and to arrive at a sense of themselves as unusually capable and resilient people.

"Just a Bunch of Fake Things and Trauma"

Jenny is dark-haired, intense olive-skinned, and articulate. When I met her she was a poised and successful student about to graduate from college, in a good relationship, and generally at ease with herself. But she had spent much of her adolescence on the edge: hanging out with volatile and dangerous men, doing hard drugs, drinking heavily—once nearly dying from an overdose of alcohol. She had also gotten trapped, while still in her teens, in a violent and emotionally draining marriage.

Jenny's father was a physician and made enough money for the family to live in a series of comfortable suburbs. But like many other troubled middle-class teenagers, she moved around a lot as a child, often because of her parents' personal problems:

The first move was when my mom was still with my biological father, and she wanted to get him clean. He was a pretty bad alcoholic and a drug addict, so she figured if they moved to Texas he wouldn't be able to find his connections. Well, he did, and he found even more, so my mom ended up, when I was like one, two, working three jobs to support my father and myself and her. And then my dad just was—he wasn't a violent drunk, but he was a drunk that would just pass out. And so my mom would go to work and expect that he could take care of me, and she came home one time and found that I had been screaming and crying, and I was actually—this is kind of gross—covered in my own feces because I was still in diapers, and I was trying desperately to wake up my dad, just like shaking him and then yelling, and I had ripped off my diaper because it started to burn.

So that was the first incident that sort of made her decide to leave him. And then the second was that she started sending me to a babysitter's, and the babysitter called her at work and said, "I am not giving Jenny to Rick because he can't even walk up the three steps to get to my front door, he's so drunk." So then she kicked him out, and I still actually remember the day he left because my mother had a broken arm. She had a cast on her arm from punching him. My mom's all of 5'1", but she's pretty feisty. And so she punched him, and she hit his shoulder. He didn't even get a bruise, and she got this big boxer's break.

And I just remember he was gone. He left. And it was really hard for me to figure out because I really blamed myself.

Her mother, who was addicted to a variety of prescription medications and perennially bouncing from one relationship to another, was also, at best, only intermittently available: "She was just a mess when I was growing up," Jenny says, "and I was sort of the adult."

And then she married my stepfather, who was another raging alcoholic, who also was really, really unfaithful and really bad about covering up his tracks. . . . To this day, I don't understand why she ever put up with that. It was OK for her if a man cheated on her. It was like he loved her

more than anything in the whole world, and it was really obvious that
for some reason he couldn't keep it in his pants.

The second marriage didn't last long, because of the stepfather's in-
stability and heavy drinking: "He tried to kill her one night. . . . Apparently he had my mom on the ground and was like just choking
her and banging her head on the floor." That was enough to precipitate another divorce, after which Jenny was sent away—in what
would become a repeated pattern—to live somewhere else, in this
instance with relatives in another state.

> And the next thing I knew it was August, and my mom made a surprise
> visit to tell me that there was this new man named Jack and I'd be meet-
> ing him as soon as I got home. And I'm ticked because she was so
> messed up my whole childhood that, you know, I was really the parent.
> It was like I would go in and get her *up*. There were times that she had
> to take hormone shots because she had these weird imbalances, and I
> would give them to her. The first time I gave her a shot I was like six
> years old.
>
> So along with that came this increased understanding that what was
> going on around me in my home life wasn't normal. But I didn't know
> any other way to be. So I was very used to taking care of her and being
> there for her when, you know, *this* guy hurt her or *that* guy hurt her, and
> she would be crying to *me*.

Though her mother leaned on Jenny regularly for both practical
and emotional assistance, the support didn't go both ways. What
Jenny remembers most about her childhood, indeed, is the peculiar
combination of being the parent and being regularly disparaged by
her mother, who criticized her appearance, told her that she'd never
amount to anything, and blamed her for the family's general disarray:

> She would go through severe depressions. And she hated me. I was the
> bane of her existence. You know, it was the little things, telling me

everything that was wrong with my face, was how she would start, because you know when you're little your mother is the most beautiful thing you've ever seen. And she'd be what I now know to be stoned out of her mind, and I'd be watching her put on makeup, and she'd look at me and she'd go, "Well, your head's way too round. Your face is just far too round. And your nose is too fat. And you're just never going to look like me, and you have these little, squinty eyes." And I'd be like . . . I was just trash.

When she was nine her mother got involved in yet another relationship, this time with a man Jenny describes as a "pedophile." Her mother, she says, was "so far gone that she wasn't really realizing what sort of situation she'd put me into. . . . I was home alone with Fred a lot during the day because he worked nights, and she worked during the day. And he—I'm fortunate to have blocked out most of what happened."

And the other thing was just how he spoke to me. My mother was always very big on, "Oh, Jenny's, you know, so smart," had my IQ tested in fourth grade, and I just went off their scale, so they sent me to [a university] for further testing, and so it was an established fact that I was a smart person. And Fred would say, "Well, it doesn't matter, because any guy's always going to look at you and think you're a fuck." You know? Nine, ten years old, and I'm going, "Oh, God." And my mother started calling me a slut. And why do you call a ten-year-old a slut? It's like there was some level that she still can't fully admit to, that she knew what was going on but she was just so messed up herself that she couldn't handle it.

The relationship with Fred, like the earlier ones, came to a stormy and traumatic end. Unable to cope, Jenny's mother sent her to live with some neighbors and shortly thereafter tried to kill herself: "She OD'd on a bunch of pills. So I didn't have a father, I didn't have a mother, and then I get this call one day. I'm at school. And the neighbor I was living with comes to get me and, 'Well, Jenny, your mom is in the hospital.'"

The suicide attempt wasn't altogether unexpected: it was the culmination of a long-standing pattern. Her mother had threatened to harm herself on several occasions. The most dramatic of them took place when they were driving back together from Jenny's school:

> She started talking about how bad she wanted to die. "I just don't want to live. I want to be dead," you know, "You'd be better off without me." So I looked at her, and I said, "Well, do it. Why do you keep *talking* to me about it? Just *do* it. I don't want to hear about it anymore." I was ten! And so we're in the car, and she starts slamming on the accelerator and driving really, really fast into oncoming traffic.
>
> And I just looked at her the whole time. I'm like, "*Do* it, *do* it." Because that's the only way I could handle it. I was so mad that she would threaten me like this. You know, I was *ten*. And as far as I could tell, the world was not a happy place. It was just all a bunch of fake things and trauma. And she finally pulled the car over, probably two seconds before we would have hit oncoming traffic and had spun into this big concrete retaining wall.

After the suicide attempt, her mother seemed to expect Jenny to resume her usual role of being the adult. But Jenny had begun to feel that there was something wrong with this emotional arrangement—that she was being asked to do a job that shouldn't really have been hers: "She expected me to be there for her, like I should just forgive her for wanting to leave me and stuff. And that didn't turn out too well":

> She became very proud of the fact that she was diagnosed as depressed and that she had this official problem that was on paper. And I was telling her that she was weak, and who cares, and she's like, "Read this!" And it was her release chart, you know, with her diagnosis on there. And I said, "So what? You're crazy? Am I supposed to *care*?"

Throughout her childhood, Jenny had done very well at school, and she was also, she says, "used to playing a part." As a result, no one outside the family (and the neighbors who had taken Jenny in) had any inkling that anything was wrong at home. But all this changed after the breakup with Fred and her mother's suicide attempt. The family wound up without a regular income and ultimately went on welfare: "All of a sudden we were poor. And when we went to the grocery store, she would pay with food stamps." Jenny was no longer able to hide "that dysfunctional family difference": the situation at home had become exposed, "and this was just horrible to me."

In junior high school she took a job in a fast food restaurant so that she could afford to have the same clothes as everyone else at her school and they wouldn't realize how bad off the family had become. But she also started hanging out with the local "stoner crowd" and discovered that she felt oddly at home with them, despite the fact that most of them were from poorer backgrounds: "You know, they sort of lived on the edge, and people were scared of them, so I found them comforting. I didn't relate to what their goals were or anything like that. It was just that they were tough, and I knew that they wouldn't judge me for having such a screwed-up family."

Her mother continued to get involved with questionable men, many of whom took an unhealthy interest in Jenny, who was now thirteen, developing, and very attractive. There were several traumatic situations, but Jenny was never able to get her mother to pay much attention to what was going on, much less to intervene. Once one of her mother's male friends came to take them both out to dinner:

And I had just begun puberty and stuff and was changing. And Jerry followed me into my room after taking me to dinner, and then he turned around, and he hands me a fifty and starts shoving his tongue down my throat. And this is a man who, you know, I've known since I was a baby. He was my mother's high school friend. And I just really flipped out. I

didn't even know how to handle that. And I didn't tell my mother because I just assumed she wouldn't do anything about it anyways, or she
wouldn't care, or she'd blame it on me.

She managed to ward Jerry off, but soon afterward began having
sex regularly:

Here I was, getting accosted left and right and not even understanding
anything. So then I lost my virginity at thirteen. And I was actually with
that guy for like three years, so it wasn't that I became promiscuous. I
just think that I became sexually active before I even understood what it
was or what I should have been doing.

As before, she managed in junior high to do well in school and
"sort of stay functional," even though her life at home felt increasingly out of control. Yet despite being able to keep up an appearance
of stability, she felt more and more like an outsider, crucially different from the more "normal" kids around her:

I've always been able to blend into the sort of cheerleader-jock, popular,
"we're perfect" crowd, even though I knew that I never belonged, and I
was always more comfortable with the rough people, the people with
problems, 'cause they reminded me of my family and everybody that I'd
ever known.
    It was very odd for me to go to my friends' houses and have the mom
and dad and everyone *sit down for dinner!* It freaked me out. I just
couldn't handle it. It's like what are they doing? They're going to know
that I don't belong here.

Still, she was able to "keep it together" through her first two years
of high school. She maintained a four-point grade average, did public speaking and debate, was on the student council, and generally
shone: "I was like freshman princess." But halfway through her junior year, her mother decided to move to a city several hundred miles

away in order to attend school. Jenny was left to live with her mother's current boyfriend. On the weekends he would drive off to visit her mother, leaving Jenny with the keys, some money, and instructions to "have fun." At this point, on her own for all practical purposes at sixteen, Jenny began to spin out of control:

> I just started partying, a lot, and all the time. And I had done different drugs. I had smoked pot and drank alcohol, and I never really cared for any of those feelings. But then one of my friends invited me over, and she had me try meth—or, as we called it, crank—and I'd never felt like that before. 'Cause I felt in *control*, but I had all this *energy*. And I felt very thin, which is always a good thing if you're a girl. And it was great.

At first, she found the methamphetamine helpful in her effort to stay "functional," because it focused her and gave her a feeling of having unlimited energy to accomplish all sorts of things at once (a reaction shared by a number of the striving middle-class adolescents in this book, which helps explain the strong appeal to them of methamphetamine and other stimulant drugs). She didn't feel that the drug controlled *her*; on the contrary, she thought she could use it to stay on top of things, even in the midst of a chaotic and unpredictable environment. But the drug had a darker side: "The high is like about eight hours, but it has these horrible periods where it just drops you. And you're paranoid, and you're depressed, and that was like one of the blackest feelings."

She began to identify herself, even more than before, with the heaviest "stoners" in town, "going to crack houses and dating these guys that I shouldn't have been dating":

> I got busted for shoplifting during this time, and mostly it was just a lot of drugs and a lot of violence. . . . You'd go down to the parks, and there were always bums there that would go into the liquor stores and buy you alcohol, and there was always somewhere that you could go that was

highly unsafe that you could get meth or anything else. There were just always drugs around me.

Yet she says that she felt less frightened and vulnerable, not more, in these situations. As before, she found herself oddly comforted being surrounded by a crowd of extraordinarily volatile people. The rougher her crowd became, the safer she felt:

> I had dated this guy who . . . had covered up his White Power tattoos by the time I knew him, but he still had a record for getting in a fight with this thirty-five-year-old man. He was sixteen and being so nuts that he had him on the ground, and he started stomping on his head, jumping on his head with his big Doc Martens sort of boots, that when the guy came in to trial, he still had the imprints on his face. And these were the people that I wanted to be around. You know, nothing could harm you if you were with the worst of the worst.

Because she had always managed to deal with traumatic situations on her own in the past, she assumed that she could handle her new life in the same way:

> I didn't consider what I was doing, and I didn't think that it would ever turn into something long-term bad because I could always find my way. You know, I always knew that I could take care of myself, so I could hang out with drug dealers and I could be involved in these things, and shoplift, and just do all this insanely crazy stuff that I'm so lucky to be alive for.

But her confidence turned out to be misplaced, or at least exaggerated. During her senior year in high school Jenny hit the wall. She hung out with more and more desperate people and moved deeper and deeper into the local culture of drugs, heavy drinking, and violence. With her mother still mostly out of town, she partied more and more heavily. On one especially wild night, she OD'd at the home of one of her girlfriends, who, at sixteen, had recently moved to town on her own:

> Her parents gave her an apartment because they didn't want to deal with her. So it was just party central. And I had a screwdriver that was probably mostly vodka, and then a bottle of Jack Daniels. And I wasn't able to breathe. I just passed out. I'm there with a bunch of sixteen-year-old kids that have no idea what to do. And I'm vomiting . . . and the paramedics came to take me, and they kept having to thump me on my chest because I wouldn't breathe. And when they got to the hospital, I actually flatlined. One of my lungs was collapsed, and my heart stopped, and I hear the monitor go off, and I hear them yelling, "She's flatlining, she's flatlining." And that's the last thing I remember until I woke up in the hospital bed the next day. And that should have been a wake-up call, but it wasn't, and things just got worse.

———•———

This kind of systematic abandonment by parents—emotional, physical, or both—is a recurrent theme among troubled middle-class adolescents. In every culture, of course, becoming progressively able to take on responsibility is an important facet of growing up, indeed a considerable part of what we *mean* by growing up. But in what I call "sink or swim" families it happens too early, too drastically, and too carelessly. It is not a mindful process in which adults gradually relinquish some responsibility as their children in these families learn to take it on but a kind of withdrawal in which the growing child is simply set adrift.

When things start to go wrong, accordingly, children are likely to feel—often correctly—that they have only themselves to rely on. If you ask them who stood by them when things got rough, they will say "nobody" or "my friends." Indeed, by early adolescence, if not before, some are willing to suffer almost anything, face almost any risk, before asking for help from the adults around them. They often feel exposed and vulnerable if they do ask for it, having come to expect not only that their parents will be unable or unwilling to provide it but that their requests will be met with rejection, scorn, or even punishment. As Jenny put it, "I just assumed she wouldn't do anything about it anyways, or she wouldn't care, or she'd blame it on me." So they try to go it alone—to cope on their own with chaotic environments and perilous relationships, as well as with their fears and self-doubts.

The problem with that strategy, of course, is that not many *adults*, much less vulnerable thirteen- or fourteen-year-olds, can successfully manage life wholly on their own for long. Without outside support, those adolescents who try will fail more often than not, and that repeated failure can deepen their sense of being inadequate or morally flawed. Some, as we'll see, do manage, against the odds, to take hold of their lives and change them for the better. For others, the too-early effort to maintain control over themselves and over an unstable environment backfires, plunging them into a profound sense of worthlessness and despair.

"It Was Normal to Me"

When I first talked with Alyssa she was sixteen and about to finish a stint in a drug treatment program. She had grown up in the suburbs of a large and generally affluent midwestern city where she was, like Jenny, a standout in many ways through the beginning of junior high: a cheerleader, good at sports, indeed already a highly regarded athlete by seventh grade. But in eighth grade she began drinking heavily, hanging out with hard-core gang kids from a poor neighborhood across town, and getting "taken advantage of, a lot," by men. She'd always gotten good grades in the past but was now failing most of her classes.

For a while, sports allowed her to maintain some semblance of being together even though everything else in her life was slipping badly. She loved playing baseball—she was a starter on the team— and during the season she tried to keep her drug use under control:

"I'd still use, but I'd be like 'I'm not gonna use before my game,' blah blah blah. And I was doing really well. . . . And after it was over, it was like, all right, I can go back to this and just keep going." Soon, however, she was showing up drunk or stoned at games. "I don't think anybody really knew what was going on with me. But they noticed that my performance had just decreased immensely. Like I could barely make it to the games. . . . It just was horrible."

She wasn't able to talk to anyone about what was happening, least of all to her parents. She didn't feel "safe" with them, even though she described their relationship as "not so bad" and had moments when she felt close to them: "I don't like people to see what's going on with me. It makes me feel, you know, out of control and vulnerable, and I don't like doing that." So even when she was falling down drunk on the baseball field, she kept things to herself. As a small child, she had concluded that "if I can show them I'm in control of things, nobody will come after me, nobody will threaten me. I'll be all right. And I won't have to be scared." When there was conflict at home, she says, she would often become "nonemotional." She would look "straight through people, with no emotion on my face or in my eyes or anything. I'd shut down. 'Everything's fine.'"

When I asked Alyssa, at sixteen, where she thought that need to be always in control had come from, she spoke of having grown up in a home where "no one was paying attention":

I've always been too independent. That's how my mom raised me. That's how I was when I was little. . . . She would go to work, and my biological father would be passed out drunk, and I was five years old, and I'd go and make my little sister a peanut butter sandwich, and clean up the cigarettes that fell on the ground, and this and that. I'd climb in the cupboard to get peanut butter, and stuff like that.

And it was *normal* to me. It shouldn't happen, it shouldn't be normal to do that, you know? I would put our biological father's vodka up so my three-year-old sister wouldn't get it. And that was normal! For me it was normal, but it shouldn't be normal, because a five-year-old shouldn't know that that's what that is and that little kids shouldn't drink it.

At the time, she tried to persuade herself that she liked having this kind of responsibility, and even thought it was sort of fun:

I just remember that she was always at work, and he was always home. And he never paid attention to us. And it didn't really bug me. At all. Like, I didn't care. I liked being able to take control of the house. . . . It was kind of like playing house. It was fun for me. And I've kind of grown up that way.

Ultimately her parents divorced, and her mother remarried, this time to a much more stable and responsible man. But Alyssa was still unable to feel "safe" at home or to reveal any kind of need or vulnerability. She assumed that her parents would punish her if she came to them with a problem or admitted that she had done something wrong, rather than hear her out or help her figure out what to do. She felt that they were always "hanging over her shoulder," whether they were there or not—always watching her. From seventh grade on, she felt as if she were ready to "bolt" from home at any moment. So when, at thirteen, things began to get out of hand for her, she still thought that it was her job to deal with them. Because she'd been used to handling things on her own for so long, she believed—or wanted to believe—that she could handle alcohol the same way: "I had the attitude, it's my life, I can handle everything, I didn't need anybody's help, I can do it by myself." Indeed, she often deliberately put herself in situations where her ability to control herself was severely tested, just to prove to herself and anyone who was watching that she could. Early on, she cultivated a reputation as someone who could drink everyone else under the table:

I've been drinking and smoking weed since I was thirteen. A really, really heavy drinker. . . . I was the kind that could drink with the football players, drink with the guys, and I could just hold it, up to whatever limit that I had to. And still people wouldn't really realize how far gone I was.

The strategy worked only for a while. She oscillated between periods in which she managed to maintain her customary tight control and times when her control broke down altogether, and it was at that point that she began showing up drunk on the baseball field. She dropped out of school at fourteen and became deeply depressed and badly strung out. Her parents decided to send her away to another state to live with a relative for several months, telling her that being completely away from her usual influences and under the watchful eye of her aunt would help her make better choices in her life. The stay was supposed to last only a few weeks, but when the time was almost up Alyssa's parents announced that she wouldn't be allowed to come home after all: she would have to stay with her aunt for several more months. Alyssa was devastated by what she took to be a major rejection. Her first response, as usual, was to try to remain in control and to suppress her feelings of abandonment and betrayal. But it didn't hold: she partied heavily and blew a couple of months of being clean. "We went out, and for some reason I was just like *forget it*, you know? And I drank, and I used, and it was a school night . . . and I was drunk, and I was doing this and that."

She fell back into using and drinking heavily. When she was fifteen, she went into drug rehab for a month but never really felt engaged with the program and had little confidence that it prepared her to deal with the issues that had driven her drug use in the first place. She was right: when she got back home, she "went out"—meaning both that she physically went out, running away from home, and that she went out of control—even harder.

When I caught up with Alyssa some weeks later, I asked her why, when she "went out" this time, it was "ten times harder and faster," as she put it, than before she went into rehab. She told me that after she left treatment she returned to a troubled and unsettled life at home: she felt mistrusted and put down by her parents, and the hopelessness she'd been trying to suppress erupted to the surface. Soon she "didn't care about anything." As in the past, her first response was to redouble her efforts to prove to herself (and others) that she could handle whatever life, or her parents, threw at her—including her growing drug habit:

> When I went back out it was like all or nothing. . . . I was thinking, "I'm an alcoholic, not a drug addict, so it's OK to do drugs. . . . No problem, I can handle it." The guy I was with was a very big addict, was a dealer. I had it all there, you know. I was gonna do everything to a huge extent.

But she couldn't handle doing "everything to a huge extent" by herself. The effort to steel herself against the chaos around her and the pain inside her disintegrated, and she "went out" once more.

This time, Alyssa disappeared for several months. When she surfaced again, she told me she was doing better. She'd gotten into a stable relationship with a guy who didn't use hard drugs, and she hadn't touched them herself for weeks. But though in her eyes things were starting to improve, her parents disagreed, and they ultimately tricked her into going to a closed drug rehabilitation program in another state. She was told the family was going camping, and she felt buoyed and reassured by what appeared to be her parents' desire to spend quality time with her. Instead they drove directly to the treatment facility. When Alyssa figured out what was happening, she tried to run away down the highway but was tackled and dragged into the place by the program's staff. As is often the case in such facilities, she was allowed no outside contact for several months. When I was finally able to speak with her, she told me that she was frightened and unsure of herself. She felt her customary control had broken down altogether: if she were to "go out" now, she said, she would almost certainly do "more and more drugs" and would probably "end up dead."

During the time Alyssa was in this program, I spoke with her mother on several occasions. She was articulate and talkative but also capable of carrying on a running critique of her daughter's character that made Alyssa's unwillingness to turn to her rather understandable. She was convinced that Alyssa was not really trying to deal with her problems; she said that Alyssa was "in denial" and prone to the "lying that goes with her disease—little lies, big lies, which are part of the disease of alcoholism." Despite appearances, Alyssa was still "full of crap," manipulative toward her parents and everyone else: "She writes letters, 'Oh, I'm doing fine. I love you, Mom,' but it's just bogus and I know it's bullshit." Alyssa would write, her mother said in a sarcastic singsong, " 'I love you mom, I miss you mom.' I thought, 'What a crock,' but I had to stifle my resentments."

Alyssa's mother spoke enthusiastically of having learned in a self-help group she'd recently joined that it was necessary for parents to be able to "detach" from their children, or, more precisely, to detach from what she and others in her group regarded as an excessive sense of responsibility toward them. She was learning, she said, how to "detach with love" from Alyssa—and from Alyssa's younger brother, who had also wound up in an out-of-state drug treatment facility where he was being held under tight surveillance. She was, she said, coming to understand how to be more at ease with herself in the face of these disappointments, learning to find her own "serenity," and part of this journey toward serenity was to lower her expectations about her own capacity, as a parent, to do much about her children's behavior. The idea that her children were suffering from a disease was helpful in this effort to loosen her sense of responsibility toward them: if they were genetically prone to the "disease of substance abuse," her ability to influence what happened to them was necessarily limited, and she had to accept that—to stop trying to "control that which can't be controlled." Instead she could now begin to focus more on her "own issues" and attend to her own physical and emotional health. (A similar outlook pervades the "parents' rights" movement. One of the frequently asked questions on the Web site of Tough Love International is, "Is it my fault that my child is in trouble?" The answer, unsurprisingly, is no: "We know you have done the best that you can with the tools that you have.")

The connection between her mother's explicit rejection of responsibility and her own failing attempts to control her life on her own was not lost on Alyssa. She was keenly aware of her mother's disparaging attitudes and deeply hurt by them: the knowledge that her mother had largely withdrawn at this critical time contributed greatly to her desperation and her desire to get high enough to recreate the illusion of control. "The other day," she said, "I got a letter from my mom saying that she still thinks I'm full of crap, not having a lot of trust in me. . . . I felt out of control and my first feeling was, 'I want a drug.'"

———•———

With Alyssa, then, there is always some kind of parental absence. Obviously the drunken father who can't get it together even to feed the children is absent in the most basic sense, but so is the parent who swerves from controlling and punitive to self-servingly "detached." In both instances, the child is forced to cope with life mostly on her own. This pattern of premature self-control is pervasive among troubled middle-class adolescents, and it is one of the predictable costs of a culture of irresponsible individualism marked by the ideological rejection of parental responsibility. But, as Alyssa's case shows, the too early effort at control almost always breaks down: children may succeed at it some of the time or even most of the time, but they can seldom pull it off all the time, because their ability to control themselves and the environment around them is inherently limited. That is true for all of us, but even more so for the young, especially those whose environments are so thoroughly *out* of control. The effort is bound to fail at least occasionally, and when it does, it tends to fail utterly, like a dam breaking. When teenagers who have tried mightily to hold things together in this way begin to "lose it," they often conclude that they might as well lose it altogether. They cannot slip a *little*, because there is no one to catch them if they do.

"What I Felt Was Good Was Never Good Enough": The Problem of Contingent Worth

A second theme in the family lives of many troubled middle-class adolescents is what I call the problem of contingent worth. By that I mean that the culture that surrounds them is one in which individuals' value—in their own eyes and those of others—is, to an unusual extent, conditional on their meeting certain narrow standards of performance. It is not sufficient to be simply a "good kid"—or to be hardworking, courageous, or generous, all qualities that might be expected to give adolescents a firm sense that they are fundamentally worthwhile. Instead, too much rides on their ability to rank high on just a few scales of worth, which, in the American middle class, typically involve some sort of competitive achievement—outdoing others in school, sports, or whatever arena is considered most important in the struggle for status and prestige. For adolescents who grow up in the culture of contingent worth, it is rarely good enough merely to do well; they have to do better than others. As a result, there is always hanging over their heads the worry that someone out there is doing even better. For them adolescent life is experienced as, in Kafka's phrase, a "court in perpetual session."

The fundamental problem for youth raised in such a culture is that not everyone can beat everyone else: only a few can win even most of the time. Thus, this value system sets up most of its adherents for failure. Where personal worth is necessarily a scarce commodity, there will inevitably be a great many people who think of themselves as relatively worthless. Every culture, to be sure, has standards by which its members are ranked, and in every culture it is possible to fail, to fall short. But what is unusual about the culture in which many American adolescents grow up is how narrowly the standards of success are drawn and how total the effect of failing to meet them can be, how completely one is defined by one's relative position in this competitive struggle for preeminence. There is no natural limit to the number of children who can be loyal, honest, caring, or many other things that a less constricted culture might deem important and worthy of respect. But in a struggle *against* others—a struggle to be on top in just one dimension or two of life—many must lose, and some must lose badly. And when they do, there are few alternative sources of self-respect to turn to.

The unusual prominence of the struggle for individual success in America has often been invoked to explain the behavior of people at the *bottom* of the social ladder. In the 1930s, the sociologist Robert K. Merton famously argued that American culture was peculiarly focused on the goals of material success to the exclusion of other measures of personal worth and social prestige. To be able to feel truly worthy, Americans had to achieve (or be born with) substantial material evidence that they had "made it." The problem, for Merton, was that a variety of barriers prevented those who started at the bottom from attaining the level of economic success that the culture held out as a universal measuring stick. Blocked by poor education and few skills, most lower-class people would never rise far and as a result would suffer not only material deprivation but the even more devastating psychological deprivation that comes from being defined as failures in a society fixated on success. Merton argued that this "strain" between the universal pressure toward success and the limited means of achieving it generates many forms of deviant behavior, from property crime to drug abuse, and a host of followers have elaborated on this idea, especially to explain juvenile delinquency among the urban poor.

This lens hasn't often been used to explore the problems of the better-off. But it could be argued that the psychological pressures bred by the uniquely American emphasis on competitive success are actually worse for the children of the middle class, precisely because there are fewer external barriers they can point to as explanations or justifications for their inability to make it to the highest rungs of a narrow ladder of social performance. Poor youth can—and often do—point to discrimination or lack of resources or connections to explain why they haven't done more or done better. Middle-class adolescents are largely denied those structural excuses and are indeed typically taught to blame themselves for their real or imagined failure to stand out in the realms where their performance is most crucially judged—school, athletics, social status. (The dilemma may have become sharper in recent years, as the paths to economic success, in particular, have shrunk even for much of the traditional middle class, thus intensifying the competitive pressures.)

The problem of how to cope with losing, accordingly, is a pervasive and pressing one in mainstream American culture—and especially so for adolescents, because they are in the midst of an already tricky and sometimes painful process of defining who they are. In every society, coming to that definition is a major part of what adolescence is about. But in the relentless ranking scheme that characterizes an individualistic and narrowly competitive culture, many will emerge from that process having defined themselves as people who do not measure up.

One way to cope with the potentially intolerable sense of being worthless and a loser is to stop caring—or to try with all your might to find ways not to care, to block the nagging pain and humiliation of feeling yourself a failure in the eyes of those whose opinion most matters. Another is to change the frame of reference—to look outside your family and community for approval and respect—or to change the terms of the game by challenging the legitimacy of the ranking system itself and replacing it with a new one. As we'll see, this strategy can help adolescents escape from feelings of failure and despair and begin to turn their lives around. But it can also work the other way: the search for alternative sources of approval and esteem can lead them to dangerous places indeed.

In contrast to Jenny, Alyssa, and others whose parents essentially abandoned responsibility for their well-being, the teenagers most affected by the culture of invidious ranking usually face a different, though related, problem at home. Their parents are, on the whole, more competent and are often quite successful in conventional terms. And they are, in their own way, more involved with their children—more likely to monitor their behavior and to engage in what the sociologist Annette Larreau calls "concerted cultivation." But they do so in ways that profoundly undermine their children's sense of being capable people whose lives count for much. Among the adolescents I spoke with, those who grew up in such families were often the ones who, when they fell, fell the hardest and fastest.

"I Was Pretty Much a Nice Kid"

I met Rick a year or so after he had stopped drinking himself into unconsciousness several nights a week. Bright, engaging, and talented, he grew up in an affluent suburb with parents who were both driven, successful businesspeople. But by the middle of high school he'd gotten to the point where he would regularly drink until he blacked out and would wake up barely remembering what else he'd done. "I ended up getting a reputation," he says. "Actually I don't really like running into people from high school because they remember me as 'that guy who can drink.'"

Rick describes himself, along with many of his equally hard-drinking high school friends, as having been "lost and confused" and profoundly unhappy in those years; they were really not, he says, "bad kids." He started drinking because it seemed like people who drank had fun, and he wasn't having any. But the drinking soon "kind of snowballed" and he began to drink for the express purpose of achieving unconsciousness, or, as he put it, "to get out of reality": "I'd just drink huge amounts of hard liquor just until I could pass out, basically. And it got to the point where I couldn't really drink at all without blacking out and then waking up and finding out I'd done a lot of serious stuff."

When I asked Rick what it was about reality that he was trying to avoid, he told me that growing up he'd always had the nagging sense of being "already in trouble." No matter what he did, he seemed never able to measure up. His parents had little tolerance for anything but the very top performance from him, especially at school, and were routinely punitive and critical if they felt he'd failed them, which was often. On top of that, he was sent to a strict and rather harsh private high school, because his parents felt that the public schools were insufficiently challenging and that Rick needed a strong dose of discipline to live up to his potential. Between the school and his parents, he began to feel that he was "getting it" from all sides: "So by the time I was done with my day of getting punished by my parents and punished by the school, I just wanted to go out and get in trouble."

In high school he "felt stress and tension everywhere, whether it was coming from home, coming from school." There was no one to provide a respite from what he experienced as an unending barrage of criticism:

> At some point I got sick of just having enormous pressure put on me. . . . I realized it was making me severely depressed, and I think that it was probably doing that for a long time. That was one of the key things. It's just I didn't get much support as far as—constructive criticism isn't the right word, but more of like appreciation for what I was doing *right*.

Of his parents he says:

> We're very different actually. We, to this day, still have the same fundamental problems that we've been arguing about since fourth grade. . . . I always had to be doing excellent in school. I mean, I remember in junior high getting in trouble for an A–! So I had a lot of expectations. And my parents went to Harvard, so they were successful. And they both work very hard, very organized. They're dedicated. And I've always been the opposite of that.

In fact, Rick wasn't the opposite of dedicated and organized: he did very well in school—well enough, in fact, to be admitted to a highly competitive university. But he couldn't escape the feeling that his achievements were never enough in his parents' eyes. It was always, he says, " 'Oh, you could have done more work.' "

What particularly got to him was that he did far better in school than most of his friends, whose parents were far more accepting:

> I was in all the AP Honors classes, and every semester I had to take the hardest schedule possible. And my friends were all in just the normal run-of-the-mill classes. They're, you know, normal—they're at colleges, but the normal colleges. My friends' families would always be . . . telling me that they would love if their kids were doing what I was doing. You know, I was on a sports team. I was doing really well in school. . . . I was pretty much a nice kid, and they were always wondering why I seemed to be getting into big fights with my parents all the time, being grounded all the time. They told me if *their* kids got my grades, they'd be allowed to do whatever they want! A lot of parents, you know, give the kids twenty bucks an A and all that stuff? *My* parents . . . I mean if I got money for *my* grades, I'd be doing *good*.

The sense that they cannot be just normal, without being criticized for not being more, is common among adolescents in the culture of contingent worth. Most parents, to be sure, want to see their children do well. But what distinguishes this strand of American middle-class culture is that the standard of what it means to do well is both unusually high and unusually narrow—and that failing to meet that standard can lead to a totalizing rejection, a fundamental critique of the adolescent's character as a whole. The result is the sense of "constant stress" Rick describes: the inability to ever really relax and simply be yourself, to get outside the struggle for preeminence, to feel confident that you are cared for and appreciated all of the time, rather than just when you win.

"Out There They Accept Anybody"

Rick got past his period of wanting to be "out of reality" by dint of being extremely capable and having, in fact, worked very hard, which allowed him to get into a good college and far enough away from his parents to find his feet and recover his self-respect. Things do not always work out so well. The crushing sense of failure in the face of high and narrow expectations can push middle-class adolescents into seeking out people with different expectations, in what can become a desperate and destructive quest for some kind of success.

Tracy, who bounced back and forth from her comfortable suburban home to a deeply self-destructive life on the street, illustrates this pattern in a particularly stark way. When we first talked, she had found it impossible to explain why she had spun downward, in her early teens, into a nightmarish world of hard drugs, careless sex, and intermittent homelessness:

> I've sat there, and I'm like where did this all begin? Where did it start at? And the weird thing is, I can't think of anywhere where it could have started.
>
> I remember the first time I tried [speed]. I remember who I was with. I remember how things were at home. I mean, nothing serious happened. . . . Like a lot of people become addicted to drugs and stuff because their families are drug addicts or because they've been raped or sexually abused or something, but nothing—it's weird. Nothing triggered my life to make me want to go use.

Nevertheless, by age fourteen she was regularly getting so stoned that she could barely think. Indeed, one of the main reasons she wanted to "get more and more tweaked out and tweaked out and tweaked out" was precisely to avoid thinking:

> I just had a lot of feelings that it's still hard for me to get out. It's like I don't know *what* I'm feeling. Sometimes I feel like I'm crazy because my head just goes and goes and goes. I really feel like I just—I just want to stop thinking. I get sick and tired of thinking, and so when I run out to go use, it just all goes away.

As she got deeper and deeper into speed, she often felt as if she couldn't get high enough, that every day she wanted to get higher than the day before. If she could get high enough, she thought, she could "get away from feelings." She told me that the feelings were mostly about "shame and guilt"—but she couldn't, at first, say what she was ashamed of. She felt sure that the feelings couldn't have anything to do with her family life, which she described as a suburban idyll: "My family's like wonderful. I had this big, beautiful home." Her background made her very different, she felt, from most of the other kids she knew who'd gotten heavily into drugs:

> Either the moms didn't care about them or they just—there's something wrong with everybody's families. Their parents split up. Something. Just something. But I'd look at my life, and it was fine, but I didn't care at the time. I was just like, screw my mom, screw my dad, you know?

A clue to that apparent paradox came later, some weeks after Tracy had gotten clean, when we talked about what it was that had drawn her so powerfully to the drug world—in spite of how dangerous and degrading it was and how "scummy" she found some of the people she had been involved with. She "glamorized" her drug-using past, she said, because she was "high up in the drug world." Now that she was clean and had started to move away from that world, she had lost a great deal: "Now I'm in the normal life, and I have nothing. I have no job. I know nobody, besides my family and the people I go to NA meetings with and stuff, and it's just like—what do I do? You know what I'm saying? Nobody's praising me anymore."

Her affluent background and her looks—she was tall, blond, and athletic—had made her a "star" in the drug world:

> When I was out there, people would look at me and say like, "What are *you* doing here?" You know what I'm saying? 'Cause I'm cute and stuff, and there's not a lot of nice-looking girls out there. At all, you know? They're all scummy looking and *old*, and I think it was the fame, the attention I got from the guys. I liked it because I got a lot of it. It wasn't good attention. They all wanted to get in my pants. But it was just the thought of it, you know?

Besides the fame and the praise, there was another, equally paradoxical emotional benefit of living in the drug world. When I asked Tracy if she hadn't been frightened to be living in a drug house, with police raids and strange things going on around her, people putting guns in her face, and all the rest of it, she said no, "I felt *safe*":

> I don't know—My head felt at ease, I guess, when I was there. I mean, not in a good way really, because I was still all messed up and stuff. . . . It got scary at points, it really did. I was mainly scared of people stealing from me and stuff. Paranoid. But I don't know. I felt more at ease. Where at my house, I'd be like antsy and just trippin' and moody, and just constantly frustrated. It was home, you know? It was home. And I could do whatever I want and say whatever I want . . . but I didn't feel at ease. I wasn't comfortable there.

So she was oddly at ease in one of the most dangerous and chaotic places she could possibly have encountered, while there was something about her parents' home, however solid and "beautiful" it may have been, that made her distinctly uncomfortable (recall Alyssa's comment that she couldn't feel "safe" at home, and Jenny's feeling safest when she was with the "worst of the worst"). Tracy's counterintuitive sense of emotional security in the midst of chaos and danger was linked to the distinct feeling of accomplishment she had gained after several months in the "using" life—a new sense of efficacy, an unfamiliar self-confidence:

> I felt scared, paranoid, because that's what the drugs do. But I did it good, you know? I guess I was scared inside because I never knew what could happen. But I made this face—that I could handle this shit. I may be this little girl that looks all innocent and cute and sweet. But I tried to make people think different. Like, "don't mess with me, I'll take your shit"–type thing, you know? I was trying to be a badass. I adapted to it very well.

It was as if she had taken a particularly difficult and challenging test and passed with flying colors.

Her newfound sense of competence contrasted sharply with how she'd felt when she was living at home. When we last talked, Tracy had been clean for several weeks—though she was no closer to being ready to go back to her parents—and she had a clearer sense of why she'd felt it necessary to leave home in the first place. "There's just something in there," she said, "that pushes me away from them":

> I didn't like myself, and I'm still trying to like myself. I think I had a lot of jealousy in me. I don't know where it came from. But I think a lot of it was my older sister. She had a full scholarship to state, 4.0 all her life. And I'm just like the younger one, so I can't really meet up to that. And never have. Never have. Dropped out of school when I was a freshman, you know?

It wasn't that she hadn't tried, at least until her freshman year:

> I was the MVP in soccer. I mean, I was in middle school, but I played tennis competitively. So it's like I did a lot. But I think a lot of that, my dad pressured me: "You gotta do this." He made me play tennis every day, every *day*, rather than just letting me grow up and be who I want to be. It's like you have to do it or else, you know, "you're not my daughter"–type thing.

She remembered her parents constantly "hounding" her about her performance in academics and competitive sports. But the message they gave her was confusing and undercutting. On the one hand, she had to be a standout in order to really be her father's daughter, but on the other, her parents let her know that she probably wouldn't be able to pull it off: "Like, 'You'll never be any good,' you know?" After a while, she says, "I got burned out of it. I stopped doing it for myself. I was just doing it to make him happy. It wasn't making *me* happy anymore."

Her father was himself an excellent athlete and a successful research physician in a medical school: "Golf, basketball, he's all into sports. He's like the macho man. He has a big ego. *Big*. Big temper, big ego. Very controlling man. Very." The kids were supposed to compete well and win in whatever they did. Even as a child, she felt that these expectations were unrealistic:

> I can't meet them. I was just like, *whoa* there. What I felt was good was never good enough, you know? And then when I was all in the drug world, it's like everything I did was good. And I was good at doing bad stuff, you know? Somebody was always like, "All right! That's good enough. That's fine. That'll do." You know, *everything* was good. It's like, "OK!"
>
> But nothing was good enough at home. That's a lot of it. Out there they accept anybody. They don't care who you are. You know? Who you are, as long as you're doing drugs or getting *them* drugs, helping them get drugs, letting them smoke your drugs. They'll accept you for anything.

Jumping headfirst into the drug life, then, was both empowering and comforting, partly because being high allowed her to "get rid of feelings" of failure and partly because the drug scene offered her the chance not only to do something well but to have her performance recognized—to show what she was made of in a different but undeniably challenging arena and before a more appreciative audience. Similar motives help explain why Tracy hooked up with an older drug dealer after she dropped out of school at fourteen. Looking back on the relationship, she said she didn't know what she was thinking. The boyfriend was "scummy" and exploitative and was heavily responsible for her becoming addicted to drugs. For a while, though, he allowed her to feel OK about herself:

> He got me sprung off him. To do anything for him. Made me think I was the world. Used me, really bad. I felt like him and the drugs were

the only things that made me OK. I didn't care if I got good grades. I figured he'd take care of me for the rest of my life.

Even when she agreed to enter drug treatment, her parents continued to let her know that they thought she was "doing it all wrong" and disappointing them. Tracy started using heavily again only a few weeks after leaving rehab; in response, her parents first stopped speaking to her and then threw her out of the house: "They said 'We love you. We can't take this no more. You're on your own.'" She was fifteen.

The result was to push Tracy back into the street drug life, since it was the only alternative she knew. And because she had so thoroughly absorbed her family's performance ethic, she now needed to prove to them (and to herself) that she could be "on her own," that she could handle being kicked out and left to her own resources, just as she needed to prove that she could handle heavy drugs and the drug lifestyle with the best of them. It became a matter of pride, a fundamental defense of her conception of herself as capable and, above all, not dependent—on her parents or anyone else:

> My parents always say that they're the only ones that are gonna be there, but then when I get mad at them, I say, "I don't care," and I guess it's like I try to show them I'm OK and I could be on my own. I just leave. Even though it's not the right way to do it. I just pack my bags.

———•———

Middle-class adolescents who go overboard into the worst kinds of self-destructive behavior, then, often come from families in which approval is both grudging and conditional. They are not praised for being "who they are," but only for doing well according to rigid norms of performance. Being unable—or perhaps unwilling—to perform well enough can lead to quick and definitive exclusion from the ranks of those who are truly "OK," as Tracy might have put it. Losing the sense of being "good enough" is often devastating for adolescents who have absorbed these values, and virtually impossible to live with for very long. So they are drawn to situations and companions that enable them to recoup a lost sense of competence and esteem in any way they can or, failing that, to stop caring about what others think of their performance or what they think about it themselves.

"There's Only a Short Period of Time Where I'm Perfect"

At the extreme, adolescents can become caught up in an exaggerated version of this quest for preeminence, in which they truly feel that they have to be better than everyone else in order to feel good about themselves. They have few emotional props to fall back on when the effort to be the best at everything inevitably fails, so they are set up from the start for a disastrous crisis of self-esteem.

Laurie was sixteen when she landed in a psychiatric hospital ward after overdosing on prescription drugs and cocaine. Her parents were self-employed businesspeople who had moved to the suburbs to get away from the congestion and crime of a large midwestern city. She had been a standout through grammar school and junior high, getting mostly straight As and participating in numerous sports and extracurricular activities. But by the time she was fifteen she was doing "huge amounts" of whatever drugs she could lay her hands on: "If I could classify myself as to what kind of an addict I was, I would say that I was a cokehead/crank/alcoholic/pill popper. You know, and doing anything else that came along."

How exactly she got to the hospital is, she says, "kind of a blur to me, because I was so strung out and fucked up." She remembers coming home early from school; she wasn't feeling well, she says, because "I had not gotten high all day and I wasn't coming down and I wasn't going up." She shut herself up in her room and took a lot of Xanax, along with many other things, including a great deal of cocaine:

And my mom and dad found me in the morning in my room and there was puke all over the place with lots of little pills, and I was talking to myself, talking to people who weren't there, and like seeing all sorts of shit. . . . You know, I was talking about people, and my friends being over—I was just totally psychotic.

She stayed in the hospital for several weeks. "I was hallucinating for a long time," she says. "I just remember looking up and seeing blood dripping from the ceiling, and just absolutely weird shit."

This was the first time she'd ever landed in a hospital but by no means the first time she'd overdosed—on pills, alcohol, cocaine, or some combination. Before, she had always managed to get through these crises on her own or with the help of friends. She hadn't been afraid at these times. In fact, she had felt a certain excitement, even comfort, in being on the edge of disaster:

> I liked being out of control. I didn't want to stop being out of control. I liked living my life like that. I liked living on the edge and getting into situations, and seeing how many drugs I could do was always fun for me. I'd do 'shrooms in the morning, and I could do a bunch of crank later, and then when I'm finally ready to go to sleep, I'll drop some Valium.

She had felt vaguely suicidal many times, and by the second year of high school had reached the point where, she says, "I didn't care if I woke up the next day or not." She didn't think that she was making a conscious effort to die; it was more that it mattered little to her one way or another: "If I do, I do." She told me that if she had been seriously trying to kill herself, she would have tried harder, because doing it halfway was extremely unpleasant: " 'Cause I wouldn't want to have to go through all that and then still be alive, you know. Fuck that." But she was more than willing to tolerate feeling desperately ill, as well as the possibility that her drug use would cause long-term damage. "I *liked* being strung out," she told me. "Kind of weird. I don't know what it was about it. I *like* to feel like shit for some reason":

> I used to self-mutilate all the time. I bashed myself emotionally and physically all the time.... That kind of depressed, self-destructive stuff, I liked it in a weird way. Not because I wanted people to give me attention for it. Just because I—I grew to not like myself, so I kind of did it on purpose. I knew that it was really really not good for me and my body to be doing all these drugs, but I liked the way it made me feel and I liked being in my own little dark hole, you know. Where it was like, nobody could come in, and this is my world.

It had been a dramatic journey from being the most popular kid in junior high school to finding pleasure in being so strung out that she "felt like shit" on a regular basis. When I first asked Laurie why she thought that had happened—why she had come to not like herself—she said that she was at a loss to understand it: "I used to ask myself why. But I don't fuckin' know." But as we talked more over the course of a year, the reasons became much clearer.

The change had come toward the end of her first year of high school:

> I started not caring about things when I was in my freshman year. I wasn't really conscious of it. And finally I just said fuck it, because I'd lost so many things, you know, let go of so many things, I was just like, fuck it. I'm not going to try to get any of my old friends back. I didn't care. I'm not gonna try to do well in school. I didn't care.

She went from caring too much about too many things to not caring at all, and the shift was in many ways a relief:

> 'Cause my freshman year I did it all. I went to all the games, I went to all the dances. Dated all the seniors, played all the sports, took all the hard classes, got all the good grades. Most loudest girl at the high school party on the weekends. But I don't know. I think I just got so sick of it. 'Cause for a long time I was just—when I look back on it, I just realize that so many people wanted a piece of me.

She began using drugs initially because she thought they would help her in the quest to "do it all." The first drug she seriously abused was over-the-counter caffeine pills:

> I was in all these really hard classes and I was finding that I didn't have time to do my homework, because I'd get home at six after—because I had soccer practice every day after school. And I started taking them and I'd stay up. . . . I took like two every hour just to be able to function, you know, hold my head up.

From the caffeine pills, it was only a short step to cocaine, because it accomplished the same thing, only more so. Switching to cocaine, of course, upped the ante considerably: "By the end of three days doing constant coke intake, physically you'll be so fucked up that you'll overdose . . . 'cause for me it was all day long, and all night long and all day long and all night long again. And after three days I'd get so sick."

When I asked what would have happened to her if she *had* gone to sleep—why she felt such an urgent need to stay awake—she explained that she had to "get some stuff done." She was "quite the perfectionist," she said: in addition to staying up to do her schoolwork, she exercised at night, too, which helped her stay awake and focused. She also needed to be wide awake early so she could start what became an increasingly elaborate process of getting ready for school. It was "easier to get *no* sleep than to get three hours, two hours of sleep, you know, and then have to get up in the morning. I'd start getting ready for school at five-thirty. I'd get all pretty, do my makeup perfectly, you know. I always wanted to look perfect." I asked whom she was trying to be perfect *for*:

> For everybody. Well, and to be the skinniest. I was the most popular freshman girl, the best in soccer, turned in the best reports. I wanted to look the cutest, and I cared a lot about what other people thought, and also I just wanted to be better than everybody else. And I was, for

a while. But God, it was hard to maintain. . . . I can't maintain it. I just keep going and going and going to the point where it's not perfect anymore, you know. So there's only a short period of time where I am perfect.

It wasn't tolerable for Laurie to feel just normal, to be a person with some terrific qualities and some that were not so remarkable. It wasn't possible to accept ordinary limitations. It was all or nothing, and when she couldn't maintain the impossibly high standards she had set for herself, she found solace in turning the standards upside down. If she couldn't be consistently perfect, she could at least be perfectly awful. When I last talked with Laurie she had been out of the hospital for more than a year. She had been off drugs for several months, except for an occasional relapse with the caffeine pills, and was back in school. But it was hard for her to shake the burden of wanting to be better than everybody else: she'd overloaded herself with too many classes and was already feeling stressed out. She was still occasionally plagued by the feeling of "not wanting to be in the real world and not wanting to have to think, because the real world can suck sometimes, you know?" She felt that she hadn't yet found a happy medium—an equilibrium somewhere between trying to be perfect and wanting to throw it all out the window:

> It's what I've been trying to do for a really long time. But I'm still look-ing for it. Still trying to train myself, because what happens is, I try to be that perfectionist, and I get there, and then it takes me the other way, because I try hard to do that and then I get done, and it just happens. Like even with school, I overload myself so that I almost set myself up for failure . . . but you don't have to live like that.

"I Was Here, I Was Alive"

Lacey's experience illuminates the problem of contingent worth from another angle. As we've seen, even when she'd been generally adrift and confused as a teenager, she had always been able to pull herself back if things got too dangerous. Even when everyone around her had lost control, she "would be thinking and reflecting about what this would mean over time." Looking back on those years, she thought that one reason she was able to keep from going over the edge was that she had never been consumed by the feelings of failure that engulfed many others in her circle: "Me, I was sort of like, well, I don't know who I am, I don't know *what* I am. I'm still *whatever.* . . . I didn't feel like I was complete. I didn't hate myself."

Not feeling "complete" meant seeing herself as not having exhausted her possibilities, as having fallen short of what was expected of her. She regarded herself as a work in progress. Since childhood, she had thought of her life as a "mission," a "sort of journey that I was on," rather than a ladder that she had to climb. She attributed her attitude partly to her mother, who had instilled in her a sense "that I had some value that wasn't related to what I did statuswise. It was more just intrinsic. Like I was here, I was alive, I could speak. I could care for things, people." She had also had a very different, and much rougher, childhood than most of her upper-middle-class friends: she'd been raised in a series of foster homes and shifted from one placement to another for years before her mother adopted her. Although she spent her adolescence in the heart of the upper middle class, she hadn't started there and wasn't burdened by its often overwhelming standards:

> There was very little put out for me, because I was considered a failure anyway. Growing up in foster care, I didn't have parents constantly telling me what I was going to be and what I was going to do. I believed I had value in who I was, but I didn't necessarily believe I had value in terms of, like, my intelligence or what I was going to become.

As we'll see, that feeling of being fundamentally worthwhile simply because of "who I was" is often crucial in helping troubled adolescents take hold of their lives and recast their futures, in enabling them to care more about what happens to them and to take themselves more seriously. Lacey contrasts her experience with that of one of her high school friends who "spiraled really bad":

> Her parents had intensive expectations of her. She was supposed to be this big achiever and blah blah blah, and that had a huge impact on her. And so her coke abuse was just one way she felt—I don't know—special, different, and also probably a way to undermine her parents. She ended up finally graduating, but she just turned into a very weird, nasty person later.

Her friend's reliance on cocaine to feel "special" or "different" illustrates a phenomenon that appears again and again among troubled mainstream teenagers. One measure of the grip of the cultural emphasis on being the "best" is that when middle-class youth cross the line into being seriously "bad," they typically want to be the *best* at being bad. They want to stand out. If they drink, they want to be able—like Alyssa or Laurie—to drink everyone else under the table. If they do hard drugs, they want to be known as the one who can do the most lines on Friday night and still get up for soccer practice on Saturday. And if their thing is to race cars on suburban streets at night with the lights off, they want, of course, to win the race—every time. Having grown up in a culture that penalizes not only the real failures but often the merely ordinary as well, they can stand being practically anything—including being viewed as *very* bad apples—more than they can stand being seen as nobody or not being seen at all. And the fact that it is not easy to win in this kind of contest either is one of the most dangerous aspects of the culture of middle-class deviance because it can spur adolescents on to ever higher levels of risk. "My ability to be self-destructive probably equals my ability to be driven," Lacey says. "I can be driven in a self-destructive way and really get the job done!" The trick to getting one's life straight is "to flip that into something else"—to turn the "driven" quality back toward some kind of productive purpose. Laurie felt the same way: "I've always been an overachiever. Lately I've been overachieving in a negative way and not positive ways. I could always drink more than any other people. I'm kind of competitive." Once she had rejected the conventional avenues of achievement, she was determined to excel in illegal ones, and she took up the challenge of doing more drugs than everyone else with typical enthusiasm.

B.J., another sixteen-year-old cheerleader and honor student who began carving herself in her sophomore year of high school and simultaneously became badly strung out on drugs, also exemplifies that competitive drive to succeed at being the baddest of the bad. She told me that she had always felt like a nonentity, both in her family and at school. At home, she was "the little whatever child," the one who couldn't boast of being anything in particular:

There was nothing significant about me. Like everybody in my family, all the kids did sports, so there was nothing special about that. Me and my sister were both girl scouts. There was nothing special about *that*. You know? I was a cheerleader, but that was the only glory I had, that was the only thing different about me. But even then I just got complained at for how much money it cost.

My brother was a big star in baseball. He was a really good ballplayer. And he's very intelligent . . . and they didn't have a school smart enough for him. They didn't have any teachers that could teach him, 'cause he was so smart. . . . Every swim meet, everything, he's got records. . . . So if I wasn't something else, I would never feel like I was anything in that family.

Cheerleading helped, but not enough:

I became cool 'cause, *boom*, that's like instant popularity, man. But other than that, there was nothing coming my way. And I guess I just have to feel like I mean something to be somewhere. That's just how I am. Because if I'm not doing something for this place, I'm out.

Quite consciously, she went out of her way to achieve some version of "glory" by being more spectacularly "out there" than anyone else she knew: "If I was gonna drink, I was gonna *drink*. I was gonna smoke everybody under the table. I was gonna pop three more pills than everybody there. And I was going to be able to handle it, too."

"The Middle Doesn't Take You to Heaven": The Intolerance of Transgression

A closely related theme in the lives of troubled middle-class adolescents is the cultural narrowing of the boundaries of morally acceptable behavior. Just as they are subjected to rigid standards of *performance* that make it easy to fail in the struggle for esteem and self-respect, so too they often confront rigid *moral* standards that make it easy to cross over into the ranks of the bad, the flawed, or the sinful. The culture they grow up in is one in which people are quickly and sharply defined as either "in" or "out." There is little tolerance for legitimate mistakes (or even a concept of "legitimate" mistakes), or occasional moral stumbling.

This worldview is reflected in a variety of American social policies that are distinguished from those of other advanced societies by a sort of totalizing moralism that excludes the possibility of a middle ground. In drug policy, we have strenuously resisted many of the so-called harm-reduction strategies that are now standard practice in Europe, like needle exchanges and the decriminalization of minor drug use, because they appear to express tolerance of drug use. Our approach to teenage sexuality is to demand abstinence, where other countries have opted to provide extensive sex education and readily available birth control, because we think that sexuality itself is the problem and we do not want to appear to encourage it by making it less risky. Where many other countries carefully differentiate between more and less serious versions of deviance, and treat them in different ways, we tend to lump them together and to approach them as if they were equally pernicious.

This rather Manichean attitude creates special difficulties for adolescents because they are at a stage of life when making mistakes, doing fairly stupid things, and stumbling at least a little are virtually inevitable and may indeed be necessary for them to develop a firm sense of who they are. So the tendency to quickly define people as beyond the pale if they slip up or break the rules is another way of setting teenagers up for failure, and it can produce a series of escalating consequences. To the degree that they internalize a sharp division of "good kids" from "bad kids," adolescents who begin to get into *some* trouble may soon come to define themselves as definitively, and perhaps irrevocably, on the wrong side of the moral ledger. And having defined themselves this way, they may begin to despair of ever being anything else and to feel that anything goes: since they are already over the line, they conclude that what they do now can't matter very much. Farther along that road, they may begin to work up a full-scale negative identity, with its own inverted standards—and they may try to live up to those standards with a vengeance. They move from being barely distinguishable from other teenagers who sometimes do dumb things to being people whose lives revolve around the situations and relationships that come with being truly bad.

The tendency to define acceptable behavior both narrowly and rigidly is rooted in religious traditions that have always been prominent in America but have spread with the rise of religious conservatism. Roughly two-thirds of American teenagers say that religion is "very" or at least "pretty" important to them; almost two in five eighth graders describe their religious affiliation as "conservative." Great numbers of middle-class adolescents are brought up in highly religious (and often fundamentalist) families and communities, and it is difficult to understand the contours of adolescent "trouble" today without taking that context into account. Even those who are not explicitly religious are surrounded by secular versions of the same intolerance toward deviance.

B.J., whom I introduced in the last section, lived with her mother, a brother, and two sisters in an affluent but troubled suburb with a reputation for drugs, teen pregnancy, and gang violence. She had a relatively uneventful childhood and, until she hit high school, was—like Alyssa and Laurie—the image of an all-American teenager: an honor student, an athlete who went out for several sports, a regular churchgoer. But in her second year of high school she fell very fast and very hard, eagerly trying every drug that anyone gave her. She spent much of her leisure time at raves, where she often got so "out of it" that she was taken advantage of sexually, sometimes by much older men. She also began carving her arms and legs routinely and at one point, in despair, tried to kill herself.

B.J.'s family had struggled with alcohol abuse for generations. Her parents divorced over her father's drinking when she was in junior high school, and shortly thereafter her mother became a born-again Christian. "I wouldn't say she converted, but she gave her heart to God, or whatever." Impressed by her mother's "awesome" transformation, B.J. soon followed her into the church. But not long after her conversion, there was "a big fat change":

> When I hit sophomore year in high school I was like, "I'm tired of being good." 'Cause I was going to church every Sunday, and for a whole year I was Jesus freak B.J., you know? Like I loved God, and after that, sophomore year hit, and I was "Get down and party!" I was a cheerleader in high school. I was blond. I was cute. I wouldn't have a boyfriend because I didn't think it was right in the Bible, you know, to have a boyfriend. And that sucked, man. I mean, you gotta put up with a lot of stuff.
>
> So I was like, "You know what? Screw this whole Jesus thing. I want to go have fun. I can use what I have to my advantage." And I did.

The Christian life was difficult from the start and grew increasingly so. It wasn't just the boyfriend issue but the overall narrowness of the life that B.J.'s version of "loving God" imposed on her. Over time, she developed what she called "a resentment against God":

The Jesus church I was going to was like holy and perfect, and I was trying so hard to live the life that I thought God wanted me to live. I wouldn't use a cuss word. I wouldn't take the Lord's name in vain. I was being honest with myself and other people. I was like true in my heart. And I was looking at all these other people, and they looked so much more happy than I am. And it looked like it was so much easier to do what they were doing. You know? And so I decided to switch friends a little bit, to see what it's like, and pretty soon I'm like, "Yeah, this is *much* better than trying so hard." Why not just sin? Why not just *do* all this? And eventually it's like, why do the God thing at all?

And after a while, drugs became a priority, and it's like, well, no more cheerleading, no more sports, let's just do drugs! Let's just rave!

B.J. continued, however, to view the world through the same moral lens as before: she had simply switched sides. At one point I told her that it seemed to me that her strict interpretation of what God wanted created an either/or approach to behavior that would be very hard to live with. B.J. agreed but insisted that it was nevertheless the right way to think about life:

And I still think that way. Like it's either good or it's bad. You gotta choose one or the other. If I'm gonna stop using, it's not gonna do me any good with God if I *just* stop using. I can't just stop in my tracks. I gotta turn around and go the other way. I gotta fix things.

Fix things. Fix what?

All the stuff I screwed up. I was living this really great life, and then all of a sudden I just went *vrrroom*, and I just went straight downhill. And now I gotta walk back up the hill to where I was, like in my life with God and my relationship with my family, how good I was in school, all the things I was accomplishing. I gotta get back up there, and then go on. And that's gonna take *forever* to do.

The thought of it's "taking forever" to get back to where she was acceptable in God's sight seemed extraordinarily daunting, especially at sixteen. I said it sounded like she felt she'd have to be almost perfect in the eyes of God in order to feel OK about herself. Wouldn't it be all right to be kind of in the middle? Her response was quick: "The middle doesn't take you to heaven, though. There's no middle ground. It's yes or no."

But wouldn't this mean that only a few people would ever get to heaven, since most people are more or less in the middle?

Yeah, most people that are in the middle, I don't think are going to heaven now. I don't know. I just think if you're gonna do it, you're gonna do it. If you want to live in God's heaven, you're gonna do what God wants. You're not gonna compromise like, well, "We could only go to church on holidays or something." He made you, you know? If you're gonna live in his heaven, you'd better do what he wants.

B.J. said that while you didn't necessarily have to be perfect to get to heaven, "your heart has to be in the right place." I responded that I thought your heart could be in the right place and you could still acknowledge that making some mistakes was only human. I said I thought there was a danger in being too hard on yourself, too intolerant of your failings: you might conclude that, since you were already a sinner, you might as well just sin all the time. Her reply was again quick and forceful:

Well, you *should* feel that way, though. If you fuck up, you should feel bad about fucking up, and you should repent. Like, one sin is as bad as all of them. So you lie, you've like murdered someone in your heart. I don't know. I think that sinning *is* a big deal. I think that if people took their love of God seriously, they wouldn't sin as much. You can make mistakes. But it's all about where your heart's at, and if your heart really is where it should be, then sin's not gonna pop up every five minutes. Like it does for me. It just would not.

If "one sin is as bad as all of them," relatively minor transgressions can force the adolescent to adopt a new and decidedly negative identity. At the time I met her, B.J. had done this with a vengeance. She had clearly defined herself as a "bad girl" and now fully expected to do all the things bad girls did—heavy drugs, risky and degrading sex, cutting themselves, hanging out with new and equally bad friends. There is a classically Calvinist quality to this outlook: sinning at all seriously or often is a sign that your heart isn't in the right place, for how could you sin so badly if it were? And once you're given that sign, there are no more limits, nothing to keep you from falling all the way. The psychological distance between caring too much about conforming to narrow imperatives of behavior and not caring at all is very short; and that helps explain why many middle-class teenagers go so completely overboard once they begin to stray from the path at all.

In America it is common to hear that teenagers make "bad choices" because they are not brought up to understand the difference between right and wrong or made to suffer the consequences of bad behavior. But as B.J.'s account suggests, the problem is often the opposite—not misguided tolerance but the unforgiving rigidity of a cultural outlook that permits few shades of gray. It's noteworthy that when I next spoke with B.J., about a year later, she had begun to take control of her life and was feeling generally good about herself: she was no longer using, no longer letting men take advantage of her, and beginning to think seriously about finishing high school and going on to college. It seemed clear that one of the things that was making this turn possible was that she had begun to abandon her earlier "yes or no" approach to life. She had come to accept the idea that she was only human and that staying clean was "really hard." She seemed less tormented by the thought that having done drugs and had sex made her intrinsically sinful, and less inclined to kick over the traces altogether as a result. She had apparently begun, at seventeen, to define herself as someone who was capable of both making mistakes and doing important and worthy things in the future. As we will see, this process of redefining oneself from being inherently sinful or flawed to being simply human and perhaps not so bad after all appears again and again among adolescents who manage to turn troubled lives around.

B.J.'s version of this narrowly judgmental worldview was explicitly Protestant; many adolescents encounter a secular variant of the same outlook. The blurring of distinctions between minor and major problems, for example, suffuses the literature of the parents' rights movement and of the burgeoning for-profit adolescent treatment industry as well. The Tough Love organization, for example, offers a "Crisis Assessment" test that lists various problem behaviors at home, at school, and with the law and asks parents to check off those that their teenager has exhibited. Parents are told that if they check two behaviors in the "home" category, two in the "school" category, and one "legal" problem, "Your crisis is building." But the home category includes everything from coming home late or missing dinner to being drunk and not coming home at all. The school category includes both "being tardy" and being suspended, while problems with the law range from getting a parking ticket to being arrested. Thus it is possible to conclude that a "crisis is building" on the basis of incidents that may be nothing more than predictable adolescent lapses, and there is no line separating those lapses from serious delinquency. An organization called Teens in Crisis Inc., similarly, offers to help refer stressed parents to facilities for teenagers "that need 24/7 supervision" for a variety of problems: "drug abuse, depression, defiant, failing school, ran away from home, motivation, self-esteem issues, adoption issues etc." It is not made clear why problems with "motivation" or "adoption issues" would require 24/7 supervision or why they would be considered on the same level as serious drug abuse or depression. But similar pitches are a common feature of advertisements touting "boarding schools" or "behavior modification" facilities for what are frequently described as "struggling" or "problem" teens.

As with the explicitly religious attitude that one sin is as bad as another, the problem with this mentality is that lumping minor lapses or routine issues together with major problems may lead the offending adolescent to conclude that he or she might as well do something really serious, since doing the little stuff brings such heavy consequences. Rick, for example, remembers that his parents treated less than stellar grades or body piercing as seriously as they did his habitual heavy drinking. "Actually, now that I think about it, I might have gotten in trouble *more* for getting pierced than for showing up drunk every night when I'd come home":

> I mean I obviously gave them enough reasons to be angry with me once I started getting in trouble. I never really denied that a good half of that was my fault. They'd tell me, "Don't go out and get drunk," and I'd do it the next night anyway. Don't go out and get this pierce, and I'd do it anyway. But I mean they told me don't do *everything*, so I'd just pick and choose from stuff.

As a result of Rick's parents' tendency to treat his infractions as all of a piece, the distinction between small transgressions and big ones began to blur in his mind as well. It was as if there was no gradation, no scale of moral priorities. If he was going to be hanged anyway, he might as well be hanged for a sheep as a goat: "You know, the line— I was going to cross it anyway with everything I did. I might as well just disregard it." But coming to disregard that line so completely meant there was nothing to stop his slide into even more serious drinking.

Another, more subtle consequence was that after a while the indiscriminate quality of his parents' response undermined their credibility. Rick came to view his parents' excessively rigid reactions as both demeaning and a little silly, and he began to disengage from them altogether, to not care about what they thought and to discount what they had to say about almost everything. He was appalled, for example, that his father's response to his drinking was not to sit him down to talk about what was wrong but to test him for drugs night after night when he came in the door drunk: "I mean I would come in and like fall down, and it was quite obvious to anyone. . . . I wasn't going to deny it, but they still wanted proof. . . . I've had friends of mine tell me that it really makes no sense, you know, using a drug test to parent me."

Once they arrive at the point of disregarding their parents' norms for behavior, adolescents must either create new standards of their own or live without clear standards altogether. Unless there are other adults in their lives who are respected in a way their parents no longer are, they are likely to learn how to deal with issues like drugs, drinking, and sex largely through painful experience. What guidance they receive comes mainly from siblings or friends who have been through it all themselves. "I think that's pretty much how I went about things is trial and error," Rick says. The danger, of course, is that learning about the consequences of binge drinking or "slamming" heroin through experience alone can be a ticket to disaster.

The Punitive Reflex and the Rejection of Nurturance

All societies must draw lines that define the boundaries of the acceptable. But there is a strain of American culture that is remarkably intolerant of what we might call "normal deviance"—of routine mistakes of judgment and minor moral lapses. Since those are such an inevitable (and perhaps even necessary) part of growing up, it is perilously easy for adolescents to become defined as beyond the pale, and once that happens, it is highly likely that many of them will accept that definition and begin to behave accordingly. They may feel that they've "blown it" irrevocably, that it will be difficult, if not impossible, for them to regain a more positive identity in the eyes of those around them—or in their own. This breeds the sense of care-lessness I've described, crippling their self-esteem, blurring the distinction in their own mind between actions that are really dangerous or destructive and those that are merely frowned on, and encouraging them to feel that nothing they do matters much because they are already lost.

These effects are compounded by the peculiarly punitive and rejecting sanctions that middle-class parents often invoke when their children begin to cross the line into serious trouble. Again and again, troubled adolescents describe their parents as both quick to find things wrong and quick to inflict punishment when they do. But not just any kind of punishment. What is remarkable about the discipline they impose is that it so often involves systematic exclusion and the withholding of assistance. These parents respond to their children's problems not by making extra efforts to pull them more closely into the orbit of the family but by pushing them out of it—and simultaneously denying them emotional and practical support, sometimes even the most basic kinds. At the extreme, they are essentially read out of the family altogether.

Sometimes this is the result of sheer desperation, the reaction of parents who are simply overwhelmed and cannot think of anything else to do with a troublesome son or daughter. But for many parents, something more is involved. Their response reflects a deep ideological current in which exclusion and the withdrawal of support are regarded as not only acceptable but laudable ways of dealing with those who fail or who break the rules. That moral outlook influences much more than the way parents deal with troublesome teenagers: it shapes how we characteristically deal, as a society, with people whom we find problematic. Whether it is the welfare poor, petty criminals, drug users, or the mentally ill, our dominant response has been to cut the offending individual off from participation in the legitimate institutions that define who "we" are—to impose and enforce a sharp distinction between "us" and "them." It would be difficult to overstate how profoundly this mentality shaped the lives of the adolescents in this book. Repeatedly, the chief response—indeed sometimes virtually the only response—of parents, school authorities, and others in the adult world to their mistakes and "bad choices" was to send them away, always figuratively and often literally. But this strategy exacerbates the problems it is ostensibly designed to correct, in mutually reinforcing ways. Some of them involve changes in the adolescent's self-conception; others involve the structural changes in their lives once they are pushed out of the family orbit—changes in whom they hang out with and where, in the opportunities that close to them and those that perilously open.

"She Just Got Sick of It"

One of the most striking commonalities among the adolescents I spoke with was how often their parents resorted to simply throwing them out of their home when things became difficult. Sometimes, as I've suggested, the parents could think of nothing else to do, and their incapacity was compounded because they usually had little outside help to call on. When Danny began to spin out of control after his parents divorced, his mother, who was working extra hours to pay the bills, "just got sick of it" and began routinely calling the police, "like twenty-something times in two years." It wasn't, he says, so much about his drug use as "about fighting and arguing and shit." He acknowledges that he was hard to handle, but he was still hurt and bewildered by his mother's response. He felt she had little patience for working with him on the issues in his life or even talking to him about what was wrong: "I love her. She's my mom. I needed to respect her more, but honestly, I think she does need to respect *me* more if I'm gonna respect *her*. I did do some fucked-up shit, but I think my mom needs to change some, too."

Since he was a small child, Danny says, he had gotten the message that he was a screwup and an endless source of hassle for his parents. The family lived in a fairly affluent suburb made up of row after row of freshly built middle-class developments, but after the divorce Danny's mother was always pinched economically and Danny began to feel increasingly like an outsider in his neighborhood. By thirteen he was talking and dressing like a kid from the ghetto; he wore baggy pants that were falling off his rear end and spoke an exaggerated version of rap lingo that could be difficult for the uninitiated to understand: "It was hard because she didn't give me no respect, you know? All I'd ever hear in my whole life was I was a piece of shit and mmm, 'Fuck you, you fuckin' asshole, get out the fuckin' house,' you know, 'you're on the streets now.'"

His mother was perennially frustrated by the fact that when she called the police they usually told her politely that they couldn't legally take Danny off her hands unless he'd actually committed a crime: "Every time the police would come down, she'd be like, 'Take him to juvenile hall.' And they'd be like, 'Well, he has to commit a crime for us to lock him up, you know, we can't just lock the kid up.' And she was like, 'He's incorrigible, woo woo woo.' And I was like, 'This is fuckin' bullshit.'" She threw Danny out of the house for the first time when he had just turned fifteen. After that, "for two years it's been off and on like that, you know, boom, you're out, boom back in, boom, you're out, boom, back in":

We'd get in an argument. "Well, fuck you." "Well, fuck *you*. What the hell you're gonna tell me fuck *me*, when I didn't even do shit?" "You always flash on me. It's my sisters be doing shit wrong, and you don't do a damn thing, but I do one thing wrong, and you flash on me like *that*." "Well, get the fuck out." "Well, fine then, fuck you." And I'd walk out the door, and I'd be gone for a week.

Danny spent his sixteenth birthday alone in a motel room drinking beer. He'd come home late the night before—sober, he insists—and had gotten into another argument with his mother, who told him once again to get out:

> I was like, "Dude, whatever. It was a great sixteenth birthday. I'll talk to you later." And then I went to the motel room, I got a six-pack, and I got drunk, and I just picked up the phone and I started calling everybody, like "What's up, dude? It's my sixteenth fuckin' birthday right now, you know, it's twelve o'clock. Sixteen, and I'm in a motel room."
>
> I was like, any other fucking birthday . . . but I thought, this is my *sixteenth*, man—it's supposed to be cool, you know?

Danny's mother was clearly at the end of her rope. Other parents, by contrast, throw their children out of the house not because they are desperate but because they no longer want to be bothered by what they regard as the undue amount of trouble and hassle the child is causing them. That seemed the case with Dale's parents, who were fed up with his inability to "deal with his mental illness." It was also true for the parents of a sixteen-year-old I will call Stephanie, who when I first spoke with her had recently been released from emergency hospital care. She had nearly died after some of her friends accidentally overdosed her on heroin, along with other drugs that she couldn't even identify. She was still showing the effects of the overdose, speaking with considerable difficulty and often "zoning out" of our conversation altogether. Before the incident, she had lived mostly with her father in his tidy suburban neighborhood but now didn't know exactly where she'd be living, because, she said, her dad no longer wanted to put up with her:

> He just kind of says he's not sure if he wants me to live at home after I get out of here, because he feels like there's crisis after crisis with me living at his house and I'm causing him to waste his time, and it'd be easier if he could just like send me to a boarding school or something.

Her father, a busy professional, had also recently acquired a new girlfriend, and neither of them wanted to be with Stephanie much: "It's pretty funny, but when I was at his house . . . my cat would spend more time around me than my dad. Well, that's not really that funny because I can't like *talk* to it." In theory, she could have gone to live with her mother in another part of town, but they weren't getting along well and, in any case, she had periodically been thrown out of that house as well. The first time was when she was thirteen and had come home late after staying out with friends. There had been a bad argument, and finally her mother had said, "Well, there's the door. You can just leave." So she did, and stayed away for several weeks.

Now, not feeling welcome at either house, Stephanie wound up, after leaving the hospital, living for several months on the streets of a large and dangerous city. Her mother, she believes, did try to find her during this time; her father did not. She mostly liked being on the street, partying heavily and enjoying the freedom to do practically anything she wanted without having to be accountable to anyone. But there was a downside:

> Most of the time I had a good time, but there's been some experiences I didn't like. . . . I've gotten really drunk, where I felt I was gonna pass out and get sick. And I've been raped . . . like twice. That was just, you know, times when I'm really messed up. It just like sucks.

For some teenagers, getting thrown out of the house is the culmination of a long process in which parents oscillate between stubbornly denying that anything is wrong and lashing out when the denial can no longer be sustained. Not knowing how to react to early signs of trouble and typically having too little rapport with the adolescent to talk things out and arrive at more constructive solutions, parents look the other way for as long as they can, often allowing troubles to fester and deepen, before booting the child out in exasperation.

That is how B.J.'s parents responded when she began doing drugs heavily. She says she was never really able to talk to her mother about what was troubling her: "If I talked to anybody, it would be my friends, because I'm really close to my friends rather than my family." Nevertheless, she and her mother got along "really well" as long as B.J. was going to church; after that, things started to "go downhill" and soon "all my trust just went down the drain":

> At first she was like, "OK, she doesn't want to do the God thing. That's fine." But then she realized the difference in my behavior. Difference in my friends. And she just kind of went through this whole denial thing. I was using for a year and a half and she actually put her foot down and said, "You're using, and this is gonna stop." It was like, dude! You know, it took her long enough.
>
> She went into fat denial. She went into major denial. . . . She just majorly denied everything. I mean, I came home loaded so many times. And I came home coming down. And she had been around drug addicts her whole life. She knows what it's like when you're using. She saw behavior changes. She found drugs in my purse. And she's like—"It's just a teenager thing, it's gonna pass, this is not a big deal." You know, I'm using hella drugs and she tries to let it slide.

B.J. went into drug rehab for a few weeks but started using again even before she left the program. Yet her mother continued to persuade herself that nothing was the matter: "She did the denial thing again. Like, 'No, no, I'm just imagining it.' She *didn't* smell like pot when she came home. Her eyes were *not* dilated.' You know?" When further denial became impossible, her mother kicked her out of the house for the weekend:

> And this was right when the whole acid thing was happening. I was doing acid a lot, and I was doing lots of drugs again, and she finally said, "You know what? This is gonna stop." And I went out the next night and just friggin'—I don't even remember what drugs I did. I did every type of drugs. And I came home the next morning, and she's like, "Get out of my house. I don't want to see you until Monday when your plane

leaves." And I was like, "My *plane* leaves?" And she was like, "To Indiana." My aunt lives in Indiana.

It was Saturday, and she said, "I don't want to see you until Monday." So I just got back in my friend's car and we bounced. . . . I came back on Monday, like at 12:00, and my mom wasn't there. And so I didn't even say good-bye to her. But that weekend I just went out and partied basically, and then I went to Indiana, and then after I came back, my mom just acted like nothing happened, until I came home really loaded one night.

From a pragmatic viewpoint, the logic behind this response on the part of parents is difficult to grasp. Presumably, the reason they are angry in the first place is that their children have caused them worry and anguish by putting themselves at risk. Why then would they deliberately expose their children to precisely the conditions that put them at risk to begin with by forcing them out of the home? Yet this happens routinely among middle-class parents in America. A recent survey by Murray A. Straus and Carolyn J. Field of the Family Research Laboratory at the University of New Hampshire discovered that nearly one parent in five had threatened to throw a teenaged child out of the house during the previous year alone. Those who had done so averaged four such threats a year. Straus and Field found that this and other forms of what they call "psychological aggression" were most common among parents in the middle of the income scale.

What explains the use of what would appear to be transparently self-defeating strategies is that, for many parents, deeper cultural imperatives frequently trump more practical considerations about their children's welfare. The almost reflexive tendency to respond to their children's troubles by kicking them out reflects a broader worldview in which a deliberate and calculated distancing in response to deviance plays a central role. Throwing their children out of the house is not just a relinquishing of responsibility. It is an expression of an intensely punitive view of human behavior in which pushing people away in times of trouble or need is regarded not only as necessary but as deserved, one facet of a moral vision in which anything resembling "softness" toward those who deviate—even one's own children, or perhaps especially one's own children—is seen as both wrong and ultimately counterproductive.

Unlike parents who, like Jenny's, have essentially collapsed and abandoned their role as guardians altogether, those who adopt these self-conscious strategies of punishment and exclusion may be quite functional in the outside world. But they are equally willing to sever connections with children who stray beyond certain boundaries. That readiness to abandon children when things go wrong is, curiously, often combined with a profoundly controlling approach to parenting. They may monitor their children's behavior closely—even intrusively—on a day-to-day basis. On the surface, this may resemble a laudable degree of concern and engagement. But these parents are perpetually on the lookout for signs of trouble and are startlingly quick to wash their hands of responsibility for their children if they find it. And this stance can contribute to adolescents' descent into deeper trouble in several ways.

When I met Sean, he was close to graduating from college after having spent more than two years in prison for nearly killing another teenager in a brawl. He grew up in a deteriorating suburban neighborhood that was beginning to suffer from gang problems and a flourishing drug culture. A self-described punk rocker and high school outcast, he had pulled a gun when he and a friend were confronted, as happened often in his milieu, by a group of hostile "jocks"; when it was all over, one of the jocks lay bleeding on the street and Sean was charged with attempted murder.

Sean told me that what he called the "long road" to youth prison had begun in his family. His mother in particular, he says, "had this constant thing of finding problems in her children." Her response to any sign of trouble was to adopt a sort of hypervigilance and to rush to medicate him whenever he seemed not to be performing to expectations:

> She was always just incredibly involved, so if I wasn't getting straight As, it meant that I needed to be on Ritalin and all this stuff, so first, second grade, maybe third grade I was on Ritalin. I mean I was in therapy or on some kind of medication or undergoing this or that test, or put on whatever the latest New Age diet was since I could walk.

Sean's parents divorced when he was in elementary school, and he spent several years bouncing from one parent's house to the other. He was always somewhat disaffected and felt like a bit of a misfit once he hit junior high school, but he didn't, at first, get into serious trouble and he felt not that different from other mildly alienated kids in the suburb where he lived. But in high school, his life started to spiral downward. When he was fifteen, he wound up living in a car on the street:

> I had gotten in some argument with my father, who I was living with now. . . . He picked up one of my boots and was trying to hit me with it or something. . . . It was a very loud, violent confrontation, and it was, "Get the hell out of my house." So I had a gym bag and threw a couple things in it and split. And it was the winter . . . and I was living in my friend's grandmother's broken-down—I think '82 Buick or something like that. Sleeping in the back of that.

This wasn't the first time he'd been kicked out of one or the other of his parents' homes: "I had heard that from both of them previously, had been thrown out of one house or the other. In which case the solution was just to go to the *other* house." But this time, after living in the car for several days, "I called my mother and told her, and in a very typical response from her, she gave me the number of the local homeless shelter as a solution."

Neither of his parents, he says, tried to sit down with him to resolve the issue that had led to the altercation in the first place, and neither came looking for him after he'd left the house with nothing but his gym bag:

> My dad, I'm sure, wanted me back. Or, you know, he would have wanted to know where I was and that I was safe and that sort of thing. My father can be very temperamental, but he calms down and would probably reassess the situation and want me to come back. But my mother is very persistent and methodical, and if I had called two weeks later, she would have given me the number of the homeless shelter again.

Whatever his mother may have hoped to accomplish by refusing to let him come home, Sean took his new circumstances in stride. He already knew many other kids who had been kicked out by their parents, some of whom had wound up running away to the city and being sucked into a "bad, bad world" on the streets. He felt that, even though he was living in a car, he was actually in a far better situation than most of them: "I had someplace local to go, and I wasn't really desperate, so it could have been worse."

The idea that the backseat of a car qualifies as "someplace local to go" suggests the extraordinary marginalization that many adolescents suffer when they are forced out of their homes. For Sean, the result of that marginalization was to accelerate his transformation from being mildly alienated to being rather proudly "hard-core." He found that living in the Buick and being homeless and without prospects was more interesting than frightening:

> I mean, I didn't *like* that. It was, you know, a particularly cold winter. But I don't remember feeling particularly worried about my future at the time, because I don't know how much fifteen-year-olds think about the future in general. And in a way—of course I wouldn't have said this then—but in a way I can look back and see that I thought it was maybe kind of cool because I was gaining credibility in certain circles, as so

hard-core. I was living in a broken-down 1982 Buick...not even a working one! I mean, it was slightly adventurous, actually.

For teenagers who have begun, like Sean, to feel estranged and disconnected, the emotional and physical rejection by parents provides further reason to think of themselves as people on the outside, since, in fact, they *are* on the outside. In Sean's case, it contributed to his sense of himself as a "badass," fit to associate mainly with other "badasses," and confirmed his belief that there was no one, outside himself and a few friends, he could rely on to protect him in the face of the violence that had begun to permeate his neighborhood—a belief that helps explain why he was carrying a gun in the first place on the night of the incident that sent him to prison.

For others, the parental rejection has different, though related, effects. Unsurprisingly, it can make adolescents who already feel bad about themselves feel worse and therefore even less inclined to care about what happens to them. It can also help breed the artificially shortened time perspective that is such an important feature of the feeling of "whatever." For one of the things that families do, ideally, is to cultivate an appreciation of the future in the young, to encourage them to think about the steps they need to take—and to avoid—in order to attain a respected place in the community as adults. Exclusion from the family, accordingly, weakens adolescents' sense of connection with a meaningful future and intensifies their inability to focus beyond the immediate.

At fifteen, Josh was slight and small for his age. He had been drifting aimlessly and doing a lot of dope for some months when his mother threw him out of her house. The immediate reason was that he'd been seen smoking dope with a friend he'd gotten in trouble with in the past. Josh asked his mother what he was supposed to do now that he was kicked out: "And she said, 'Well, you can just tell your dad you have nowhere to live.' So I went to live with my dad." Things worked out badly at his father's house, however, in part because his dad was also doing drugs and offered little by way of attention or supervision; he was out of work and spent a lot of time either riding his new motorcycle or hanging out in bars. Josh was still using as well, and generally not being "a good house guest," so after a few weeks he was kicked out of that house, too.

With no place to live and bereft of competent adult engagement, Josh, who had been depressed for some time, fell into a deeper depression and started doing drugs even more heavily. He told me that the experience of being kicked out by both parents had affected him profoundly, worsening his already nagging feelings of estrangement from people, of being "disconnected" and unable to care much about anything. It also fueled a certain "screw you" attitude, a visceral feeling of opposition:

> When I first got kicked out, I was kind of shocked. I was like, "You're kicking me out of the house? Well, fine." I was like, "Fuck it, I don't care." My friends would be like, "Well, why don't you go talk to your mom, try to fix it?" And I don't even care. I don't even *want* to.

His first reaction, indeed, was one of liberation: "I was like, 'Well, this is a good thing. Now I got complete freedom. I could do drugs *all day*. No one's gonna be on my back.' But then it didn't get so fun after a while."

If being thrown out of his home gave him more freedom to do what had gotten him into trouble in the first place, it also caused him to be even less concerned than before with the potential consequences. Like Sean, Josh wasn't especially worried during the time he had "nowhere to live":

> Like, I didn't really have any feelings. I was always messed up. So if I *was* frightened I wouldn't remember or I just never even felt it. I mean, I guess it was kind of frightening, the fact that I had to support myself and stuff. But, I don't know, it seemed like there was nothing I could do about it. It was like, well, I got kicked out, this is what I have to do now.

It was all day to day. I didn't think about tomorrow or anything, or think about yesterday. It was, what am I going to do *today*? When I was living on my own I didn't really have time to think about the future 'cause I was just worried about getting more drugs and stuff. And getting them at the moment.

Being focused on the moment meant, almost inevitably, that Josh's drug use got worse—which deepened his depression and further undermined his ability to care about what was happening to his life. The less he cared, the more drugs he did; the more drugs he did, the less he cared about anything else. Some of his friends tried to intervene: "They're like, 'All right, well, maybe you shouldn't be doing so much dope' or 'Watch what you're doing.' And I just didn't really care."

Aside from that handful of friends, no one talked seriously with Josh about what he was doing to himself. He couldn't, in fact, remember a time when anyone had. He had always found it hard to talk to either of his parents, even before they divorced. His father "didn't really say much, at least not about drugs," and his mother he "didn't really talk to that much." She had never actually explained to Josh why she threw him out of the house: he thought that it was probably "just 'cause she didn't know what to do with me." There were adults who supervised him in the various low-wage jobs he took on as a teenager, but "the bosses I had, they did drugs too!"

Even as he was sinking deeper into depression and drugs, neither parent would allow Josh to return home. One day, his mother picked him up off the street, drove him to a residential drug treatment center, and unceremoniously dumped him at its door: "And she gave me two numbers to two shelters, and said, 'Here's four quarters, and here's some shelter numbers. You're on your own.' And she took off." At that point, he says, he felt "trapped." He called a friend to see if he could get a ride home; the drug rehab was a good thirty miles from his mother's house. "I said, 'Hey, my mom just *left* me here.' And I was crying and saying she kicked me out of the house again and I have nowhere to live." But his mother had called the other boy's parents and they'd taken away the car keys. His four quarters spent, Josh was stuck with no way to get back to his neighborhood, so he started walking home on the freeway. A taxi picked him up. Josh explained that he didn't have any money, but the driver took him as far as the next exit and dropped him off by the side of the road. He walked another few miles and tried to get on a commuter train, but since he had no money, he couldn't buy a ticket. For a while, he "just sat there and cried." Ultimately he talked his way onto the train. He got off at his hometown and took a bus as far as it would take him toward his mother's house. He then walked the rest of the way. When he got there, he says, "I took a bunch of pills to kill myself."

He'd been thinking about killing himself all the way home. He was wracked by the sense of having been "dumped" by his parents and was completely at a loss as to what he should do with himself now, without money, plans, or even a roof over his head. He began ruminating about friends who had betrayed him and used him to get drugs, and much else:

> That was part of it, and the fact that I got kicked out of both houses again, I wasn't gonna have anywhere to live and, I don't know, it was like an overwhelmment. And all that was repeating in my head over and over and over again, almost like so I wouldn't back out of it.

Josh's attempt to kill himself failed, but that seems to have been purely a matter of luck. What is remarkable in this series of events is how willing his parents were to court disaster in the name of forcing him to "confront his choices." If his parents were aware of how dangerous it might be to put a severely depressed boy on the street with nowhere to live, an out-of-control drug problem, and no one to talk to, they certainly did not let that awareness get in the way of enforcing their moral vision.

Some months after this incident, Josh told me that although he had hated this treatment at the time and that it had brought him to the point of suicidal despair, he had come to believe that the "tough love" his mother had imposed was a good thing, that it "worked." He was now living back at home and had more or less gotten on top of his drug habit. He had so far stayed away from his "drug of choice," though he was still depressed and still had no sense of what he might want to do in the future. I pointed out to him that the strategy had "worked" only because his effort to kill himself had narrowly failed and that it could just as well have meant his not being alive to tell the story—a reality that Josh acknowledged with considerable discomfort.

———•———

Most often, attitudes like Josh's parents' are so blended into the culture that they are barely visible. Occasionally, an extreme example brings the underlying mentality to light. During the time I was interviewing the teenagers in this book, one such case reached the courts in California. A fifteen-year-old boy had been routinely locked out of his home in an affluent suburb and sometimes forced to sleep outside on a dog mat. He was often rousted out of bed at four o'clock in the morning, forced out of the house, and not allowed back in until his father returned from work late in the afternoon. Once he appeared at a friend's home at one in the morning soaking wet: his father had "awakened him by dousing him with several gallons of water to punish him for returning home late from school the day before." On many nights the boy wandered to other friends' homes because he had no place to go. Once, when he neglected one of his chores—picking up the family dog's droppings from the backyard—his mother deposited the feces in his room; the next time, she made him walk around with them in his backpack. His parents were acquitted of misdemeanor child abuse: one of their attorneys described their actions as evidence that they were parents who "cared," and that view apparently prevailed.

The strategies of exclusion and occasional humiliation that appear so often in these stories are routinely justified as being both morally appropriate and ultimately for the child's own good. But the practical results are almost always counterproductive. At worst, the systematic withdrawal of nurturance can have cascading effects that progressively push adolescents into ever riskier situations and ever more dangerous states of mind. It loosens their connections with the social institutions that could, in theory, provide them with guidance and help them develop a sense of larger purpose. It often forces them to make dangerous alliances with other troubled people in order to survive, while exacerbating their sense of being people of little value. In combination, these effects can lead—as in Josh's case—to a potentially catastrophic sense of isolation and desperation.

Often, adolescents are aware of being caught in this downward spiral and may try to extricate themselves by reconnecting with their families. What is striking is how often their parents resist their pleas for help. In the moral calculus of many middle-class families, once adolescents have passed beyond a certain threshold of troublesomeness, they cannot go home—literally or figuratively—unless they have, in effect, solved their problems on their own first. They have forfeited their right to nurturance and assistance by their bad behavior, and, in any case, too much help would be bad for them. In the real world, however, this stance usually worsens the problems it is designed to correct.

"Lose My Phone Number"

Like Tracy, Tori is a child of the suburban middle class who descended into a nightmarish world of addiction and abandonment on the streets of a large and dangerous city. By the time I met her she had managed—almost entirely on her own—to conquer her addiction, had been clean for several years, and was about to graduate from college. But more than once she'd come close to killing herself as a teenager and still bore many scars from her essentially lost years.

"Pretty much from the time I was sixteen to the time I was twenty is like a blur," she says, " 'cause I don't think I have a sober day in there."

Tori's childhood was spent in a suburb she describes as "a really horrible, horrible place to grow up." She felt painfully disconnected from the social world around her and couldn't fathom its priorities or share its enthusiasms:

> I didn't fit in at my high school. I didn't have the same interests as people—like I didn't want to play sports, and I didn't want to be a cheerleader, and I didn't want to go to after-school clubs. I just wanted to go home and listen to my stereo or go to concerts. I didn't want to do any of the things that the people my age were supposed to be doing. I didn't want to be on the yearbook committee. . . . I just absolutely never had an interest in that stuff, and I don't know if I was just born who I was born as or what it was, but I just never felt like I fit in.

Since junior high school she had only felt at home with other kids who felt the same way: "It's kind of cliché, but I was always drawn to the misfits in the neighborhood." All of her first friends, she says, were "burnouts" like herself:

> There's this vocational school that I went to . . . 'cause I didn't think I was ever gonna make it to college, so I was tracked. And it was called BOCES, which stands for Board of Cooperative Educational Services, but we used to refer to it as Burnouts Can't Even Spell, because that's where all the burnouts went. You know, I guess everyone figured like *us*, *those* kids, were never going to make it to college, so they'd teach us how to do something productive. So I went to cosmetology school. They always send the girls to cosmetology school.

When she was fifteen, Tori moved to a very similar community in a nearby state: "Another horrible place to live. Went from bad to worse." She was devastated at losing the few friends she had; she says she "couldn't imagine anything worse you can do to your child." She felt equally isolated and different but was now also terribly lonely. This time, however, she was only a short drive away from a big-city neighborhood that was well known for its street culture of drug use and teenage prostitution, and "things took a real big turn for the worst":

> As soon as I got a car, it was the first place I went. And it was weird. When I got there, I kind of felt like at home. Like I finally felt like I fit in with the people I was seeing around me. And I'd go to clubs and people there looked like me, and they looked like they might have felt like me and stuff.

Unfortunately, the people she felt most at home with were junkies, and she was increasingly unable to sustain that unaccustomed feeling of belonging unless she was high herself: "It's kind of sucky, and it's not very good, that the only time you fit in is when you're a junkie, but that's kind of how I felt."

In the beginning, she says, her drug use was primarily a "social thing," a way of enjoying the rare experience of being with people who were like her. But after a while, the drugs took over, "and then I started feeling normal when I was doing drugs and even more weird when I wasn't." She began doing drugs by herself, alone in her room, and spending less time with her user friends.

The extent to which the drugs were taking over her life was masked, she says, because she'd always been inclined to "medicate" herself in one way or another in order to cope with troubles: "Whether I was drinking in high school or smoking pot or shooting heroin when I was older, I never dealt with stuff. I just erased it from my mind." Convinced that if she opened herself up to her parents they would be judgmental rather than supportive, she had never felt able to turn to them with a problem: they would treat it as a moral failing, "a blame kind of thing." Her mother's response in particular was "just really, really, really punitive":

I felt like if I went to my mom and said, "You know, Mom, I'm drinking a lot, and I'm really nervous," or whatever it was that I'd say to her, she wouldn't say, "OK, let's try to work it out." I'd get punished, you know, because I was drinking and I wasn't allowed to drink. That's all she would see, is that it was against the rules, and I broke the rules, and that I'd have to be punished for it. I didn't feel like I'd ever get help for it. Or for anything, you know. . . . There was times when I needed my mother, or *somebody*, to be able to tell them stuff that was going on. When you're sixteen—like I was sixteen and I was pregnant, and I was just freaking out. Well, my other sixteen-year-old friends can't help me, you know? It was like, what do you do?

The result was that Tori preferred to face almost any danger, risk any catastrophe, rather than approach her mother for help or advice: "I would rather have suffered whatever consequences would happen to me than call my mother for *anything*." What was missing was some sense of latitude—the confidence that she had room to "screw up" at least a little without the whole world falling on her head.

Over time she developed the conviction that neither her parents nor any other adults were on her side.

Even if something was really wrong, I don't think I would have ever told any of the adults. I always felt just alienated from everybody that wasn't, you know, in my position, I guess. I don't know if that's the right word. But my parents and the school people, they did absolutely nothing to help.

When Tori began using drugs heavily, her mother was furious that she had screwed up both their lives:

She used to say things like, you know, "I'm not gonna go through this again." And I understand that when somebody's using drugs or whatever, that they're not only affecting themselves but the people that care about them. But . . . all I ever got from her was how this was so hard on *her* and how it's so hard to watch your baby do this to themselves and blah blah blah.

Tori ran away when she was sixteen to a chaotic and transient life in the worst neighborhood in the city: "I'd just live somewhere for a month and then pack all my stuff and move somewhere else for a month, and pack all my stuff and move somewhere, and little by little I didn't *have* any more stuff." On her own, on the street, estranged from her family and more and more isolated in a world populated by other junkies, she drifted more deeply into drugs:

> I started hanging out with these people who were using IV drugs. I was like, "*I'm* never gonna do that, I'm not touching needles," you know, blah blah. But it's crap . . . because if you live with it long enough . . . for me at least, it was kind of like a natural progression. So I wound up shooting speed for a while, and that turned into shooting heroin.

During this time she often wanted to leave the street life, but her parents never made any effort to bring her back home. Tori was always the one who initiated attempts at reconciliation, always the one who picked up the phone and asked if she could come back. That wasn't easy to do, given her mother's tendency to respond with anger if she asked for help. Even years later, Tori still spoke of her requests to be allowed to come home as "groveling" or "crawling back." She couldn't altogether shake the sense that there was something inappropriate, overly dependent, about these expressions of need. Still, she came home on her own initiative periodically—when things got too scary on the street, the drugs became too much to handle, or she got really sick and had no place to stay. But she couldn't feel comfortable there, since she was given the distinct message that she wasn't welcome. So she'd "always go right back, right back out to it, as soon as I started feeling healthy again. I'd just take off." Once she was "back out to it," however, it proved impossible to stay clean for long. She tried going into a drug treatment program but soon relapsed and was kicked out. Again, Tori tried to come home, but when her mother discovered she was still using drugs, she not only threw her out of the house but forced her back into the same sordid environment where she'd gotten into heavy drug use in the first place:

> I was asleep up in her bed, and I woke up, and she was pushing my sleeves up and looking at my arm. I had really bad track marks at that time. And I guess she had looked in my backpack and saw I had a little kit full of stuff in my backpack, and then she came to look at my arms, 'cause I think she just wanted to confirm—like why else would I have, you know, syringes and spoons and whatnot in my backpack if I wasn't using? So she called my brother, and he came, and he drove me home and dropped me off in front of where I was staying.

At one point her mother told her to "never call her again if I didn't get clean this time. That she wasn't going to go through it again. Literally she said, 'If you don't do it this time, you can just lose my phone number.'" So Tori signed up with another drug treatment program but was kicked out within a couple of weeks for having a "dirty" drug test after she'd ground up some pain pills and shot them up. This sort of "one-two punch" is common in the stories of troubled adolescents: their parents' tendency to push them away when they "mess up" is repeated—and amplified—by outside "helping" agencies. The result is to throw troubled young people back on their own resources at precisely the point when they need help the most. The practical importance of keeping teenagers within range of concerned adults, for their own good and everyone else's, is overridden by a moral judgment that they have forfeited their claim to assistance. For both Tori's mother and the drug program, it wasn't enough that she was making an effort to change: she needed to be abstinent in order to get help—needed, in other words, to have largely solved the problem on her own to earn the right to assistance in dealing with it.

After she was kicked out of the drug rehab for continuing to have a drug problem, Tori desperately tried to come up with a solution to her methamphetamine addiction on her own—and did, after a fashion: "My brilliant plan to get off of speed was to start doing heroin! I was like, 'I'll stop shooting speed, but I gotta do *something*.'" Soon she was truly strung out, badly depressed, and, as it turned out, desperately ill:

> I was doing all these drugs, and I wasn't feeling *anything*. I wasn't feeling high. I wasn't feeling well. I was nothing. I was just feeling gross. I was feeling sick and miserable and horrible. And so I called my mom for like the hundredth time. I was like, "Oh, can I come home, I really don't feel good," blah blah blah. She made me swear, to promise and, you know, all these things, that I'd go into rehab. So my brother picked me up and took me home, and I wound up—it turns out the reason I was so sick is because I had hepatitis.

Tori was terribly ill by this point, but her mother continued to maintain her self-consciously "tough" response:

> I was, like, bright yellow. It was horrible. I was throwing up. And my mother had no sympathy for me. 'Cause it was like I'd brought it on myself, was how she saw it, which—it's true to a point, you know, but, shit, take me to the doctor! Do *something!*
>
> Maybe she could have just given me a hug or something, but when I had hepatitis she couldn't even bring me something to drink. She was just so angry that she couldn't even, like, bring herself to help me.

"She couldn't even, like, bring herself to help me" could serve as a theme for many of the adolescents I spoke with. Though it was not usually this extreme, they often experienced a similar withdrawal of parental support and nurturance when they began to have problems. With only a few exceptions, the inner culture of their families was not one in which help was easily or generously given.

Instead, the very idea of help was regarded with distaste, resentment, or skepticism. When trouble appeared, their parents were likely to push them away rather than reel them in. Tori thought her mother was "weird" in this respect, and certainly refusing to take a desperately sick child to the doctor because she has brought the illness on herself merits that description. But this kind of "weirdness" is not just the response of a handful of isolated parents. The degree of its acceptance in America is highlighted by the experience of one parent I came to know well who did not adopt this approach when her daughter began to spin out of control. Mandy had gotten heavily into hard drugs at fourteen, dropped out of school, and fallen into a general state of drift. She stopped snorting heroin and speed only upon learning, at fifteen, that she was pregnant. After the child was born, she returned to the drug life with her usual abandon, until she decided, when the child was two, that she wanted "to be a good mother" and that she couldn't be one if she was constantly leaving her daughter with relatives so she could go out and get stoned with her friends. She entered a drug rehab but didn't stay long, because she felt the program was shallow and unserious; instead, she went home and embarked on a concerted effort to stay clean on her own.

During this time Mandy lived with her mother, who had divorced her father several years before. Things were not always smooth; there were arguments about her occasional relapses and tension over her continuing to hang out with some of her old friends, people her mother regarded as unsavory. But in contrast to Tori's parents—or Dale's or Sean's or Josh's—Mandy's mother insisted on keeping her daughter under her roof. This decision, she told me, brought an incredulous and even angry response from many of her friends, as well as Mandy's father, who couldn't understand how she could allow Mandy to live in her home while she was still using and associating with bad kids. But it didn't make sense to her to address Mandy's problems by pushing her away from the people who cared about her the most. If she were thrown out of the house, where would she go? With few meaningful relationships outside of her somewhat questionable friends, who would provide reliable advice and guidance?

It's perhaps worth noting that Mandy's mother was born and grew up outside the United States and had come to this country shortly before her daughter was born. She simply didn't get the logic of pushing a troubled child even farther away than she already had gone on her own and denying her the support that only a parent could offer. It seemed to her that "a kid in that shape" needed more parenting, not less, and she was stubbornly committed to trying to provide it. When I last spoke with her mother, Mandy was doing OK. She was not altogether out of the woods and hadn't yet gained much sense of direction in her life. But she hadn't gotten back into hard drugs or the culture surrounding them, and she was responsibly taking care of her daughter.

———•———

I am not suggesting that the responses of these parents took place in a vacuum. The conditions many of them faced, at home and elsewhere, were often difficult. Some of the teenagers in this book were, as they themselves well understood, quite a handful. They had real problems, at least for a while, and they would have tested the skills of even the most engaged and supportive of parents. Some of these families, moreover, struggled with tough economic circumstances that would have made it difficult for the parents to find the time and energy to deal effectively with their children's troubles, even with the best will in the world. Some were periodically out of work; others endured the stresses of working too hard and too long in jobs that couldn't otherwise provide a middle-class income. Some were single parents facing the pinched finances and the constant scramble for stable housing and child care that followed a divorce. Some had bounced from place to place in search of a steady job or an affordable home, and as a result their support systems were weak or nonexistent. And, as we'll see, few could rely on help from outside agencies when their children pitched into crisis.

Thus many of these parents were as constrained by the limits of a fundamentally unsupportive society as their children were. These were, after all, what we might call post-Reagan parents. They began raising children just as many of the institutions that had traditionally helped to make the middle class middle class—affordable health care and housing, stable and well-paying jobs, well-staffed schools, predictable social benefits—were being systematically undermined in the name of "market" values. For many of these families, life was far from easy, even in a period characterized by widespread prosperity in the country as a whole. This version of prosperity masked what were often increasingly disrupted and stressed lives, and even at best it could require fairly heroic efforts to maintain. Many parents, in short, were themselves profoundly buffeted by the new American Darwinism, and their relations with their children cannot be fully understood without taking this into account.

But that is not the whole story. The Darwinian approach to child rearing these parents adopted was rarely simply a response to being harried by social and economic forces beyond their control. It was part of a belief system, a cultural and psychological orientation toward the world—especially toward the bedrock issues of responsibility and mutuality, discipline and nurturance. Most of these parents were not just victims of this belief system but subscribers to it. It was, after all, a worldview shared by the most affluent among them, who did *not* suffer from significant economic stresses, who *could* afford help, and who had sufficient resources to buy a variety of services for their children. The rejection of the idea of mutual responsibility, a righteous distaste for offering help, the acceptance or encouragement of a view of life in which a competitive scramble for individual preeminence and comfort is central, the insistence that even the most vulnerable must learn to handle life's difficulties by themselves and that if they cannot it is no one's fault but their own—these were not the idiosyncratic views of a few parents but pervasive themes in American society and culture during the years in which these teenagers were growing up. As we'll now see, those themes have also shaped the way adolescents are treated by a variety of institutions outside their families.

"THERE'S NO HELP OUT THERE":
THE WORLD OF THERAPEUTIC DARWINISM

The family was the most important locus of the cultural pressures that undermined the capacity of these adolescents to care about themselves. But their drift into care-lessness was usually accelerated by what happened to them beyond their homes. All of them had some formal contact with the "helping" professions—ranging from a few brief sessions with a therapist to a series of institutional "placements" that took up much of their adolescence. In theory, these encounters might have been able to buffer the effects of punitive or neglectful families. In practice, they often compounded them.

There were some inspiring stories—about the counselor who offered empathy and attention, the therapist who helped them to understand themselves better and gave them the confidence to become more fully who they wanted to be. But these were not their usual experience. More often, what they found in the wider world of schools and helping institutions was a version of the same culture of negligent individualism that pervaded their families. Sustained and ungrudging support was as hard to find outside their homes as inside them. "There's *no* help out there, man," B.J. told me with a brittle smile when I asked who had helped her most when she was struggling with drugs, depression, and self-mutilation. She was hardly alone in this view. Most of the teenagers in this book said some variant of the same thing: during their worst period of crisis, there was little or no help for them when they most needed it.

That might seem surprising, even overwrought, on the surface. After all, these were not poor kids. Most of them lived in relatively prosperous places, and some in extremely prosperous places. Many—though not all—of them lived in communities that would be described, in the jargon of the social services, as "service rich." They had access to school counselors and usually to outside mental health agencies as well. Some parents could afford to send them to expensive therapists, private treatment facilities, or the growing number of special for-profit schools for "difficult" adolescents.

What, then, was the problem? Why do B.J. and others say there's no help out there? The problem was actually several rolled into one—all of which reflected the culture of indifferent and punitive individualism that surrounded these young people as they were growing up. In the military, a distinction is sometimes made between the "official truth" put out by authorities and the "ground truth"—the reality as lived by the troops in the field. For most of these adolescents, the "ground truth" bore little resemblance to the "official truth" of a service-rich, indulgent society.

Part of the problem was that, despite what were often truly dire circumstances, some of these teenagers had little or no contact with any formal helping agency at all. Some, indeed, simply fell off the institutional radar screen altogether. Help may have been technically available somewhere in their communities, but no one made a serious effort to connect them with it. That was especially true if their parents had adopted the Darwinian inversion of responsibility I've described and were unable or unwilling to put much effort into providing help themselves. Such parents were often equally uninterested in making much effort to find outside help once their children began to have trouble. And since these were, after all, children, it was difficult for them to find help by themselves. There is a telling scene in the 1980s movie *River's Edge*, in which some teenagers who have just discovered that one of their friends has killed a girl come on a public telephone, and it dawns on them that it would be good to call someone to tell them about the murder. But since none of them have any idea whom they should call, they hang up the phone. The scene rings true for the teenagers in this book. If they did not have adults in their lives who were concerned enough to seek outside help for them, they rarely had any idea where to find it (finding real support was, as we will see, difficult enough even when their parents *were* trying). At the extreme, some of them became essentially invisible to the official world of the social service agencies, and sometimes to the schools as well.

The usual stance of the agencies themselves contributed to this disconnection. There are few examples here of institutions actively reaching out to troubled teenagers. The approach of even the more solid mental health or drug treatment agencies was most often passive and reactive. They would respond, most of the time, if a teenager was referred to them by parents, schools, or juvenile justice authorities or came to them on his or her own. But they rarely sought out vulnerable young people in order to forestall trouble. As a result, much damage might already have been done before any help was available at all.

A similar passivity characterized the other end of the process: when adolescents did spend some time in the care of a drug treatment center or a mental health agency, little effort was made to maintain supportive connections with them once they left. The same was true for those who left their schools, voluntarily or otherwise. In theory, some schools and treatment agencies had mechanisms in place to follow them up. In practice—"ground truth"—follow-up occurred sporadically if it happened at all. Teenagers who ended up in some kind of "treatment" were often cut loose from it very quickly, and once they were, they were usually left to manage—or to flounder—on their own. No one tracked them down after they left, no one reeled them back in if they began to sink. They might go in and out of several different "placements" during their most troubled years, but these were almost never connected to each other, as parts of a carefully considered overall plan: they were separate, disconnected experiences that rarely cumulated into anything intensive enough or sustained enough to seriously address whatever needed addressing in their lives.

There were several reasons for this passive stance. Sometimes what appeared to be unconcern actually reflected a lack of resources to do much else. By the time I was interviewing these young people it was almost universally agreed in the helping professions, for example, that even the best intervention had to be followed by systematic "aftercare" if it was to make an enduring difference. And surely many of the youth-serving agencies encountered by the adolescents in this book would have done more in this respect if they could have. Again, these were, in a very real sense, Reagan's children. They grew up in a time when public investment in social services of almost any kind, for adults as well as teenagers, was under constant siege. And though the poor suffered most from this retrenchment, the middle class was by no means spared its effects. The shift of much health and mental health care into the private, for-profit sector played a role, too: many agencies that might have wanted to provide greater continuity of services were cut off at the knees by private insurers insisting on ever shorter "lengths of stay" for troubled kids.

But once again, as with the behavior of their families, sheer economics was not the whole story. The agencies' tendency to allow youth to disappear from the radar screen also reflected an acceptance, by many of the people who staffed them and who shaped their policies, of the larger cultural attitudes about dependency and responsibility I've described. Many of them adopted an institutional form of the inversion of responsibility: often, it turned out to be simply no one's job to track down still-troubled, still-endangered children after they had been discharged from a psychiatric ward or drug treatment program. Once they left an agency, they became somebody else's problem.

I encountered a striking example of this institutional indifference once when I tried to convince the head of a treatment program that his agency might want to explore ways of keeping closer track of clients when they returned to their communities—whether they had been successfully discharged or had run away from the program. I had done several interviews with a girl, fifteen when I last spoke with her, who had fallen into desperate straits upon leaving his agency. She had disappeared for weeks at a time, ultimately surfacing on the street with an even worse drug problem than she'd had before. She had been abused and sexually exploited by a series of men and had spent months bouncing between her dysfunctional home, the streets, and juvenile hall. I thought that her experience highlighted the importance of following kids like her when they left treatment and that we could usefully brainstorm about ways of doing so and about the combination of agencies, including his own, that would best be involved.

To my surprise, my suggestion made the director quite angry. There was no need, he felt, even to talk about the issue: what I was calling for, he said, was already being done. If the girl was still under the jurisdiction of the juvenile court, then it was the job of her probation officer to organize the required "case management." I said that the girl was in fact no longer on probation and that in any event her probation officer had not seen her or spoken with her in months. In that case, the director replied, it was the responsibility of the county child welfare authorities to provide case management. I pointed out that whether the child welfare authorities even knew of the girl's existence was unclear, that indeed she had been living in several counties in the last few months, and that no one in authority from any county—or anywhere else—had been in consistent contact with her during this period, which helped explain why she was in the perilous state she was in. None of this prompted the director's agreement that there was a need—much less a responsibility on his part—to devise better ways of tracking teenagers like her. (When I last spoke with her family, she had recently been picked up by the police, after several months on the street, with a newly acquired heroin addiction and an unexplained and very serious head injury that may have caused brain damage; she was in a state of emotional crisis so severe that she was admitted to the locked ward of a psychiatric hospital.)

The inability to get help was just one expression of a broader syndrome of official attitudes toward youths in trouble. Often the problem was not that there was no one to help them at all but that the help they were offered made things worse: it exacerbated their feelings of inadequacy and alienation and thereby pushed them farther along the road to heedlessness and isolation. That is the deeper and more precise meaning of B.J.'s comment that "there's no help out there": the people who are supposed to help you are, much of the time, actually doing something altogether different.

At its worst—and, as we will see, the worst was not uncommon for these teenagers—their experience with what purported to be helping agencies was painful, intimidating, and sometimes bizarre. More frequently, help consisted mainly of a cursory interview in a psychiatrist's office and a prescription for some sort of medication. And if they did get something other than medication, what they got, all too often, was "treatment" that was overtly punitive and shaming and seemed virtually designed to undermine their sense of worth. The working ideology of many agencies emphasized the adolescents' own responsibility for what was wrong in their lives and, like their families, insisted that it was mainly their responsibility to deal with it. Teenagers were recurrently exhorted to accept the consequences of their "choices." There was a great deal of concern about the dangers of giving *too much* support: indeed, the denial of assistance on the ground that teenagers needed to experience the consequences of their bad behavior was startlingly common. Many treatment agencies created elaborate systems of rules that were hard for kids not to break, quickly punished those who broke them, and rejected altogether those who broke them too often—or who continued to suffer from the problems that had driven them to seek help in the first place.

Again, it was not always this way. A few of the teenagers I spoke with were fortunate enough to find truly caring institutions and competent, attentive therapists or counselors who could tip the balance between their remaining stuck in a precarious and unhappy life and their being able to forge a path toward a more centered and constructive one. Too often, though, the adolescents' experience with official agencies of care and control either made them feel even worse about themselves or helped convince them that the adult world was "bogus" and unreliable at best and malignly arrayed against them at worst.

"Doctors Just Shit Out the Pills"

Most of the teenagers in this book *were* seen, at some point, by psychiatrists or other mental health workers, and a number of them were seen regularly, often from an early age. Some were taken by their parents; some were forced to go by juvenile justice authorities. A few took the initiative themselves when no one else stepped in. But they did not necessarily find a willing or sympathetic ear: again and again, they complained that the helping professionals showed little interest in talking about their problems and especially in hearing their own take on the situation. Instead, the first intervention was often simply to prescribe some sort of medication. Indeed, by the time they reached high school, if not before, many were already veteran consumers of a bewildering variety of pharmaceutical drugs.

By the time B.J. got to a psychiatrist's office, she was doing Ecstasy and acid heavily, dabbling in several other drugs, scraping the skin off her arms with anything sharp she could lay her hands on, and, by her own account, feeling so depressed that she was sometimes unable to "fucking get out of bed in the morning." Her mother took her to the psychiatric service of a local HMO:

> I was diagnosed with bipolar. I was very depressed. I was just *boom*, I was down, and I was low. . . . All of sudden I'm "manic depressive." And I'm like, OK. I still sometimes can't predict my moods, but I don't know, that's what they diagnosed me with. So they were trying to fix that,

right, because, you know, doctors just shit out the pills basically. They hand them out like candy. "Here, take some . . . !" I was taking Prozac already, from the August before that, so I'd been taking it for like six months. And then they're like giving me more Prozac. Plus I'm taking these other pills for my face because I have really bad acne.

She had all of three sessions with a psychiatrist, but it "didn't work" because, among other things, her mother was in the room and she felt unable to open up: "I couldn't be totally, you know, 'This is how it is.' If I'm going through some stuff and I really want to get some help, my mom can't sit there and listen. I'm sorry." In any case, the doctor seemed uninterested in talking about the reasons for her depression:

> The first time I went in there, I said, "I'm depressed, I'd like to take some pills." He just asks me about my symptoms. He goes, "OK, so you're depressed. All right, do you feel this?" "No." "Do you need to sleep?" "Yeah." So he gave me some sleeping pills and some Prozac. Boom, that was it. He asked me a couple of questions, checked off on a chart. . . . The sleeping pills were a bad idea, because I ended up taking a *lot* of those.

I asked B.J. if the doctor ever talked with her about why, in addition to doing so many drugs, she was carving herself repeatedly. She said she'd never been able to talk about it with anyone other than a friend who was doing the same thing; because "the only guy I was talking to was a guy that was passing out pills":

> My mom told him. We were in a session and I wasn't saying all that because I didn't want to talk about it in front of my mom. And then she mentioned it. She goes, "I think she's self-mutilating," or something like that. And I was like, "Thanks!" You know? And so that's all that was said. And he was like, "Oh, here, take this! This'll help you not want to do that!" I don't think he really was that kind of a personal doctor, and he was just like, "Well, we'll just give you this pill." Like it was nothing. I didn't talk about it.

Even at fifteen, B.J. thought that pills weren't enough, that there needed to be a "real someone" to help her figure out "for real" what was going on with her and "how can we better work with it." But, she says, "I didn't get any of that. I had to figure it out myself." Unsurprisingly, the problems—the depression, the drugs, the carving—continued. She went back to the doctor, whose response was to prescribe more medication.

> And so I was taking face pills. I was taking Prozac. And they were giving me things like—what did I take, man? Depakote. I took a couple of other things. I can't even really remember. And for a while it was like, "I'll stick to my Prozac." But they all had really bad results. And also, since I was taking two other medications, they were not working right together. And I don't know if that's why one of them made me stay up all night and puke, but it was all bad. And after a while it's pretty ridiculous. And I didn't want to deal with it anymore.
>
> So I was like, "Screw the Prozac. Screw the face pills. I've had it with pills, period. I don't want them to throw another one in my face—tell me, 'Oh, this'll fix your . . . ,'" you know. So I gave up on those, and I haven't felt the need to go back to the doctor and tell them I need some more, because they weren't doing anything for me but stressing me out.

Overwhelmingly, the teenagers I spoke with resented what they regarded as the knee-jerk reliance on medication as a response to their problems. They saw it as an abdication—the reflection of a cultural predilection for the quick fix, an unwillingness to grapple with difficult issues. Sean felt that way about the care he received during a stay in a private psychiatric hospital:

> And then you have the doctors, you know, these psychiatrists who are just there a couple of hours a day. I don't know if they go from hospital to hospital or their private practice to the hospital. I don't know what their deal is. But you know, they pull up in their, sometimes literally, red convertible Corvettes, and things like that, and they come in, write a

couple prescriptions for antidepressants, and leave. I mean, you come in and they try to dope you up in some way or another. The generic diagnosis that everyone gets is depression. Because most insurance plans cover that. And it's, you know, a sort of one-size-fits-all diagnosis. It's nothing you even have to demonstrate. And what happens? You're depressed because you're in one of these stupid places!

Anna grew up in a somewhat tattered middle-class suburb that was beginning to go downhill. She described her family as "altogether dysfunctional." Her father ran a small retail business that was often on the brink financially, and her home had been a tense and sometimes violent place for as long as she could remember: "I was always in constant fear all the time. And so I constantly had headaches, stomachaches—my body had terrible pains. And we'd go to the doctor, and for some reason everybody thought I was making it up." She managed to do well in elementary school, where—like several others in this book—she was frequently enrolled in programs for gifted children. But in seventh grade things began to unravel:

For some reason, when I turned twelve, everything hit me. You know? And it was really bizarre. Before, I didn't think about the abuse as much because I would use school as an outlet. But I think also at twelve, that's the time when children become really mean towards each other, and so it was just very hard all around. And I wound up never going to class.

Her school, however, either took no notice of the change or never responded to it:

My grades suffered. I skipped school constantly. And, you know, it was going from a person who got straight As and was in advanced classes to getting Fs. And that should be a sign. But no one really recognized it. . . . And no one ever really thought, "Oh, wow, something must be wrong. You know, she went from getting straight As in advanced courses to failing the average courses."

Between the abuse and tension at home and the problems at school, and with no one in either place she could talk to, "I felt like I couldn't deal with it anymore. I couldn't reach out to anyone, so I wound up running away." She was caught and sent home after a few days. But with none of the original issues resolved, she continued to slide downhill:

> I dropped out of school. I just got really depressed and isolated myself, and things got—eventually they put me on Prozac. But it's just another part of this problem, where, you know, there's no quick resolution, and by medicating someone, it doesn't—it doesn't work. It can't make you happy when you have emotional wounds and you're still in the environment that's causing the unhappiness.

Like B.J., many of my interviewees ultimately rejected their medication. Dale, who was diagnosed as having attention-deficit/ hyperactivity disorder (ADHD) and being "oppositional" at age six and who was given Ritalin, Dexedrine, and Prozac in elementary and middle school, stopped taking most of the pills because they made him feel "weird and tired." Anna flushed her Prozac down the toilet: "Naturally, being rebellious, I just threw those away. You know, an adult's telling me I *should* take this. Of course, like, 'OK, I *shouldn't* take it.'" Others threw their pills out because they didn't want to be changed into someone who was no longer their "real" self or because they wanted to try to come to grips with their emotional issues in a deeper way: they felt that it was important to understand their problems, not simply medicate them. After Laurie overdosed and wound up in the emergency room,

> They tried to put me on all sorts of pills. I said, "Hell no, I'm not taking those pills." Because you don't want them to—I didn't want to be on

anything that altered me. I just wanted to go cold turkey. Even if they don't get you high, they still affect you. . . . If I'm moody, I'm moody. That's me.

What is especially striking is how cavalierly these powerful medications could be given out to children—despite the existence, on paper, of a complex structure of regulations and guidelines for their use. Teenagers were sometimes given Ritalin or antidepressants without a diagnostic justification, and sometimes, apparently, by people who were not qualified to prescribe them. Danny was put on Ritalin during elementary and middle school, even though, according to a later psychiatric report, "it is not clear that he had significant symptoms of ADHD." Tracy describes being put on "a whole bunch of shit" at one of the several treatment programs she cycled through in the attempt to deal with her eating disorder and drug use. Like B.J., she "couldn't even remember" all the medications she had been given: no one had explained to her what they were or even what they were for. But she was convinced that the barrage of medication hadn't helped and that the only reason the program kept giving her so many pills was that they didn't know what else to do with her:

They didn't know how to handle it. They thought I was crazy. They put me on—what did they put me on, dammit? They put me on just downers and downers. Without prescribing them to me or anything. So it was really wrong what they did. Like, we could have sued them big time, but we just dropped it. But they did some stuff just 'cause they didn't know how to handle me throwing up my food and stuff.

I was on—I don't even know *what* they had me on. I can tell you that much. I mean, my dad did not know me. My mom did not know me. Like, I don't even remember what I did out there. They gave me stuff that knocked me out for like four days straight. I slept. Oh, God! What the hell—what's that stuff called? Depakote was one of them. They gave me some drinking fluid stuff, plus my Prozac. And they gave me some other pill. My dad would know. I really don't know. But they had me on a bunch of stuff.

> I didn't know who I was. I didn't know *anything*. I was out of it. It's
> like I was at the point where I thought everybody was after me. . . . I had
> roommates, and my roommates actually wanted to move out of the
> room because I was—they had me on so much stuff. It was horrible!

Tracy says she wasn't prescribed these medications by a psychiatrist:
indeed, she hadn't seen a psychiatrist at all—or for that matter any
medical doctor—while she was enrolled in this program. This
shocked even her father, who intervened. "My dad said, 'And did
she see a psychiatrist for all this?' [The nurse] said, 'Well, we're *going* to get her one,' and my dad said, 'Oh, nuh-uh, you don't just put
my daughter on shit!' "

Prozac, Paxil, Depakote, Ritalin, Welbutrin, Dexedrine—the
brand names roll out through these stories like a series of pharmaceutical advertisements. And the quick resort to psychotropic medication was hardly unique to the young people I interviewed.
Nationally, the prescription of such medications generally for children and adolescents doubled between 1987 and 1996; the use of
antidepressants specifically increased from something over three
times in some health care systems to over ten times in others. It is
fair to say, given the widespread retreat from more expensive and
longer-term "talking" therapies in the eighties and nineties, that
medication with some sort of psychotropic drug had become the
dominant mode of treating adolescent problems by the time I began
interviewing these teenagers. By the late 1990s, some of the most
commonly prescribed childhood medications, notably Ritalin, were
significant drugs of abuse in their own right. Among my interviewees, stories of snorting ground-up Paxil or Zoloft to get high were
common.

By the turn of the new century, indeed, a growing number of
studies showed not only that psychotropic medication of troubled
children and adolescents was increasing by leaps and bounds but that
these drugs were often prescribed without careful attention to
whether they were really needed or whether some other kind of intervention would have been more appropriate. This was a problem

across many different diagnoses but was especially apparent in the case of depression and, even more, of attention-deficit/hyperactivity disorder, which a startling number of the boys in this book were said, at some point, to have suffered from, including Sean, Danny, Dale, Terry, and Rick.

A Duke University study in western North Carolina found that the number of children who were prescribed stimulants for ADHD increased two and a half times in the first half of the 1990s alone and that "stimulant treatment was being used in ways substantially inconsistent with current diagnostic guidelines." More than twice as many children were prescribed stimulants as had been given a full diagnosis of ADHD, and indeed "the majority of those who received stimulants *never* met criteria for ADHD"—that is, they "never had parent-reported impairing ADHD symptoms of any sort." The average duration of stimulant treatment for children without a diagnosis of ADHD was about two and a half years. Twenty-nine percent of this subgroup of children who were treated with stimulants even though they did not meet the criteria for a diagnosis of ADHD "had an ADHD symptom score of 0. In other words, at no time over 4 waves of observation did their parents report that they had *any* ADHD symptoms" (emphases in original). A great many children, in other words, were being fed stimulant drugs at an increasing pace during the 1990s even though they did not have the disorder for which the drugs were ostensibly being prescribed. The study found that the overprescription of stimulants was more likely among children who were not poor, a fact that the researchers wryly interpreted "as suggesting that poverty is a protection against the receipt of poorly indicated medications." They concluded that "current treatment practice in the community is far from optimal" and that their findings presented "a troubling picture of a serious mismatch between need for stimulant treatment and the provision of such treatment."

A study reported in the journal *Pediatrics* around the same time found that children diagnosed with ADHD were highly likely to be prescribed not only stimulants but a variety of nonstimulant drugs as well, often concurrently, even though "many of these [latter] drugs have little or no empirical basis in the treatment of ADHD." The authors concluded that "future research to examine the use, effectiveness, and safety of these medications alone and in combination in children with ADHD is urgently needed." A Rhode Island study of third to fifth graders similarly found that almost one child in five taking medication for ADHD was receiving "multiple psychoactive medications" in addition to stimulants; in that study, too, there was no clear reason to believe that these other medications would help—if in fact the children were actually suffering from ADHD.

A Virginia study found that the diagnosis of ADHD, and the subsequent prescription of psychotropic medications to treat it, was especially common among white boys—an astonishing 18 to 20 percent of whom were on medication for ADHD. Overall, the proportion of children receiving medication for ADHD was two to three times higher than the best estimates of the actual rate of the disorder in the school districts the researchers studied. Unsurprisingly, they concluded that the evidence pointed to "potential over-diagnosis and over-treatment of ADHD in some groups of children."

Thus, the experiences of my group were hardly unique. As these studies suggest, during the time I was interviewing these young people, psychotropic drugs were being widely prescribed, indeed systematically overprescribed, especially to deal with the problems of mainstream white youth. What is perhaps most notable about the widespread resort to pills as the first—or only—response to youthful psychological issues is that there was so little evidence that this approach would be effective in addressing the problems it was theoretically attempting to solve. At the time when these teenagers were routinely being given an array of medications, it was widely understood among serious practitioners and researchers that there was scant scientific evidence of the efficacy of most of these medications for adolescents and that very little research had ever been done on their long-term effects.

In the case of antidepressant medications, these concerns reached a climax shortly after I finished my interviews, with the revelation that some studies of SSRIs had exaggerated their beneficial effects and obscured potential risks. British authorities banned Paxil for use by children in 2003, and the following year the U.S. Food and Drug Administration required that manufacturers place warning labels on most SSRIs, noting the potential for, among other things, suicidal thinking. An Australian analysis of existing studies of the safety and efficacy of SSRIs for children and adolescents went further, pointing out that most of the positive studies were sponsored by pharmaceutical companies and that many had "exaggerated the benefits, downplayed the harms, or both." On balance, the authors concluded, there was only marginal evidence that any of the SSRIs were effective in reducing depression among the young, and no evidence whatever that they were more effective than some kinds of traditional "talking" therapy. Yet despite the weakness of the evidence that they actually worked, roughly 2.7 million children under twelve, and more than 8 million aged twelve to seventeen, were given such drugs during 2002.

The indiscriminate use of medication, as my informants suggest, involved more than the cavalier prescription of stimulants and antidepressants. A variety of other drugs, many with even less evidence of effectiveness, are routinely given to troubled children and adolescents in the United States; moreover, the conditions in which they are prescribed sometimes violate reasonable guidelines for ensuring that they are administered in ways that are both safe and developmentally appropriate. A manual called the *Concise Guide to Child and Adolescent Psychiatry*, published by the American Psychiatric Association, describes the proper approach to medication for adolescents:

All psychotropic medications have the potential for cognitive toxicity. Because some drug treatments last for years, there is a risk for chronic and cumulative effects. Cognitive blunting can impair developing academic skills, social skills, and self-esteem even before physical side effects are observed, especially in young children. Young patients may have behavioral toxicity (i.e., the worsening of preexisting behaviors or affective states or the development of new symptoms). . . . The clinician must specify target symptoms and obtain affective, behavioral, and physical baseline and post-treatment data. Treatment effects can be assessed by interviews of and rating scales for the patient, the parent, and other caregivers; . . . direct observation in the office, waiting room or classroom; and, as appropriate, laboratory tests or specific cognitive tests to measure attention or learning. The clinician must ask about and look actively for both therapeutic and adverse effects because many young patients will not report them spontaneously, and parents may not notice.

Such caution is surely appropriate, but for many of my interviewees nothing remotely approaching this level of careful monitoring took place, and indeed in many of the settings in which they were treated, it realistically *could not* have taken place. Teens were often given drugs during short-term placements in psychiatric facilities or in drug rehabs where the length of stay was limited by insurance or budget constraints to a month or so at most, and many kids ran away from these places or were kicked out even sooner. Once they left the "placement," for whatever reason, adolescents were rarely followed up, whether or not there was a formal mechanism in place for doing so. This meant that none of the monitoring of dosages, compliance, or effects outlined in the *Concise Guide* was possible and that in some cases no one had the vaguest idea what the long-term impact of the drugs were, for good or ill, on the kids to whom they were prescribed. And since there was usually no overarching case management of teenagers as they moved from one placement to the street to their homes to yet another placement, they might be prescribed an entirely different, even overlapping or conflicting, regimen of medications at several points, without anyone's monitoring the overall process.

What makes this especially troubling is that it was also universally understood among serious practitioners that most of these drugs had the potential to cause serious problems. Of Depakote, a drug initially developed to control seizures but now frequently used to moderate mood swings, the *Concise Guide* notes that "caution is indicated in the use of anticonvulsants in sexually active girls because of teratogenicity [*teratogenesis* is the production of deformity in the developing embryo, or of a monster]" and that

> before initiating anticonvulsants, the physician should measure hemoglobin, hematocrit, white blood cell count, platelets, and liver function every month for four months (more often if counts are low). . . . [Thereafter,] the clinician should monitor plasma levels routinely because children metabolize the drug more rapidly than adults do.

It is difficult to see how these precautions could have been taken with the several teenagers in this book who were given Depakote for bipolar disorder, a use for which, at the time, no credible studies of efficacy in adolescents had ever been done. Of the antidepressant desipramine, the *Concise Guide* reassures us that "the evidence appears to suggest that treatment with desipramine in usual doses is associated with *only slightly added risks of sudden death* beyond that occurring naturally," despite several reported cases of sudden unexplained death among children and young adolescents during desipramine treatment (emphasis added).

Again, a very large proportion of my male interviewees were diagnosed at some point with ADHD. The *Concise Guide* tells us that "the most common combination used currently for ADHD is probably a stimulant plus clonidine, although no trials of safety or efficacy have been published." Clonidine is a drug specifically approved for hypertension, not for adolescent psychological problems; the *Concise Guide* notes that it may be useful at bedtime to help decrease "ADHD overarousal *or oppositional behavior*" (emphasis added) and that it may also help counteract the tendency of stimulants like

Ritalin to cause insomnia. The child, in other words, is first rendered sleepless by being fed stimulants; the effect of the stimulants is then countered by a blood pressure medication whose efficacy in treating problems *other* than hypertension is acknowledged to be unknown.

The Pejorative Assumption

Beyond the issue of whether these medications were safe or effective for teenagers, the larger problem was that they so often substituted for any attempt at deeper engagement on the part of the helping professionals. The depth of this problem was brought home to me when I spoke with Laurie shortly after she had been hospitalized for her drug overdose. She had been given "a whole bunch of pills" at the time, most of which she threw away, but when I asked her how she had gotten "from there to here"—how she'd gone from being an overachiever in school, an A student and star athlete, to being strung out on multiple drugs and winding up in the emergency room—she said, "I don't know. I've never been asked that question before."

The failure to ask what would appear to be obvious questions was only one facet of the problem. Typically, when these adolescents did spend time talking with therapists or counselors, the talk remained oddly, frustratingly disconnected from the context of their trouble. From the youths' point of view, these conversations never got to the real issues and indeed weren't even directed there. Many complained that the "shrinks" tended to "put it all on *me*": issues that involved complex social or familial relationships were turned into purely personal problems. This feeling was best articulated by the college students, who were looking back at their adolescence after having learned something about the social world and the pressures that it could put on teenagers and after having had time to think through, and come to terms with, their often traumatic relations with their families and schools. But even those teenagers who were still in the throes of a current crisis often felt that the professionals wore blinders, that all of their attention was focused on the individual's "choices," none on the external forces that pushed people to act in the ways they did. In this sense, the teenagers had the beginnings of a more sociological understanding of the world of adolescence that was distinctly lacking in the people who were supposed to help them figure things out. Over and over, they said that what the professionals seemed unable to understand was that there were *reasons* people did destructive or self-destructive things. Tori puts it this way in describing what happened after her mother found out she was smoking pot in ninth grade:

> She sent me to psychiatrists and psychologists and therapists, and none of them had any idea, you know. Like, they all just wanted me to stop using drugs. None of them had any inkling about—like, no one even asked me *why* I was using drugs. They were just like, "You just need to stop."

Mental health professionals, in fact, often seemed to resist the search for reasons, thinking, apparently, that looking for causes might let adolescents off the hook, might diminish their already minimal capacity to take personal responsibility for their actions. For those who were not "personal doctors," as B.J. put it, and who were mainly or entirely in the business of providing medication, the lack of interest was even more basic, because for them the search for reasons was over before it started: the reasons were simply biochemical, and nothing more needed to be explored—it was just a question of finding the appropriate prescription and adjusting the dosage. But the pressure to internalize troubles, and the resistance to taking a more contextual view of them, was much more widespread. It operated as a kind of background ideology that pervaded the relationships these adolescents had with the helping agencies, no matter what specific problem had brought them there. Whether the issue was drugs or alcohol or risky relationships or problems at school, the lens was characteristically turned back on their own "contribution" to the problem.

Lacey, for example, went to a therapist when she was seventeen to try to understand, among other things, why she so often felt that sense of "abandonment" that led her into tricky and dangerous situations. But she felt persistently frustrated: the therapist, she complained, always "put things on me." When Lacey told her about having been sexually assaulted by a man she'd briefly dated, for example,

> her thing was like, why was I attracting men that would abuse me? And she never contextualized that within a larger social, political, economic context. And so I constantly went back to her: "What's wrong with me?" And later, as I slowly was starting to question it, it was like, "No, there's nothing necessarily wrong with *me*." OK, clearly there are many issues I could work on, certainly, but there's something else. . . . I was furious that she never asked, made it a bigger picture.

Lacey thought that the pressure to internalize problems could "make you crazy" by piling on more self-blame when you already felt inadequate. She had always been vulnerable, even as a child, to feeling guilty about real or imagined things she was doing wrong. But instead of confronting that tendency as an issue worth exploring, the therapist compounded the problem by holding up a mirror that reflected her problems "back on her":

> She made everything very individuated. . . . You couldn't talk about the structure, . . . couldn't talk about a whole system set up to do that to me, . . . [look] at it in a larger context and [say], "OK, well, you know, men and women aren't really built to interact in a really healthy, positive way in our society. What does that *mean*?"

She found the therapist's "constant focus on the inward" to be "stifling" and tried to get her to "grapple with the outward": "Just because you're in a park with a guy doesn't mean he can rape you. And that he does has nothing to do with the fact that you were *there* or that you were doing something that says, you know, 'Rape me!' " But her efforts to "broaden the scope" of her discussions with the therapist had little success. When she complained that the larger issues about men, women, and sexuality weren't being addressed, the therapist's response was, "Well, I couldn't bring all that in the room. I mean, how are we going to deal with all that other stuff?" By default, in other words, what could be "dealt with" was Lacey's own attitudes, not the cultural values that legitimated sexual assault. She later went to a therapist who took the opposite tack and encouraged her to stop blaming herself for having been assaulted. For Lacey, this was a life-changing revelation: "Being able to take it from just the 'me' experience out to the society helps me realize, oh, OK, I can understand a pattern. Although it hurt and it was very painful and very violent and really horrifying, I understand how it happened and *that it's not me.*"

Getting to the realization that "it's not me" was for many of these adolescents, as we'll see, crucial to their ability to turn their lives around for the better. But that sort of understanding was only rarely fostered by the helping agencies, which, with certain important exceptions, seemed either unable or unwilling to confront the broader social and cultural pressures that Lacey and others struggled to comprehend and wanted desperately to talk about.

That the mental health system seemed to focus reflexively on the adolescents themselves as the problem was especially puzzling—and especially frustrating to my informants—because they were, after all, children, surrounded by adults who at least in theory had responsibility for them and certainly had a great deal of power over them. The kids understood what many of the helping professionals apparently did not—that as children they were far from being the masters of their own fates. They were particularly critical of psychiatrists and social workers who ignored the role of their families in their current troubles in favor of doggedly uncovering their own deficiencies. Anna was surprised by the indifference to family problems of the psychiatrist she saw briefly after running away from home at twelve:

> It kind of amazes me, you know, that she never once questioned my mom about my siblings. . . . My sister, my oldest sister, she ran away twice, did a lot of drugs, got pregnant a couple times. . . . And she left home when she was sixteen for a while and lived outside the house. And my other siblings suffered from obesity, did terrible in school. They were failing school. And also did a lot of drugs and drinking.

But the psychiatrist, she says, never asked about any of those things:

> You know, it was all completely overlooked, as if those elements had no bearing upon my state. And that really shocks me because I feel like we're all a product of society and our environment, and yet that's so gravely overlooked. I think that they believed this was some sort of, like we're born like this, to be the problem child, and therefore we're not going to change, so we need like a kick in the pants.

Many of my informants describe a similar skewing of focus, and their experience is backed up by my own observations. It was indeed astonishing how quick the therapeutic world was to isolate and "treat" a child, often with the ubiquitous pills, as if it had been clearly established that there was something individually wrong with her. This was true even when it was widely understood that the child faced truly awful conditions at home. No matter how horrific a child's family history, for example, or how thoroughly abandoned she had been by parents or other caretakers, it was unquestioningly assumed that it was the *child* who needed to change or to be changed. Again and again, the response of the helping authorities was to insist that children "take responsibility" for situations that were, realistically, far beyond their control.

I came across a remarkable example of this mentality in looking through the voluminous official file that one fourteen-year-old girl had accumulated by the time she arrived at a psychiatric facility for adolescents. When she was about twelve, the girl, who had been severely and repeatedly abused from an early age, was kicked out of a group home where she'd been sent by the juvenile court. In recommending that she be sent back to juvenile hall, her social worker said that the girl had "chosen to disregard the tools that the placement provided to her, choosing to not internalize, or not implement, the treatment that she was offered." The social worker acknowledged that the girl had suffered an almost unbelievably traumatic childhood: she had been diagnosed at one point as suffering from "post-traumatic stress disorder" resulting from a family background of "profound chaos." But, the social worker went on, "despite the setbacks that the minor has had to endure throughout her life, she has to take responsibility for her behaviors."

This language of choice and individual responsibility and tools was repeated like a litany in the helping agencies my interviewees encountered, and the emphasis on choice often led to a somewhat paradoxical conception of the agencies' role. Since it was generally assumed that people's difficulties in life were due to their own "bad choices," the job of the helping agencies was not really to help people, for people should be held responsible for those choices, but, at most, to offer them the tools to help themselves. But the tools typically consisted of exhorting them to look inward to understand why they behaved the way they did and to work to change their own attitudes and their responses to the people around them.

Another anecdote helps illustrate just how deeply this attitude runs through the institutions that serve troubled adolescents today (assuming that they receive any formal intervention at all). In the course of studying teenagers in drug treatment, I wrote up some of the early findings in a paper I titled " 'It's Our Lives They're Dealing with Here.' " The line was taken from an interview with a fourteen-year-old girl who was highly critical of the drug program she had been forced to attend and who ran away from it after a few weeks to live a hand-to-mouth existence on the streets. She'd said to me that she felt that many of the staff in the program were "clueless" about the impact of their policies on their clients and heedless of the fact that some kids were so alienated by those policies that they resisted the program or fled from it altogether, often getting themselves in worse trouble or even sent to youth prison. In this sense, she felt, the program was insufficiently serious about consequences: the staff did not seem to understand, she said, that "it's our *lives* they're dealing with here." On learning that I planned to use this phrase in my paper, the program's director became quite angry. He felt that it gave the wrong impression: the whole point of the program was to emphasize that the clients should take responsibility for their *own* lives; they should not think of the *program* as "dealing" with their lives in any way, and neither should I.

This seemed to me to represent a worldview so deeply ideological as to be disconnected from elementary reality. The girl was surely on target, and the director was the one who was arguably in a state of denial. At fourteen, surrounded by adults in authority who had much more power over her life than she did, she was correct in her assumption that the program was "dealing with" her life and hardly unreasonable in her belief that it needed to take some responsibility for the consequences. But it could not—or would not.

The response of the helping professions to these adolescents was rooted in what we might call the pejorative assumption—the reflexive belief that if there was a problem between a child and her parents, for example, or between the child and school authorities, the problem was *inside* the child, a problem of her character or personality, not of the relationship. That assumption represents a classic example of what William Ryan, in the early 1970s, famously called "blaming the victim." Ryan was writing about the way comfortable social scientists and others in authority talked about the poor, but he could just as well have been addressing the "official" attitude toward the problems of middle-class adolescents. Central to the victim-blaming mentality, Ryan wrote, is

> the swerving away from the central target that requires systematic change and, instead, focusing in on the individual affected. The ultimate effect is always to distract attention from the basic causes and to leave the primary social injustice untouched. And, most telling, the proposed remedy for the problem is, of course, to work on the victim himself. Prescriptions for cure . . . are invariably conceived to revamp and revise the victim, never to change the surrounding circumstances.

The relentless tendency to define problems as the result of individual failure or deficiency is, in part, a reflection of the training that most practitioners in the helping professions receive. Most have been trained in identifying and addressing individual pathologies, not in understanding the problems of the family as an institution, much less those of the larger society. Few are taught much about the social forces that impinge on families and individuals in the real world. The result is often that the routine, "on the ground" assumptions of the mental health professions closely resemble the everyday individualism of the larger culture. The language may be more complicated, but the basic worldview is remarkably similar. As the old saw goes, if your only tool is a hammer, every problem begins to look like a nail: since the main tool in the kit of the conventional helping professions was some variety of individualistic theory about the causes of behavior, the focus of treatment was necessarily on the adolescent's internal problems.

The tendency to individualize problems and to wrench them out of any broader social context is, indeed, built into the technical psychiatric categories that constitute the main lens through which the helping professions viewed the troubles of these young people. A striking number of the boys in particular were, at some point in their journey through the agencies of treatment and control, diagnosed as suffering from what the standard psychiatric *Diagnostic and*

Statistical Manual (DSM-IV) calls "conduct disorder" (CD) or "oppositional defiant disorder" (ODD). But these concepts were often deployed as vague catchall categories that provided little insight into the real-world conditions in which these teenagers lived and that mainly served to individualize and pathologize problems that were invariably more complex and more grounded in social relationships.

To a striking extent, these "disorders" were invoked to describe one kind of behavior in particular: the adolescent's noncompliance with authorities of one kind or another. But they were invoked, for the most part, without any serious investigation of the context of that noncompliance or any recognition that under some circumstances the unwillingness to comply with authorities might not be a symptom of a disorder at all, but rather the opposite. This isn't to say that the concepts have no connection with the real world. Everyone knows, for example, of people who really are mindlessly, and perhaps helplessly, "oppositional" and who would have trouble getting along in any institutional setting. But as they were used in the lives of these adolescents, these categories were often simply tautological: if a boy engaged in bad conduct, it demonstrated that he had a conduct disorder. Thus, instead of explaining why a teenager behaved badly, the category only gave the bad behavior a new name that definitively located the problem inside the adolescent. And the equation of defiance with disorder also made these concepts transparently open to abuse, since it allowed what might have been healthy resistance to mistreatment to be simply defined as pathology. There was no allowance for the possibility that under some conditions opposition or resistance to authority may have been understandable and perhaps even laudable—even necessary for emotional survival.

Consider what the *Concise Guide to Child and Adolescent Psychiatry* says about the category of "disruptive behavior disorders," of which ODD and CD are subcategories. These disorders, we're told, are "characterized by willful disobedience." Along with ADHD, they are "externalizing" conditions in which the child "often denies symptoms, blames others for problems, and is reluctant to undergo treatment." There is no acknowledgment that perhaps, as several of the stories here illustrate, the child may be reluctant to undergo treatment because she does not believe that there is anything wrong with her, does not believe that she is the problem requiring "treatment," and may have very good reasons for feeling this way. It is surely true that some children, like some adults, have trouble facing up to problems and may blame others for troubles that are really of their own making. But it doesn't take great sophistication to understand that people—and especially children, who have so little ability to control their surroundings—may well be correct, at least some of the time, in attributing their troubles to people or institutions outside themselves, who do have a great deal of power to affect their lives.

The *Concise Guide* says that it is important not to ignore the context in which these behaviors take place, and the best people working in the field of mental health do indeed take a more careful and nuanced approach to these problems. But these diagnostic concepts are so vague, loose, and self-confirming that in the hands of less careful practitioners they can easily become justifications for stigmatizing and punishing adolescents whose troubles mainly reflect their treatment by irresponsible, incompetent, or resentful adults. The concepts, moreover, mesh seamlessly with the quick resort to pills as the dominant response to adolescent troubles: if the problem is a disorder within the individual child that may, as the *Concise Guide* insists, have genetic or biological origins, then it follows that chemical intervention may be the best answer, and perhaps the only answer. Thus the *Concise Guide* tells us that for children and adolescents with both ADHD and conduct disorder, the use of stimulants and/or antidepressants "may reduce oppositional behavior and improve compliance." Indeed, in the case of the strategically vague conduct disorder, it turns out that treatment "can include virtually any psychotropic drug, depending on the individual patient's neuropsychiatric findings."

It is extraordinary how much the language of these disorders is ultimately about the enforcement of compliance. The Iowa Conners Teacher Rating Scale, a checklist for teachers to monitor pupils for evidence of ADHD and other "externalizing" disorders described in the *Concise Guide*, asks teachers to rate children according to the frequency of these behaviors, among others: "Fidgeting," "Hums and makes other odd noises," "Quarrelsome," "Acts Smart," "Defiant," "Uncooperative." The authors of a generally useful guide to the DSM-IV note some of the objections to the lax use of concepts like conduct disorder but also insist that "society certainly does need to be protected from the actions of raging youth." No doubt it does, but there are two problems with that otherwise uncontroversial statement: most youth who are routinely diagnosed as "conduct disordered" hardly qualify as "raging," and there is no recognition that many youth clearly need to be protected from a raging *society*, from raging adults—and the fact that they have not been has a great deal to do with why they are having problems in the first place.

There is a sense in which the tendency to quickly define teenagers with problems as suffering from a disorder that requires medication represents a secular version of the intolerance of deviance—the narrow boundaries of the acceptable—that I described in chapter 2. Just as it was easy for teenagers like B.J. to regard themselves as sinners if they "fucked up a little," so in the psychiatric version it was easy for them to be regarded as "disordered" and in need of medication if they had virtually any problems at home or at school—if they deviated from a standard of normalcy that was, oddly, both narrow and vague. In both cases, what was missing was a more flexible and generous view of the range of behavior that could be considered tolerable or "normal." Relatively small deviations got the adolescent defined as having fallen outside acceptable boundaries and thus as a member of a distinct category of people: in the mental health world, as people in need of chemical rather than divine redemption. (It is worth noting that some studies find that the diagnosis of such "externalizing" disorders is more common in the United States than elsewhere, a fact that is said to be attributable not to differences in the actual prevalence of these problems but to differences in diagnostic practice.)

"Come Get Your Daughter. She's Loony"

The pervasive ideology of individualism within the helping institutions is closely related to another common characteristic of the world of therapeutic Darwinism—the markedly punitive quality of so much of the "help" adolescents received. As with their families and schools, intervention, when it came, often involved a predictable combination of harshness and exclusion, combined with a stunning lack of concern for the consequences. Indeed, it is difficult, from the vantage of an outside observer, to imagine how some of what passed for help in their experience could be described as help at all.

One expression of this reflexively punitive response is the oddity we've encountered already: it was curiously easy for troubled young people to be kicked out of helping programs (just as it was easy to get kicked out of school) if they demonstrated that their problem was indeed serious by continuing to have it. Tori's experience of being thrown out of drug treatment because she used drugs was matched by that of several other teenagers in this book. Tracy, for example, was kicked out of several treatment programs because she used drugs and "threw up her food," and indeed she was denied aftercare in one well-regarded drug program because she had "relapsed." "I don't really think you should ever drop someone for that, you know? But after you use three times, relapse three times, they kick you out." Presumably, the rationale for having the aftercare program was to maintain relationships with discharged clients during a potentially difficult period of transition and to help those who were still struggling: it would have made little sense to have provided aftercare only for those who had already successfully "recovered." But the inability to become drug-free was grounds for exclusion from the program and for the total withdrawal of help: "My parents even tried to get me in there again to go for another month, and they said, 'Nope, she'll never come back.' "

Shortly after this episode, Tracy was sent to another treatment program which did let her in briefly: "And they kicked me out of *there* for my bulimia! They didn't know how to handle it." I asked if the second program had referred her to some other, more appropriate agency where her eating problems would be specifically addressed. They had not: "They just called my dad up, said, 'Come get your daughter. She's loony!' Yeah! For real!"

Mandy, who despite having had a child at fifteen was still living on the edge from one high to the next, was likewise kicked out of a series of placements on the ground that she continued to have the drug problem for which she had been referred to begin with. She had already been kicked out of "regular" school at fourteen for "frequent relapsing and substance abuse problems" and soon discovered that the stubbornness of her problem routinely disqualified her from receiving help:

> The month when I was living on my own I didn't go to school 'cause I was too high. . . . Then I went to a clean and sober school. Went there stoned and everything, didn't really care. Then I got kicked out of there because they found out I was getting high every day. Not, you know, going by all the rules. I *told* them I was getting high every day. And how I relapsed and all this other stuff. But they still kicked me out.

Like Tracy, Mandy was not referred to another source of assistance once she was kicked out of the "clean and sober" school, and she spent some weeks essentially living on the street, away from almost all adult contact. Others had the same experience. They describe a social service and mental health establishment that all too often washes its hands of people if they turn out to be overly difficult—to require more help than the system is willing to give. It would seem reasonable to expect that we would put more of our resources into the more difficult cases; in practice, however, those adolescents who are deemed most difficult are the most likely to wind up having to deal with their problems essentially on their own because they have forfeited their right to assistance by their continued bad behavior. Curiously, what this means is that the amount of help troubled young people receive is often inversely proportional to the seriousness of their problems. On the other hand, since there is little effort put into preventing problems before they happen, teenagers usually have to get in *some* trouble to receive any assistance at all. As Anna put it, "It seems like in order to get any form of help, even if it isn't adequate help, you have to really screw up. It's not there in the beginning."

Some of the problem, of course, has to do with the absence of sufficient resources to take on the more difficult cases in a serious or long-term way. I don't think I ever came across a truly well-funded helping agency for adolescents in the course of this study. At times (though by no means always), the agencies charged with the care of some of the most seriously troubled, even damaged, youth in America operated not just on a shoestring but hand to mouth, warily anticipating every new funding cycle, never knowing where next year's budget for even the most basic services would come from, much less the funds to take on the really time-consuming and labor-intensive cases. The increasing shift of much adolescent treatment to a managed-care model meant that agencies were able to spend less and less time with troubled kids and that many of the most critical services—like aftercare—were cut back or eliminated.

But there was more to it than resources alone. The helping agencies most often operated with the same thin and impatient commitment shared by so many parents, and the same disinclination to roll up their sleeves and work with difficult youth over the long haul. The agencies also shared the parents' tendency to respond to adolescent troubles in ways that seemed peculiarly—and self-defeatingly—harsh. Thus, if one expression of therapeutic Darwinism was the tendency to give up on kids who could not overcome their problems, another was the readiness to shame, isolate, and punish them in the name of "treatment."

The inclination toward harsh treatment of adolescents in trouble has been dramatically exposed by revelations of mistreatment and brutality in some of the burgeoning "schools" for troubled or "defiant" teens that mushroomed during the time I was working with these adolescents and in the near-totalitarian "treatment" programs, often strategically located in third world countries, that several of my interviewees spent time in. The *New York Times* reported in 2003 that "the overseas 'specialty boarding school' industry is growing so fast that United States consular officials in overseas embassies say they have no idea how many such programs exist." A Web site offering help in placing teenagers in such schools suggests the flavor of these institutions:

> Today's teens are given more while having to do less to earn it than any previous generation. Instead of being appreciative of this generosity, many teens begin feeling an entitlement. Teens often feel they are entitled to current privileges and comforts without any effort on their part. This is far from reality.

The site makes it clear that the aim of specialty schools is to replace that sense of adolescent entitlement with unquestioning compliance:

> Specialty schools are designed to teach respect. This includes respect for others, property, self, authority figures, and more important, respect for rules and expectations. Our programs offers [*sic*] a military-type regimentation including a strong set of rules with high expectations and follow through. Failure to follow rules or commands will bring immediate consequences. Participants quickly develop a solemn respect for rules, orders, and authority figures.

This declaration is accompanied by a not-so-veiled threat: "Participants in our programs experience a lifestyle that reflects what it would be like for them if they did not have what their parents, or others have provided for them."

The site offers referral both to short-term "boot camps," where the aim is to instill "the importance of consistency and obedience," and to longer-term "behavior modification" facilities, where "teens progress and earn more privileges as good attitude, work ethic, and behavior are demonstrated" and where, "when teens make a bad choice, they are conscequented [*sic*] and redirected helping the teen make better choices." The brother of one of my interviewees was sent to one such behavior modification school; it was located in a desert setting in a third world country. Among other "consequences," participants were required to complete several laps around a track at midday under the desert sun. The boy's mother told me with considerable satisfaction that no excuses were accepted: kids had to finish the required number of laps whether they had to "walk, run, or crawl." Faced with accusations of brutality, the director of a chain of these schools responded this way in 2003:

> We run a tight ship and a tough program where inappropriate attitudes and choices are confronted and redirected and the living conditions are not as nice as the homes the parents had so kindly provided the teen before the teen sabotaged it. If these are the accusations, then we have no problem with the accusations.

Notably, though these institutions professed to be therapeutic facilities capable of dealing with a wide range of adolescent problems, including serious emotional troubles and depression, they often had few—if any—professional mental health workers of any kind on their staffs.

American-run specialty schools shut down under pressure from local authorities in Mexico, Costa Rica, and the Czech Republic, and in 2002 a California congressman called for a federal investigation of their operations both at home and abroad. But such extreme examples were just the tip of the iceberg, the visible sign of a much broader current in the American approach to troubled adolescents, a current that affected every one of the teenagers in this book.

"People Cry Here Because of the Way They Get Treated"

The treatment programs my interviewees encountered often seemed to equate treatment with the enforcement of obedience. They were shot through with arbitrary and sometimes confusing rules and relied heavily on a variety of highly public, ritualized punishments. When I first interviewed Zack, he had recently been admitted to a residential drug treatment facility, and I asked how he liked the program:

> It sucks.
> *Oh? Why does it suck?*
> Well, first of all, there are eighty-five rules and you have to learn them all.

Zack was right: the program did in fact require its young clients to memorize eighty-five rules, ranging from the obvious—like not getting in fights with other clients—to the murky, including a somewhat mysterious prohibition against looking in a mirror that was hung on the wall. Unsurprisingly, the kids routinely ran afoul of them: "You take a step, you break a rule. Take eighty-five steps, you break eighty-five rules." Zack himself spent an exorbitant amount of his time in "treatment" being publicly punished for one or another infraction and was finally thrown out of the program and sent to a juvenile detention facility, where he wound up staying for nearly a year. Stephanie found that her experience in a drug rehab that obsessively focused on rigid and sometimes incomprehensible rules made her so angry that she wanted to use drugs within two weeks of getting out:

> I was pissed off about being [there] and I didn't want to stay sober. So I was like angry that I had to be there in the first place and that I didn't feel like it helped that much. Like I felt the staff didn't really care about me and it's why I didn't follow any of the rules they had. . . . And that was their big focus. I was angry that they had all these rules. Like, you are disrespecting the mirror in the hallway if you look at it.

She understood that there needed to be rules but thought that there was something both punitive and arbitrary about the ones her program imposed:

> I mean I guess what they were trying to do is like get people used to following rules. . . . And so I understand that but I don't think they should have rules like—if you are thirty seconds late for a group, that you have to do some kinds of punishments for it. Or—don't look at the mirror that's in the hallway. Why is the mirror in the hallway if you're not supposed to look at it?

Beyond the sheer proliferation of rules, many treatment programs were given to the routine use of strategies of exclusion, humiliation, and public shaming. B.J. was sent at one point to a drug rehab that had a fairly solid reputation in its region. She went in with high hopes and a good deal of determination. But she ran into trouble early on. Once in the program, she was supposed to do the twelve steps of Alcoholics Anonymous that are ubiquitous in the adolescent treatment world. She had an emotional crisis during her fourth step, in which she was required to make "a searching and fearless moral inventory" of her shortcomings:

> Basically you have to write all the resentments you have about everything that's ever happened in your life. All your fears about your sexual conduct . . . I mean, I wrote like millions of pages on this thing. And it brings up a lot of things that have happened to you in the past. It's really hard . . . like stuff that you've done to other people, that other people have done to you. And like *everything*. So it's rough.

She ran away from the rehab for several days—"AWOLed," as the program called it—because it was hard to deal with these issues and there was no one to talk to about them: she was just supposed to make lists of them. She returned to the program after a few days but immediately began trying to get loaded again, inside the facility, in order to "kill the anger":

> And you can't. Can't kill it. And as I came back, I started like trying to get high when I was in here and like doing all kinds of stuff, like snorting like Tylenol and Prozac and huffing nail polish. And nail polish remover. All kinds of stuff, like a lot of it. But it didn't really work. It didn't work at all, actually.

I asked B.J. whether anyone in the program had sat down to talk with her about why she'd run away, why she was desperately trying to get loaded even inside the program, and why it was so hard for her to dig up her feelings. After all, as she had told me, she was clearly making a cry for help. "No," she said, "they didn't help out at all." Instead, she was assigned a special punishment status: she was not permitted to communicate or even make eye contact with anyone else. "You can't talk to people. You can't talk to anybody. And you basically isolate yourself. You go to bed early. You're not a part of the family at all, you can't pray with the family, you can't do anything with the family. So it's like you're *out*. Until they accept you back in." She had to wear a brightly colored shirt at all times, to set her off from the rest of the clients. She was also formally excluded from all the normal program activities—put "out of the family," in the jargon of her program. (It was not lost on B.J. that being put out of the family was precisely what had often happened to her before, in her real family.) B.J. told me that she had found this approach perplexing and self-defeating:

> I'd wear the orange vest, walk around by myself isolated for however many days it took me to finish my hours. That—I don't think that's a very good way to, like, deal with something when someone's going through

stuff, obviously. They throw someone in this orange vest and expect them to, like, fix everything, and it's like it didn't help me. It made it worse.

In fact, she ran away again out of frustration, "And then I came back, and they threw me right back on. And I was just like, *great policy*, you know? Obviously it's not working, you know?"

This time, in addition to being placed "out of the family," forced into silence, and made to wear special clothing that set her apart from others in the program, B.J. was required to sit motionless on a bench in the hall of the program facility, staring straight ahead of her. Her punishment was what was called "ten on ten"—ten hours of the bench alternating with ten hours of other assignments. Although this was "pretty harsh," she said, it could have been worse: other kids had gotten up to "twenty-five on twenty-five." In her case, the ten hours on the bench were split into five on each of two consecutive days. As B.J. explained, the program justified these hours on the bench as a "therapeutic" measure:

> Basically the bench is a tool for you to focus on yourself and think about yourself. You're not allowed to move. You're not allowed to talk. You're not allowed to look anywhere but straight ahead. . . . But like it's so *hard* to sit there on the bench and just focus on yourself.

Note again the language of "tools" and the imperative to look inward. The aim of this practice is to force B.J. to "focus on herself," yet from everything she has said it should be clear that most of the problem is not in herself—at least not in any simple sense. Her problems—both the out-of-control drug use and the emotional crisis brought on by her "fearless and searching moral inventory" of her shortcomings—involve her relationships with others and are unlikely to be illuminated by having her sit motionless and staring on a bench, "thinking about herself." But punishments of this kind, and with this rationale, are a staple of the adolescent treatment world, and they are sometimes taken to far greater extremes. In one

American-run treatment program strategically located in Jamaica, violation of the rules was routinely met by "Observation Placement," meaning that kids were made to "lie flat on their face, arms by their sides, on the tiled floor. Watched by a guard, they [had to] remain lying face down, forbidden to speak or move a muscle except for ten minutes every hour, when they [could] sit up and stretch before resuming the position." This "treatment," according to the program's director, was meant to give the kids "a chance to reflect on the choices they made." The record for time spent in "observation," according to this official, was held by a girl who had in the course of her stay spent a total of eighteen months on the floor.

Something like B.J.'s experience was common among the adolescents I spoke with who had been in some kind of treatment program. The operating principles—enforced silence instead of open and honest dialogue, exclusion rather than inclusion in time of need, isolation and shaming rather than understanding and firm guidance—appeared to be unquestioningly accepted in agency after agency. Indeed, the degree to which an emphasis on punishment dominated the inner culture of many "helping" programs bordered on the bizarre. Every institution that deals with troubled people, to be sure, requires some way of maintaining discipline, and achieving a balance between discipline and support is never easy. But the discipline meted out in many of the agencies encountered by these teenagers was often explicitly designed to demean and humiliate them. In one program, clients who broke the rules were made to sit or stand in a garbage can in the hall. In another program, they had to pretend to be an animal and run in circles around a room making animal noises; one was forced to wear a wet shoe on her head and run around a pool table quacking like a duck, another to bray like a donkey. Unsurprisingly, most of those who went through this treatment, or witnessed it, felt that it was counterproductive. Stephanie put it this way:

You heard about them doing that at [ ], where someone gets more than three different write-ups in a week, or whatever the number is. . . . And there's a pool table, and they have to run around it making animal sounds. Someone tell you about that? They choose which animal. It's usually like, you have to be a donkey with three legs and a broken nose and then you have to make the animal sound too.

What do you think they were trying to do with that?

Make someone regret whatever they did that was breaking the rules that week and feel embarrassed. So maybe feeling embarrassed at that time will make them not want to break the rule again because they know that if they break those rules again that they're gonna have to go back around the pool table and do that again.

Do you think that works?

No.

A common feature these teenagers encountered was the use of "confrontation" tactics in which program staff or other clients, or both, systematically criticized them in group settings. The idea was, in part, to break down their "false images" of themselves and, again, force them to acknowledge their "shortcomings"; in pursuit of those goals the sessions could be both intense and deeply humiliating. "It's hell," Terry said of his own experience. "It's just a bunch of people yelling. At least the first couple of times it was really hilarious. Like I didn't stop laughing."

Terry, as we'll see, was among those who left drug treatment with fairly positive feelings about it, who bought more of the programs' view of the world than most. Yet even he was troubled by the negative and undercutting culture that suffused his rehab program. He complained that "people get shit for just feeling the way they feel":

They say a lot of gnarly shit in that place, you know? I think there should be more positive reinforcement than there is. Or, you know, positive criticism or whatever, constructive criticism. . . . Like saying "You do this and this and this wrong, but you do this, this, and this good," you know? Instead of always "You do this, this, and this and this and this and this. You need to change that and that and that and that and that."

Like you have people go in there really fucked up, but obviously, there's *something* good about them because they're still alive, you know? And they're there, and they're trying.

Unlike Terry, the program staff did not think that "trying" was good enough to merit praise or support; indeed, the program explicitly taught its clients that "trying is lying"—that saying you were trying was nothing more than a lame excuse for laziness or avoidable failure. Like most kids I spoke with who had been through similar experiences, Terry believed that the routine harshness of the program—the fact that, as he put it, clients were "beat down all the time"—drove many kids away who might otherwise have benefited from treatment:

People cry here just because of the way they get treated here. . . . And it's not constructive. It's just kids calling each other names and like trying to put each other down. . . . I'm sure if there was a more therapeutic environment, there'd be less AWOLs. If a kid felt that he could really get something out of it and that, you know, the kids were open to what he had to say and they were understanding and stuff, then I think there would be less AWOLs.

After spending many months observing one such drug program and talking to teenagers enrolled in it, I had occasion to give a talk about what I had seen to a group that included people who ran similar treatment programs or worked in them as psychologists or psychiatrists. I noted that the program—like many others—made systematic use of public shaming of clients as an integral part of what it described as its "treatment model" and that, almost uniformly, the kids I had talked with were critical of these shaming ceremonies and felt that they had not been helpful, indeed had been a key reason some had run away and thus missed out on whatever positive assistance the program had to offer. I thought that the heavy resort to public shaming might be particularly inappropriate because so many teenagers who wound up in treatment were likely to have experienced far too *much* shame already in their lives: that was, after all, a running theme in my conversations with them.

After the talk I was approached by a psychiatrist employed by a residential drug program, who politely told me that he disagreed. The problem, he felt, with most kids who abused drugs was the opposite: they had experienced too little shaming in their lives and were inclined to act impulsively and without regard to what others thought; a good dose of shame was precisely what they needed. I pointed out that a substantial number of the kids I had talked with had been badly humiliated or abused by parents or caretakers and that deliberately piling more shame on top of those childhood experiences seemed not merely wrongheaded but potentially dangerous. He didn't see it. In his view, the problem was that most of these children had been overindulged and made to feel that there were no real consequences of their actions. A little humiliation would therefore hardly hurt at this stage and might be just what the doctor ordered.

I responded that this kind of shaming was not what most families I knew who had successfully raised competent children actually did—and was certainly not the way I would approach the drug problems of my own children, if they had them. The psychiatrist hemmed and hawed, then sputtered that perhaps the kids who wound up in drug treatment were extreme cases; the fact that they hadn't had the more supportive parenting I was describing in the first place might mean that they now needed the harsher and more humiliating treatment he felt I was unfairly criticizing.

What made this exchange particularly disturbing to me was that he was not some low-level staff person but a heavily credentialed professional who was in charge of providing treatment in a program that had a relatively solid reputation in his city. As that suggests, the strategies of deliberate shaming and strategic humiliation that my interviewees describe are not isolated peculiarities of a handful of eccentric programs; they are standard fare in many well-established treatment agencies, though the rationale for them is rarely discussed or defended in the open.

Resistance to the idea that adolescents in trouble might need a good deal of external support and that it ought not to be entirely up to them to manage their own lives was utterly pervasive in my encounters with the mental health or treatment staff who worked with the teenagers in this book. That resistance did not seem to be a carefully thought-out position grounded in theoretical understanding of the roots of adolescent problems: it was simply part of the way they looked at the world. Often, it produced an institutional indifference about consequences that closely paralleled that of the adolescents' families.

One expression of this view was an almost visceral sense that the world was necessarily a harsh place and that, accordingly, it was better to treat troubled kids with a corresponding harshness than to offer them a kind of support and nurturance that they were unlikely to find in the larger society. Once, for example, I presented some of my material on the negative reaction of many adolescents to the confrontational treatment they received in many drug programs to an audience of upper-level staff working in one of the programs in question. They met my concerns with a mixture of resentment and bewilderment. They did not deny that "tough" and often humiliating treatments took place in their agency, but they felt that I didn't understand that these practices were, in the larger perspective, not really severe at all but part of an effort to provide a "structure" their young clients had never had. When I objected that this was not the kind of "structure" that most parents I knew would want to provide for their own children, the staff responded that these were not ordinary children and therefore they needed something different. They were kids who had always "overreacted" to what this group clearly regarded as the normal, expected harshness and humiliations of life: "If they feel humiliated at school, they don't go. If they feel humiliated on the job, they quit." And so on.

I asked if this meant that the aim of the treatment was to toughen the kids up—to deliberately give them a taste of what they should expect on the outside. My audience demurred: it was not, they said, that they were trying to humiliate their charges "on purpose" but that, as one person put it, "this is life and they have never had to learn to deal with it." (Somehow, these adults in authority seemed, in their own eyes, to have no agency, no responsibility: things just sort of happened in their program, not exactly "on purpose," and when they did, it was the kids' job to "deal with it.") I repeated that it did not seem to me to be a necessary part of life to undergo public rituals of humiliation or to be forced, at thirteen or fourteen, to reveal the most intimate or scary or embarrassing aspects of one's personal life before an unsympathetic and deliberately hostile group of peers and program staff. To this, they had no answer. What, I asked, if this sort of treatment pushed kids away from the program and perhaps turned them against treatment of any kind? The response was quick and unanimous: "That's exactly their problem. They run away from things when life gets tough." (Looking around the table at the group of rather well-paid and clearly well-fed adults seated there, I found it difficult to believe that most could even imagine lives as tough as those lived by many of the children in their care.) I then asked: but what do we *do* with them then, if they reject treatment altogether, if they run away? Where will they go? What happens to them now? There was dead silence.

It was, in short, difficult for these educated mental health professionals to set out an articulate justification for these harsh and (in their clients' view) counterproductive practices—much less to seriously ask whether they worked, whether they actually helped the kids deal with their problems. The staff members' assumptions combined the foundational Darwinism of the broader middle-class culture with an institutional variant of the inversion of responsibility that characterized the parents of so many of their adolescent clients: Life is, and perhaps should be, hard. Your task, as an individual with a multitude of choices (even if you are, say, a fourteen-year-old girl who has been abandoned by both parents and is scrambling for survival on the street), is to acquire the emotional tools to navigate a world whose fundamental harshness and absence of concern is a given. It is certainly not *our* job to make things easy for you; if anything, that would hurt your chances in the future because it would raise expectations that the outside world will not, and perhaps should not, meet.

This attitude often involved a remarkable disconnect between the professionals' image of their clients and the reality of the adolescents' lives. Overwhelmingly, the conventional wisdom among the providers of services for troubled youth was that their charges had had it too easy and, accordingly, had never learned to accept limits or take responsibility. In fact, as we've seen, most of these teenagers had been forced to take on too much responsibility too early, and some had been forced to take care of themselves, for all practical purposes, since they were small children. It is hard to see how a child of five or six who has had to learn how to fix lunch for her little sister because their father is routinely passed out drunk on the living room floor can be said to have been coddled. Yet I cannot overstate how common this view was among the staff of "helping" agencies. And it could persist in the face of the most compelling evidence to the contrary.

Given the spectacularly bad and punitive character of some of these agencies, it is reasonable to ask why parents bought into them. Part of the answer is that some of the parents' own views about discipline and responsibility were very much in tune with those of even the most extreme of the youth control agencies. The ideology of the conventional mental health professions closely tracked the broader individualism of the culture, and many parents found it both familiar and appropriate.

But there was another reason as well. For some parents, parking their kids in a somewhat troubling placement was more a matter of acquiescence to practical realities than a sign of agreement with the philosophy of these agencies. They put their children in these places because they didn't know what else to do, and they sometimes did so with real trepidation. In this, they faced the same dilemma that confronted the adolescents themselves. Lacking more solid alternatives, parents were often grasping at straws. They ultimately put their children in places that worried them because they had no other choice, or at least no way of knowing if other choices existed. There was, in short, not much help out there for parents, either. Forced into a situation where they felt that they couldn't handle the problems on their own but unsure how to get help, they often accepted alternatives that they would have rejected had more choices been available. And a few parents—including Tracy's and Lacey's—stepped in to remove their children from placements that they had come to realize were treating them in ways that were simply unacceptable.

Therapeutic Darwinism and the Road to Whatever

What makes this institutional failure so troubling is that many of these teenagers really needed help at some point in their adolescence. They were at best overwhelmed and adrift, and often in peril. Some had been genuinely damaged by their treatment at the hands of abusive, neglectful, or dysfunctional adults. Over and over again, the teenagers I spoke with said that what they most needed during their periods of crisis was basic: they needed someone to listen to them, pay attention, take them seriously, not put them down or humiliate them. They needed people who were sufficiently engaged to help them figure out what to do next and strong enough to be flexible and understanding rather than reflexively judgmental—people who could help them understand their mistakes while acknowledging their good qualities and who could help them build on their strengths and potential. When they got that kind of response, they appreciated it and usually responded in kind. But they rarely got it. What they got too often was an ideologically grounded regime of punishment and blame that seemed designed to break their "oppositional" nature and force them to accept demeaning or even destructive circumstances in other realms of their lives.

This contributed to their descent into deeper trouble in several ways.

On the simplest level, it meant that opportunities to intervene seriously and to alter dangerous states of mind and courses of action were missed. These teenagers frequently went to helping agencies with high hopes and with a clear understanding that they were on a bad track and needed help. (Not always: sometimes they weren't ready to think about these things and were coerced into going. But even then, most became receptive to help if they received it.) They were often primed and ready to accept the assistance of sympathetic adults. When it was not forthcoming, their troubles were likely to fester and get worse, at least for a while. Listening to many of their stories, it is hard not to feel a sense of the sheer waste this neglect represented: it is clear that it would have taken very little to have helped many of these teenagers avoid the worst troubles they fell into. Instead, they were likely to be bounced from one ineffective placement to another, back to their problematic families, and often to the streets, in a depressingly meaningless cycle.

Beyond simply denying them help when they needed it, the stance of the helping agencies accelerated adolescents' descent into trouble in other ways as well. One we've seen already: the punitive character of so much "treatment" often drove kids away in anger, leaving them back out on the street without any help at all and sometimes making them mad enough to want to get in trouble again, out of spite if nothing else. This helps explain why adolescent drug treatment in particular has such a discouraging record: studies repeatedly find that most who begin treatment never finish it. Paradoxically, the fact that so many run away or drop out ends up making drug treatment appear more effective than it really is because most studies of the outcome of treatment look only at those who finish it and ignore the dropouts. But that statistical sleight of hand masks a system that works for only a minority of teenagers with drug problems and works least of all for those whose problems are most serious. Whatever help such programs are able to offer is undercut by their tendency to alienate those who could most benefit from it.

The "shaming and blaming" stance also meant that the contacts these adolescents had with adults who were theoretically there to help them were often fraught with frustration and even fear, and sometimes a sense of profound injustice. Not surprisingly, they felt inhibited from opening up about what was really bothering them, which left them even more convinced that they had no one to talk to, that there was nowhere to turn, and that they had to cope with their problems on their own. Anna's visits to a psychiatrist after she ran away from home at twelve illustrate the pattern:

> It was just a terrible experience for me. I was traumatized by it because the woman . . . walked in there with this attitude of *I know what you're all about.* And she had this very jaded sense about her, and she just *knew* everything about me. I was a problem child. She was convinced I was in a gang, which I wasn't, you know. . . . And so basically the whole session was her interrogating me and trying to humiliate me enough to convince—to try to get me to confess to being in a gang. . . .
>
> And I believe maybe she did ask me why I ran away, and my response was I didn't know, although inside I did know. But I was so scared, you know, because my mom's right there, and she's the perpetrator! And then I have this woman who's treating me like my mother, you know, being abusive towards me like my mother. And so, naturally, any child who's twelve years old, is scared, fearful what their mom's going to do to them once we arrive home, is not going to say anything. Especially with this woman humiliating me. I didn't feel safe to say anything. And it was just really frustrating and hard because I felt like no one's there for me. I can't reach out to anyone.

Many of the adolescents I spoke with told me that their encounters with mental health or treatment professionals had eroded whatever trust they still had in other people in general and adults in particular and helped cement their sense that authorities were not on their side, even when—or perhaps especially when—they claimed to be. As a result, some teenagers who really needed help and knew it would not bring themselves to seek it out or even to accept it if it was offered. As Anna says,

> It's not necessarily that adults are bad people. It's just I have had the experience so many times that I just don't trust adults. When I was that age, that was my overall mentality towards people who weren't—well, I didn't really even feel like I could trust people my *own* age. But I knew adults were capable of really bad things. So I just avoided being vulnerable— and I couldn't tell them what I was going through.

Tori, similarly, told me that even when she was in college, and years after she had beaten her heroin addiction, she still couldn't open up to others about her problems:

> I guess I should have taken the opportunity when I was there, but I just didn't, didn't trust them at all. . . . I mean, until this day I still don't trust people like that. Like, I tried to go to therapy to deal with my father's death, and then my grandfather just died, and I'm trying to deal with all this crap, and then graduating from school, and my mother's dating now, and all this stuff, so I tried to go to therapy to work out some of these feelings, and I still—I couldn't tell her the truth. . . . 'Cause, you know, she'd probably just think I was a junkie anyway. . . . Or "she's a *wacko*," or she's this or she's that, or whatever the judgment is.

Lacey was sent to a private psychiatric facility at seventeen because she "had another year of high school left, and my mother didn't know what to do with me." She describes her several months there as "hell, constant, constant hell." The program was "run like a military place": it was "very hierarchical, very stratified," its staff "very aggressive with us." The director told her from the start, she says, that she had a chip on her shoulder that he was determined to knock off. It was a place, she felt, where you could easily get in trouble and be punished if you revealed too much about yourself or dared to be critical. The program offered regular therapy sessions, but she didn't feel safe opening up in them:

> I hated therapy. I hated it. You couldn't criticize anything. You couldn't say what you felt. They wanted a puppet show. That was one of the things that destroyed the trust, I think. In this place everything you said to the therapist was told to the head guy. There was no privacy. And I found out, you know, the hard way. If I felt things or told things to her, she would immediately tell him.

While she was in the program, in fact, she often drew pictures in which she appeared either as a puppet on strings or as a child who had literally been burned by the authorities. The burned child represented what happened when she tried to be herself—when she ceased being an obedient puppet:

> Yeah, who I am fundamentally. You've been burned your whole life by what you are, and who you are has been charcoaled. You've been set on fire and burned because of who you are and what you are. . . . And it's like you have no skin, no hair. There's no feature that is distinguished on some level. . . . It's kinda weird. And then right next to it is the puppet.

Lacey's response was first to withdraw and then to shut down altogether, ultimately refusing to speak to the staff at all:

> That experience scared me so much. I think that was just like the worst. It was horrifying. I hated it. But I was very quiet, and I just sort of retreated. . . . I knew that I was going to be eighteen very shortly, so just shut up and put up would be better. So I just became nonresponsive. And that's one of the places I stopped talking.

Even if it did not cause most of the adolescents to shut down so completely, the sense that help was often a mask for unjust punishment or was fundamentally bogus deepened the alienation that already afflicted them and intensified their belief that the adult world was untrustworthy and unserious. It thus helped push them even farther beyond the orbit of "legitimate" adult institutions and deeper into worlds that were more congenial but more dangerous. It also encouraged the enforced self-reliance that so many of them had adopted—their conviction that no one but themselves was really there for them, that no one else was able or willing to protect them.

Some chose to take their defense into their own hands, but the consequences of that decision could be catastrophic. Sean's experience after he got kicked out of his parents' house illustrates this with particular clarity. While he was living in his friend's grandmother's Buick, his mother called the police on him and had him arrested as a runaway. After the arrest, he was sent to "one of those private adolescent hospitals." The experience left him thoroughly disgusted and even angrier than when he went in:

> You know, these moneymaking scams. They're ridiculous. They're absolutely useless. They don't do anything. And, you know, cost a couple hundred dollars a day. And I was in there for three months. And I got out, you know, just went back to things just as they were before, just a lot more resentful of my parents now.
>
> Your therapy was, you know, you'd sit with a psychologist or somebody in a big round room, and people would be, "So, Timmy, how was your day today?" "Like, I hear this place sucks and *you* suck." "Oh, that's very nice" and [moving on to the next patient] "How are *you*?" Just this sort of thing, that's your therapy. And . . . art therapy time, which was just draw pictures and have some like, you know, charlatan analyze it. They'd charge you a lot of money for everything. You know, a big waste of three months.

Sean felt that the staff systematically avoided confronting the underlying problems that had brought most of the patients to the hospital in the first place and indeed colluded with many of their parents in sweeping difficult issues under the rug:

It's just a lot of screwed-up kids mostly. A good percentage of them had problems because they were abused in some way by their parents or a relative or something like that. And then usually as soon as something like that would come up, the parents would pull them out of the hospital. . . . You know, at first both my parents would come, and you'd get in fights with them, tell them to take you out of there, and they'd say no, but the doctors have told them already ahead of time that that's a sign of your— you know, they're going to attempt to make you feel guilty and this and that —it "fits the profile of the troubled adolescent."

So I mean they had briefed them ahead of time what to expect. And then, you know, as soon as attention began sort of focusing on my mother, she stopped coming!

Sean believed that "warehousing" troubled kids in what he called "these mills" was worse than useless. It was self-defeating, because it concentrated the "screwups" together and was guaranteed to make them worse: "Almost everyone who got out, you'd wind up hearing about them getting in trouble or being back on drugs or running away or doing something." The sociologist Howard S. Becker pointed out fifty years ago, in studies of how people learn to become marijuana users, that becoming a full-fledged "deviant," and coming to think of oneself as such, requires learning the ropes that enable one to participate in the disapproved activity. This pattern was shared by several of my informants. The time Sean and others spent in places designed to hold troubled youth—especially in the absence of a culture of support and genuine adult involvement—typically taught them how to become more competent participants in adolescent deviance and firmed up their emerging sense of themselves as members of a community of outsiders that existed in opposition to the "normal" world of parents, school authorities, and "straight" kids. Sean said of the psychiatric hospital that

it has a similar effect as jail, in that you meet with lots of other kids who are doing all kinds of other things, and you talk to each other and exchange ideas about how to get in more trouble, and they tell you, "Oh, this is how you beat a drug test" and "This is how you do this, and this is how you do that." You know, which is this sort of exchange of bad ideas for the most part.

Sean left the hospital with nothing improved in his life and a heightened feeling that he was on his own in what had become an increasingly dangerous situation at school and in his neighborhood, fraught with drugs, gun-carrying gangs, and entrenched rivalries between "jocks" and "punks" like himself. He drifted steadily into worse trouble, without any clear sense of what he was doing or why. He began using a lot of LSD as well as selling it—not, he says, to make money but because "it was something to do, pretty much." He increasingly identified with his small and beleaguered subculture of oppositional "screwups," who were edging closer and closer to serious violence. The fear of being attacked was on his mind almost constantly, and he bought a gun on the street for fifty dollars—the one he was carrying when he got into the confrontation that landed him in prison.

At the extreme, the sense of injustice bred by the punitive approach of the helping agencies could trap teenagers in a fruitless cycle of punishment, resistance, and further punishment, so that some who had initially committed relatively minor offenses wound up spending months or even years in confinement. This is what happened to Zack: though he was first arrested for a minor incident involving drugs and fighting, he ultimately spent much of his adolescence in some sort of custody—not because he committed further crimes but because he kept getting in trouble with the authorities in the various institutions he ended up in. Sent to drug rehab after spending time in juvenile hall for the initial incident, he was constantly running afoul of its labyrinthine rules and finding himself on the "bench." "I tell you, I hated it there," he told me once. He thought it was possible to make it through the program without getting in trouble by being carefully compliant, "putting your head down," and "not making a commotion," but despite his awareness of the consequences he just couldn't do it. During his several months in rehab he was kicked out once and bounced back to juvenile hall for mouthing off at one of the staff members. Then he was sent back to the program for more "rehabilitation," only to be kicked out for good for refusing to sit on the bench. Several more months in a new juvenile facility followed and then a stint in a private youth "camp" for "defiant" teens.

When I last spoke with Zack he had finally been released from custody and was back at his parents' home, but only because he had turned eighteen and was no longer a juvenile, and the authorities had no reasonable justification for sending him on to adult prison. He had been incarcerated without a break since he was fifteen. And he had lost, as he was painfully aware, much of the experience that "normal" kids could take for granted. He had never been to a prom, had never had a "real" girlfriend or an after-school job, and of course didn't have a high school diploma. He wanted very much to go to college and was certainly smart enough to do so, but he was understandably apprehensive about what would happen to him there—a kid who had missed out on most of the skills that his peers had acquired and was returning to normal life with a distinctly ab-normal history. When we talked, Zack straightforwardly acknowl-edged that he had gone back to "doing what I do," by which he meant dealing drugs; our conversation was interrupted several times by the urgent jangling of his cell phone.

Zack was by no means an easy kid to deal with: he had trouble avoiding conflict and he kept tripping himself up because he found it hard to back down when challenged by authorities who "got in his face." He could be sullen and uncommunicative, and his ghetto-suburban style could be intimidating at first. But it is hard to believe that these qualities made him so difficult that no response was pos-sible other than cycling him from one form of confinement to an-other. What appears to have happened in each of his various placements was that he was quickly labeled as an enemy, not as a boy with considerable potential who was struggling with deep issues in his life. After many months of being defined as an opponent, he became one. He couldn't escape from this dynamic, even though he was bitterly aware that it was hurting his own chances.

"I Just Felt Very Incriminated"

By routinely generating mistrust and resistance the helping agencies often promoted what sociologists call "secondary deviance"—the tendency for the response to problems by officials or authorities to generate new, and frequently worse, problems. The constant pressure on kids to internalize their troubles had a similar effect. Many of these teenagers had endured a steady diet of blame and criticism at home and often at school as well, and their tendency to accept the view of themselves as "the problem" was already a punishing one, part of the reason they had descended into care-lessness in the first place. That many of the people who were supposed to help them and to whom they looked for expert guidance also told them, in essence, that their problems were their own fault made things that much worse. It could pitch the adolescent into a crisis of despair and self-loathing and solidify the negative identity that had already begun to develop. As Anna said of her experience with the mental health system, "I just felt very incriminated." Others felt the same way, and once they perceived themselves as incriminated by the system, there was little to keep them from living up, or down, to that feeling.

Some of them consciously fought against that definition of themselves, but the fight was likely to be a losing one, given the power of the institutions that were sometimes arrayed against them. They were, after all, only children when this process of negative definition began, and those doing the defining were not only much older than they were but also in positions of authority. The result was that they frequently gave in to that definition, at least for a while, with what were usually highly destructive consequences. This is strikingly clear in Anna's account of her trajectory from a mental hospital to several years of hard drugs and crippling depression. She was just thirteen when she was sent to the hospital, where she stayed for three months:

> It was just a very scary place. Everything was so sterile and—oh, my God, it just gives me the chills when I think about it. The other patients there were very suicidal. So constantly, this chaos around. . . . I'd pass by this kid on the ground being held down by doctors, and that was kind of a normal thing, or hearing screaming at night because if for some reason you are rebellious there, they put you in this little room and strap you down. And they'd have a doctor watch you at all times, and so the person screams the whole night. And it's really close. . . . We're right next to it, so we can hear the screaming. And I believe that that room was placed there just to put fear in us, . . . that there is this attitude of, oh, if you rebel, this is going to be *you*, and *you* are going to be scream-ing here all night.

If the aim of the hospital stay was to frighten Anna into good be-havior, it backfired. The day she got out, she says, "was probably the happiest day of my life." But soon after, "things got progressively worse":

> I got very depressed there. It just kind of *broke* me, in a sense. It wasn't helpful. It was just very scary for me, very traumatic. And I basically had gotten nowhere with my therapist, and so I just left there worse, much worse. And at that point I felt very suicidal. But, you know, luckily that never occurred. I still had a *little* bit of will in me. But, yeah, things got much worse.

I asked if there had been anyone she could talk to once she was re-leased from the hospital—had anyone followed up with her, main-tained some sort of connection? Anna laughed at this: "No, there wasn't anyone at all." She left home for good when she turned fif-teen. This time, she told her mother she was leaving, and her mother, she says, was hardly unhappy at the news: her response was "basically, 'OK, see ya.'" She moved in with a relative in another city, where she spent two years sleeping on the living room floor. She enrolled, for the first time, in regular high school and took a full-time job to support herself at the same time. But there was still no one to talk to, and she remained alone with her depression and saddled with the profound sense of "incrimination" that had been exacerbated by her stint in the mental hospital. She sank into the heavy drug use that was to consume her spirit and energy for several years.

She started using speed, in part simply to stay awake as she struggled with a forty-hour work week and a full load at school but also because the stay in the mental hospital had helped convince her that she had "nothing to lose":

> I felt so empty and dead that it didn't matter to me if I was sabotaging myself or, you know, whatever the negative repercussions were. It didn't matter. I just felt a void within from—you know, I still was really affected at that point from the mental hospital. I mean it took me a lot of therapy sessions to finally become calm and harmonious with that.

Anna had effectively bought the definition of herself that both her mother and the mental health system were offering, one that left her with no reason *not* to become a methamphetamine addict. Stuck with that definition, she took on its responsibilities with a vengeance. She began shoplifting. "I had no reason really to steal that stuff," she says.

> I didn't even need the stuff I stole. . . . I just figured, hey, I'm going to be rebellious. I'm going to do as much as I can to rebel. I didn't have integrity for myself, so I could justify turning around and hurting someone or, you know, stealing something. I was basically treating people in the outside world the way I treated myself within.

The stealing, she agreed, was mostly a way to establish her identity as a truly bad girl, a way of saying "Oh yeah, you think I'm a screwup, so I'll show you; I'm very good at screwing up."

You do tend to take on that persona. If you're treated like that enough, you're going to take it on. I just feel like when you're treated like you're the problem, you become convinced that you *are* the problem. No matter how cocky you are with adults, you, deep down inside, don't have love for yourself. You are stripped of that. Any sort of self-worth, dignity, you're completely stripped of. And as a result, when you have such little respect for yourself because you were never treated with respect, you were never taught to love yourself, you don't care. There's nothing to lose.

"You become convinced that you *are* the problem," so you have "nothing to lose." That, in a nutshell, is the logic that brought many of the adolescents in this book to the point of a profound and dangerous care-lessness.

"The World Don't Change for You"

The tendency of therapeutic Darwinism to encourage youth to internalize their problems had more subtle effects as well. Some of the saddest of my encounters with troubled adolescents involved those who had bought in to the pervasive ethos of Darwinian individualism that dominated the world of the helping agencies. By the conventional measures, they were considered to be successes of the system, at least for a while: they had, by virtue of "putting their head down and getting through it" (as Josh put it), managed to complete some sort of treatment and return to their communities. In the process, they had come to accept the agencies' view that their problems were theirs and only theirs to deal with, the consequence of their own "bad choices," and that the only way to surmount them was to start making "good choices." But "success" often came with a price, for the acceptance of this relentlessly individualistic ideology set them up for a sense of failure when they tried to put it into action. Several left drug treatment, for example, armed with little more than the implanted conviction that they could handle their drinking problem or the temptations of their "drug of choice" (an oddly revealing phrase in itself!) or their conflicts with their families if they just chose to do so. If they relapsed into drugs or drink, it was because they weren't making use of the tools that authorities had generously made available for them. Certainly, they should not expect much help from the outside or hope for change in the conditions of their lives. "The world don't change for you, you change for the world," Zack told me once, parroting a platitude he'd learned in one of his several placements. But they rarely had the capacity, realistically, to "change for the world" on their own, because to do so would have required having control over forces much larger than themselves—in their families, schools, and communities—that profoundly influenced their risks of falling back into dangerous or destructive behavior.

The tools that they had been given by their various programs, accordingly, proved to be very slender reeds for them to lean on. Typically, they had precious little time for in-depth exploration of their troubles while in treatment, and they usually left with not enough changed in the environment around them to significantly improve their chances of staying healthy and out of danger. Often, their treatment programs specifically admonished them not to think about the past, which meant that they were discouraged from examining deeply the reasons why they had gotten into drugs or drink or become depressed. As a result, they were no more prepared to understand their propensity for self-destruction than they had been before their treatment, and often less so. When they went back into their old lives believing that they were now supposed to triumph over their troubles alone and largely unaided, they often failed. When they did, they blamed themselves and took the failure as further evidence of their fundamental inadequacy, and that could bring them crashing down into even more destructive behavior than before.

Terry was a prime example of this pattern. When I met him, he was certainly deeply troubled—a heavy drinker, a user of multiple illicit drugs, an intermittently homeless fifteen-year-old who drove cars at breakneck speed while he was stoned or drunk and broke into stores to get money for drugs and gasoline. But he was also spirited, feisty, and keenly aware that he'd often gotten a raw deal from his collapsed family and the stunningly negligent schools he'd attended. After many months in treatment, he'd changed. He seemed less vital, less savvy, more depressed. He was also given to regurgitating the program's line: he did not think it was useful to talk about why he was still depressed. He thought what was important was that he make good use of the tools that the program had given him ("It's all there for you if you decide to use it" was his mantra) once he returned to his suburban community.

On one occasion, after he'd been out of treatment for several months, I asked Terry, as I had many others, if there was anything he would suggest to the mayor or the city council about ways to improve his community's capacity to help kids in trouble. Despite his lengthy experience with the limitations of the schools and social services in his city, he found it hard to think of anything or even to accept the legitimacy of the question. He thought in general that it was not the community's responsibility to provide things for people and that in any case the people who really wanted to change would find ways whether they had help or not, while those who didn't want to change probably wouldn't, no matter how much help they received from outside. I reminded Terry that, according to what he'd told me, a treatment program had helped *him*. Shouldn't we then invest in more such programs so other kids could benefit from a similar experience? He responded this way:

> I don't know. I'm not one to judge what the community needs or not because I know usually what it comes down to is what *I'm* willing to do. You know? Like, you can make every program in the world and every service in the world, but it's like, no matter where you are or what it is or what there is to offer, it's always going to be the same people that succeed.

Terry went on to say that he didn't think that existing treatment programs helped very many people, since only "two out of about three hundred" kids he'd been in treatment with had gotten clean. But he wasn't able to think about how the programs might be made better in order to improve those percentages. He complained, on the one hand, that there was realistically no way for him to make use of his treatment center's aftercare program, because nothing was available in his own city or for many miles around and getting to the program facility to take part in aftercare had taken him over three hours the one time he'd gone. On the other hand, he said that he didn't believe that his community had any responsibility to offer more accessible care or that anyone would necessarily avail themselves of it if they did.

Terry was consistent in this view: he applied the same principles to his own situation. He didn't expect anyone to change things for his benefit. He was, in short, committed to going it alone when it came to addressing the depression and drift that still dogged him after he left treatment. This seemed to me like a recipe for disaster once Terry hit the street, and it was. He did all right for a few weeks after he came home, but soon things began to fall apart. He became deeply depressed about things that were going on in his family and in his relationships with other kids, and he began doing heroin in a big way for the first time. Before his treatment he had used it sporadically, but he had never come close to getting hooked and indeed regarded people who were as "kind of pathetic." He now, at sixteen, spent most of his time holed up alone in a cheap motel room shooting heroin or out on the street hustling and stealing to pay for it.

Obviously, there is truth to the idea that adolescents, like everyone else, need to accept responsibility for their lives, to learn from mistakes, to do the best they can in the circumstances they are in. But for Terry, as for most of the other teenagers in this book, the balance was out of kilter. They had already been burdened with far too much of the responsibility of managing their own lives and too little assistance in doing so. That had been a main reason why they had fallen into trouble in the first place. Now they were also being told that they had to pull themselves out of trouble on their own, that they shouldn't expect much help in this effort, and that this was the way it *should* be, the natural order of things. Help, in effect, had been oddly redefined for them as its own negation, as the therapeutic withdrawal of assistance. Some, like Terry, fell especially hard when they could not maintain this coerced and premature independence. Others, as we'll see, managed to keep their heads above water and ultimately found their way to a more centered and productive adulthood. But it was often just the luck of the draw if they did.

THE SCHOOL AS OPPONENT

Until Mickey was thrown out of the house for the third and final time, she lived in a rapidly growing suburban town that had once been pretty and even bucolic but has been increasingly engulfed by the relentless sprawl of a large and rather faceless city several miles farther down the freeway. The village center still has the look of a classic American small town, but it is now surrounded by new developments—upscale gated communities, a stunning shopping mall with a movie theater boasting twelve screens. A flood of traffic roars along the wide streets leading into town. There is a general air of busyness and prosperity but also a certain chaotic and unformed quality to the place, a sense that it has grown too fast, that too much is going on too quickly, and that its various pieces fit together only haphazardly. Mickey lived in one of the newer neighborhoods, where spacious homes have sprouted on streets that are still bare of vegetation. Construction seems to be going on everywhere: piles of building materials are stacked in driveways, and a constant din of hammering and machinery can be heard during the day.

Mickey is blond, tiny, with almost angelic features, and looks like she might be a stalwart in her high school chorus. But when I met her, when she was fifteen, she hadn't been to "regular" high school for more than two years. She had been using alcohol and drugs since she was ten and was now heavily into both methamphetamine and heroin. When we first spoke, Mickey was about to be released from a drug treatment center, where she'd been for about a month. She was afraid to leave: she felt that if she were back at home, she'd probably start using again, "because of what I'm feeling inside. I just don't want to deal with anything right now." When I asked what it was she didn't want to deal with, she said, "It's just frustration and fear and—I don't know. I'm depressed." I asked what it was that was making her afraid: "I have really high expectations of myself, for some reason. I don't know why. But I never seem to meet anything, so that kind of like really lowers my self-esteem. And I'm afraid that if I try to do something, I will fail."

She had felt isolated and adrift ever since her parents broke up when she was a small child. The divorce had been very hard on her: "I missed my dad, and I was really lonely. I felt like I was all alone. I didn't have anybody to talk to." Her mother was a computer consultant and was in high demand; Mickey says that she was "always at work." Her father moved to another state after the divorce, and Mickey hadn't seen him for years. Starting school, even though it took her out of a lonely house, only made things worse:

> When I started going to school, I felt very different. I've always been really shy and introverted, so I had a hard time making friends. I was always really depressed. I remember feeling like I was floating above my body, like people were, you know, going on and living their lives, and I would sit there, and I would watch them. And they would make fun of me and, you know, do things to me or whatever. And it wouldn't affect me because I was kind of—I was disconnected completely somehow. I don't really know how I did that, but I remember feeling very disconnected about that.

She found it difficult to keep up with schoolwork as well, " 'cause I wasn't intelligent enough." Early on, she says, "I knew that there was something wrong with me but I didn't know what it was":

I never did well in school. I went through my elementary school and my junior high and like another half a year of not knowing that I have a learning disability, so I thought I was stupid. And even my teachers thought I was stupid because they didn't understand why I couldn't do the simple things that everybody else could do.

Still, she worked hard up until fifth grade. At that point, she says, "I stopped trying":

That was the first time that my teacher called me stupid, several times, like in front of the class. And then after that I kind of just like kept to myself. I stopped doing homework because I didn't want to be confronted by the teachers. I thought I was stupid, and I didn't want anybody to know I was stupid except for me. And even then I wanted to forget.

No one at her school, she says, tried to figure out why she was having so much trouble keeping up:

My fifth-grade teacher, I remember, was the first like confrontation I had with the whole thing. We were doing math and she kept asking me what school I came from. "What school did you come from? Why are you so far behind?" And I knew everything they were doing, but I *didn't* know it. Do you know what I'm saying? Like I had seen it all before, but I didn't know how to do it.

The school didn't test her to see what might be wrong:

That costs money for them, to have somebody tested. So they never did that. My mom finally decided to have me tested in the ninth grade, and then that's when I found out. And still, like they had the test results and everything, and the school still tried to deny, you know, I'm just lazy, I'm just—if I tried a little harder, you know? But it was on the test that I had. It came up pretty clear.

After the fifth-grade teacher told her she was stupid, school "scared" her; she still went, but she was afraid to open her mouth in class, stopped doing homework, and started hanging out with the "bad kids," who, she said, were the first friends she'd ever had:

> I just started acting up, because it was easier. 'Cause then I was belonging with the bad kids. That made me feel not as different, I guess, because they didn't know that I was not very intelligent. They just thought that I was—I fit in with them because I didn't want to do my work or I was rebelling. I was only rebelling because I didn't feel I was smart.

She started drinking in fifth grade, was smoking dope in sixth, and was doing crystal meth by seventh. "Tweaking" on meth was especially appealing because, she said, it took her out of herself, but in a good way: it overcame her shyness and her fear of other people. It also gave her a sense that nothing could hurt her anymore and, above all, made her feel not stupid. "I felt like I could do more stuff. I could deal with more things. That I could—anything could happen to me, and I still wouldn't be able to feel anything":

> It gave me energy to do things, you know. Like I never really *completed* anything. But I don't know. It just—it made me feel like I was *doing* something instead of just watching everybody all the time, like I was used to doing. Like I had been introverted all my life, and then when I was on crank or crystal, it allowed me to talk to people that I didn't know, and start conversations, and I'd be outgoing, like being everything that I've always wanted to be, you know?
>
> Also, I felt like I was more intelligent. Like I don't even know where the intelligence came from when I was on drugs, but I was—I would shoot things out of my mouth without even thinking, and I would have the answer to something, and I never even knew where it came from.

She continued to do poorly in school but was passed along anyway until she reached her first year of high school:

And then when I got to ninth grade, I just didn't go to school any-more. Like I'd show up to get high or whatever. But I'd just ditch school like every day. And at Cedar Ridge High they have a hard time dealing with people who don't want to go to school. So the first initial reaction for them is to kick them out. Or make them go to some kind of a community school or continuation school or home studies or something.

She was indeed expelled from school—"because I wasn't going to school"—and sent to the local continuation school. I asked if the school had made an effort to work with her to try to understand why she wasn't going to school before they expelled her; she said that nothing like that had happened, and she believed that it very rarely did happen for people like her or like her friends, most of whom had also either dropped out of school or been expelled:

I think that the more intelligent people got the more—the more attention, I guess. Like the attention was more on them because the teachers knew that they would be the easiest kids to teach, whereas the people that weren't as intelligent or the people that weren't really trying to do the work or whatever, as far as the behavioral problems or just, you know, they just kind of ignored them.

She thought the kids who were less intelligent or who otherwise had problems were generally allowed to "fall through the cracks":

And I think that the people who fall out of the regular school education system, like whether they're having behavioral problems or because of—just whatever might be going on, whether they're bad kids or whether they just don't fit into the mold of what a regular teenager should be and do, you know? They were sent to this continuation school or they were put on home studies. And if they can't—if they weren't smart enough or if they just weren't able to do that, then they were screwed.

Mickey fell into the category of the "screwed": sent to continuation school, she floundered there too, partly because the school lasted only three hours a day and partly because many of the kids showed up high and sometimes did drugs "before, during, and after" school. She was still afraid to talk in class, even though there were some supportive teachers at this school, because she worried that she would again be revealed as being "different." Soon she stopped going to the continuation school as well and became convinced that she wouldn't go back to school "ever again":   "I was just scared, and I—I felt like a failure. I don't think anybody should have to feel like that, even if they are stupid. I think everybody has a right to their education, however they have to do that."

"Legally, I think, your parents are supposed to take care of you"

Around this time, her mother "got fed up with it" and threw Mickey out of the house. She was fourteen. "It was because of what I was doing. Drugs in the house, and not coming home when I was supposed to, leaving for a couple of days at a time without even calling to say where I was, if I was alive. And I can understand that." I told Mickey that, from the perspective of a parent, her behavior would certainly be upsetting but that I didn't think my own response would have been to kick her out of the house and tell her she couldn't come home until she straightened out. "I don't think it would be my response either," she said, "but I guess you gotta do what you gotta do. I think a lot of the reason she did it was for tough love or whatever. And I don't really know a lot about tough love, but oooh—it didn't make me want to change any faster, I can tell you that."

Her mother had remarried shortly before this incident. Mickey got along poorly with her new stepfather, who, she said, rarely spoke to her at all. She began more and more to feel that, like the schools, her mother and stepfather wanted nothing more than to wash their hands of her:

> I felt like, if I had a problem, they just didn't want to deal with it. Like if I couldn't be responsible and basically take care of myself and still live in my house, then they weren't going to have anything to do with me. And that really, really hurt me.

Part of her understood her parents' point of view, and she often blamed herself for her failure to make "better choices." She felt very lonely during the time she was living away from home, especially since she'd been booted out by her school as well. But she was half convinced that she might just be using this feeling as a way of avoiding responsibility. "I feel pretty much on my own," she told me, "but it's because I make myself feel that way. I *make* myself feel like I don't belong, you know? I do it on purpose where I can have an excuse to go and use. So I can't really use that as an excuse." But sometimes she did feel that there was another side to the matter: that it shouldn't all be up to her and that her mother bore some responsibility too. Just as she thought that everyone had a right to an education, she believed that they had a right to parenting as well: "Legally, I think, your parents are supposed to take care of you." At one point, while she was bouncing from friends' homes to the street and back again and finding herself in situations that were "definitely, definitely scary," she called the county child welfare authorities, in a rare display of initiative, and tried to get them to force her mother to take her back in. But nothing came of it:

> Yeah, CPS just kind of said, you know, whatever. They came to the house I was staying at for a while and did a couple interviews, but nothing happened with that. I think they wanted some kind of abuse to be going on, like physical abuse. Otherwise I don't think it was very important to them. I'm sure a lot of that stuff happens all over the place, that it just wasn't a big enough deal to them.

At fifteen, strung out, lonely, and increasingly frightened by the bad scenes around her, Mickey checked herself into a drug program. It was during her time there that she told me that she was afraid to come out because she was terrified that she would fail again. Her prediction was accurate. When she came out of rehab, she was determined to "go on and move forward" with her life. "And do good things, you know, make good choices." She went back to another continuation school and tried to stay sober, but it was hard because "basically everybody that goes there was using drugs." Meanwhile, she was still "not welcome" at home; she "felt like an outsider" in her family. She soon began using again, and shortly thereafter her mother kicked her out for the second time. When I caught up with her around that time, this is how she described her days:

> I'd get up and sometimes I'd go to school. I'd meet my friends at the Burger King, which was just down the road from Cedar Ridge High. That's where everybody met before and after school to get high, and meet up and go ditch school or something. And meet up with my friends, and go over to people's houses or to parks or whatever and drink and smoke and just kick it. And when school got out, go back up to the Burger King, meet everybody else, and go do it all again. Then find a place to sleep or go home. And get up and do it all again.

———•———

Other than the family, the school is the most significant adult institution most adolescents encounter as they grow up. Indeed, in some places the school is, for all practical purposes, the *only* other adult institution with which teenagers have much contact. And for most of the teenagers in this book, the "ground truth" about school—at least from middle school onward, and sometimes earlier—was astonishingly bleak. Many describe high school in particular as a "horrible" experience; some spent little time in high school at all and were bored, angry, and disengaged when they were there. The schools, at best, failed to engage their interest or mobilize their abilities and, at worst, bred a painful sense of injustice that compounded the anger and alienation they felt as a result of their treatment at home.

Like Mickey, most encountered in the schools the same neglectful individualism they had found in their families, and this experience affected their lives in several destructive and mutually reinforcing ways. It made them feel worse about themselves at a time when they desperately needed to feel better. It helped confirm their sense of themselves as failures, screwups, or outsiders. It added a geographic dimension to that emerging identity by actively pushing many of them outside the schools' orbit altogether or into "alternative" schools that they most often (though not always) regarded as both a form of punishment and a waste of time—places to hang out with other screwups and do drugs. Accordingly, it put them even more beyond the range of potential engagement and support from competent and responsible adults and thus solidified their sense that they were mostly on their own, with few people to lean on or ask for guidance. It often exacerbated their feeling that the adult world was hostile, untrustworthy, and generally "full of shit" and left them with that much less reason to care about what adults thought of them. It chipped away at their expectation of a clear and attainable future of increasing competence, of steady integration into a stable and approving society, and thus contributed to their sense that what they did with their lives didn't matter much one way or another. More subtly, by failing to engage their spirits or tap their abilities, the school deprived them of the emotional sustenance and self-esteem that the life of the mind and creative achievement can bring (and later did bring, for some of them). It helped strand them in a limbo of isolation, self-loathing, and catastrophic boredom that placed them at great risk of drifting into behavior that could destroy them—or others.

The problem with school, for most of them, was twofold. On the one hand, school authorities often seemed peculiarly unaware of their problems and generally passive and disengaged when signs of trouble arose. The schools were often inept and desultory in their few attempts to intervene, even when problems had become obvious.

On the other hand, they were quick to label kids as troublemakers, the ones to watch out for—and quick to punish them, generally by suspension or expulsion, when trouble rather predictably occurred. These may seem to be contradictory responses, but they were actually two sides of the same coin, two facets of a larger culture of institutional indifference that pervaded many of their schools. The bottom line was that the schools functioned less as actively nurturing institutions, committed to building the competence and intellectual capacity of all their students, than as instruments for sorting and categorizing them—sifting the good from the bad, the promising from the "losers," the troublesome from the "OK."

"That Kind of Stuff Doesn't Happen"

Like Mickey, Terry had a hard time at school from the beginning. By the time he started elementary school, his mother was so depressed that she could barely get up in the morning; as Terry puts it, "she just kicked back all the time." He was sympathetic to her condition, which he explained as "a chemical imbalance kind of thing." But by third grade he was often depressed and angry himself, and he brought those feelings to school. He acknowledges that he didn't make things easy for his teachers: "I never listened to any of my teachers really. I used to yell at them and tell them to shut the fuck up. In elementary school I did it all the time. They'd tell me to go outside or like go to the office, and I'd say, 'Fuck you,' and start crying and walk away."

As at Mickey's school, no one worked with him to figure out what was going on. I told Terry I thought this was unusual. If it had been me, I said, and a little kid at my school was constantly crying and telling the teachers to shut up, I would have wanted to find out what was up. At this Terry laughed out loud. "That kind of stuff doesn't happen," he said. "That's like a fantasy."

What happened instead was that the school punished him regularly—but also fruitlessly:

If you look at my school record, it's pretty damn thick. . . . I've been expelled like at least six times. I've had like 30 million suspensions. When I was in elementary school, I'd go to school every other day! 'Cause I'd go to school and get suspended, and I would skip a day 'cause I got suspended for that day. And then I'd come back and then get suspended *that* day. I'd be there for like three half days a week. And I didn't even care.

This meaningless and wholly predictable ritual produced in Terry a profound estrangement from school and deepened his feeling that he really "didn't give a shit" about things in general:

I get to school, get kicked out and go home, and then do whatever the fuck I want, you know? I don't really care. I knew how to read better than anyone in my class anyways. I could do math. I wasn't worried about, you know, being *stupid* for the rest of my life.

By eighth grade he was regularly coming to school drunk or stoned: "When I had PE first period, I'd go high all the time. And like I'd get drunk *in* PE and stuff." I asked Terry if anyone at school noticed. "People noticed," he said, but "they didn't even trip about it." On the other hand, the school expelled him on the spot for being caught with a small pocketknife that he used to clean his pipe. People were carrying around guns, he pointed out, "and they're like tripping out about some little pothead and his pocketknife."

The school held an expulsion hearing: " 'Well, you're expelled.' And so I was like, 'OK, fuck it then.' " He was ultimately sent to a continuation school but quit going after a few weeks, and when I met him, when he had just turned fifteen, he'd had no contact with any school at all for several months. By this point, his estrangement from the very idea of school was complete. This came out strikingly in one of our discussions shortly after we'd met. I had read a news article reporting on a study suggesting that teenagers were doing fewer drugs because of antidrug education programs in the schools, and I asked Terry if he thought that was true. He became uncharacteristically angry:

Who the hell said that? No one gives a flying about the drug education programs. I started using when I was six years old. And the shit they say in school never would stop me from using. I'd have to be really stupid. If anything, it's the parents. If people started hanging out with their kids more and getting them involved in stuff. . . . Whoever said that needs to be *decapitated*. I mean—who the fuck would think—seriously, kids don't listen to school. Even the *good* kids don't. . . . They don't give a flying fuck.

School is such the smallest thing in a teenager's life as far as they're concerned. They don't even teach you anything in school. . . . You know, it's like, you're a fuckin' teacher and your job is to piss off kids all day! Why the hell should I listen to *you*?

Terry was hardly alone in this feeling. Most of the adolescents in this book found the schools both disengaged and hostile, and many came to respond in kind. They felt that it was difficult to get attention from school authorities when things began to go bad for them, but if they ultimately went very bad—or if they simply crossed an arbitrary behavioral line drawn by their teachers or principals—the school was quick to exclude them altogether. I asked Laurie, for example, if anyone at her high school had ever asked what was going on with her during the time when her grades, which had been stellar for years, suddenly plummeted in her sophomore year as she began doing drugs heavily:

Not really. I mean, I never—maybe back at junior high that would have happened, but not at *high school*. No. I mean, I stopped going to all my classes. . . . Teachers in high school don't really care that much, I don't think, individually about their students.

Zack, who was routinely placed in classes for gifted students in elementary school, became a bored, angry, drug-addled student in high school and ultimately left altogether during his second year:

I used to be a great student. I used to win championships and shit like that all. It was cool. Doing all that shit with science fairs. Whatever, you know what I'm saying? And then I just—schools became boring to me. They couldn't teach me nothing new. I wasn't really learning nothing new in the last couple of years of school.

And then I just started doing drugs. I could keep up, but then I just couldn't keep up 'cause it just wasn't no point to do homework if you was never in class. And when you *was* in class, I was in there talking about what are we going to do, how are we going to get drugs? I would be kicking it with my partners. It's like, "What do you want to do after class? Fuck seventh period, let's cut."

Not a single teacher or administrator asked what was up, even though Zack was going to class with bloodshot eyes, "high as fuck":

I used to go into classes sometimes, the class right after lunch, science, I'd go in there and she'd just go, "Zack, put your head down and go to sleep." I wasn't trippin'. Know what I'm saying? Let me go to sleep.

Again and again, the schools' response to such evidence of trouble vacillated between a startlingly laissez-faire attitude and the repeated but ineffective use of suspension and expulsion. What was missing was a middle ground, a strategy of firm but constructive engagement. This wasn't simply because the schools were so large or the teachers so overwhelmed that kids with problems went unnoticed: in fact, they usually *were* noticed. Neither Zack's high school nor Terry's nor Laurie's was the kind of impersonal place with thousands of students that critics sometimes single out for allowing students to fall through the cracks. Yet all three found the idea that teachers in a high school might actually care about their students' difficulties to be slightly strange and even amusing.

It might be argued that the view of school offered by adolescents like Zack, Laurie, or Terry has to be taken with a grain of salt: after all, these are disaffected and troubled teenagers who, for the most part, did poorly in high school and, unsurprisingly, had a sour attitude toward it. But there are several reasons why it would be a mistake to discount their perceptions.

For one thing, as we'll see, the college students I spoke with, all of whom were ultimately quite successful academically, described remarkably similar experiences with high school; some of them, indeed, had done well even while attending high schools that they generally loathed and that, apparently, loathed them. And it would be gravely misleading to dismiss those who were still high school age when I talked with them as a bunch of academic losers. Most were thoroughly estranged from school but, with only a few exceptions, they hadn't always been. Several, like Zack, had been in special classes or tracks for gifted and talented students before they hit middle school; some, like Laurie, had been star students into their early high school years. Whatever happened to them later in school was not a reflection of low abilities or the absence of potential.

There is also broader evidence that their experience is far from unusual. The common pattern I heard so often from my informants—the routine neglect of highly visible problems, coupled with peremptory exclusion from school over what could be quite minor infractions—turns up regularly in scholarly studies of the schools' response to troubled or failing students. A review of a number of such studies that appeared in the staid *Journal of the American Academy of Child and Adolescent Psychiatry* around the time I was interviewing these teenagers is instructive. The review points out that most studies of schools' responses to discipline problems and academic failure show that students in trouble often have a range of remediable problems that appear early in their school careers, and it suggests that schools could benefit by taking a more attentive approach to those problems and developing strategies to prevent them before students get in serious trouble or drop out. The author notes that these studies generally recommend "early intervention, specific diagnosis and intervention planning, and sustained involvement" with students in trouble, "in contrast to common school reactions of delayed or even absent response, uninformed intervention, or erratic punishment."

Some findings from specific studies are revealing. One study of disciplinary referrals in middle schools, for example, concluded that such referrals "are common practice in middle schools, especially for non-compliance and disrespect, i.e., problems with authority, which may often be developmentally appropriate behavior." A survey of students suspended from middle and high schools found that the majority "have serious problems, for which suspension will have little effect." Similarly, a study of students recommended for expulsion in a suburban California high school district found that most had clear academic problems that had apparently been largely unaddressed by the schools before they were singled out for potential expulsion. Their mean grade point average was a D+ and their average scores on various tests of achievement in reading, math, and language were well below the 50th percentile. Such students, the study noted, are hardly difficult to spot: they "should be obvious to schools before they present with an expulsion incident."

A large-scale longitudinal study of factors leading students to drop out of school found that "most students who dropped out did not commonly receive school interventions to help them not drop out, e.g., only 39% indicated that school staff had tried to talk them into staying." This despite the fact that, as another study indicates, the typical high school dropout, like those with serious discipline problems, presents a variety of academic problems by the third grade, notably "underachievement and poor attendance." The review concludes by saying that current research suggests the need for "active, sustained, relevant intervention with such at-risk children" but also makes it abundantly clear that such intervention is now very far from the norm. Note that many of these studies were done in mixed-race or largely white or suburban schools; expulsion and dropping out are even more severe problems among disadvantaged minority children, but the pattern of systematic neglect coupled with reactive harshness toward troubled or floundering students shows up again and again for those who are white and middle class as well.

These long-standing tendencies were exacerbated by the spread of so-called zero-tolerance policies in the public schools, which spread throughout the country during the 1990s and were a pervasive feature of the educational landscape during the years I was inter-viewing the teenagers in this book. The federal Gun-Free Schools Act of 1994 mandated that schools expel children for a year if they brought a weapon to school, but many school districts went much farther, adopting policies that could cause students to be expelled for bringing over-the-counter medications to school or talking back to a teacher; the vast majority of expulsions and suspensions in the era of zero tolerance were not for serious incidents or threats of vi-olence. Of the more than three million suspensions from public schools in 1997, according to a review of such policies by the Amer-ican Academy of Pediatrics, the vast majority involved "nonviolent and noncriminal acts." Roughly 10 percent of expulsions or suspen-sions that year involved the possession of weapons. Rates of expul-sion and suspension, moreover, were several times higher in smaller towns than in large cities, even though rates of student violence were generally lower. As the pediatricians point out, suspension and expulsion were being used primarily as a general disciplinary mea-sure to rid school districts of troublesome students, not as a specific response to the threat of violence. At the same time, however, many school districts were neither trying to prevent kids from getting to the stage of expulsion nor developing serious alternative programs for them if they *were* kicked out. Indeed, the Gun-Free Schools Act, while making expulsion mandatory for students bringing a weapon to school, made the creation of such alternative programs voluntary for school districts. The result was that significant numbers of youths booted out of schools received no educational services at all. There were of course exceptions to this pattern: some school dis-tricts created innovative alternatives for suspended or expelled stu-dents, and indeed a few of my informants had their *best* school experiences in such alternative programs. But that was not the usual pattern.

The pediatricians suggest, with some exasperation, that there is a disturbingly heedless quality to these policies; indeed, they run counter to both scientific evidence and common sense:

Children who use illicit substances, commit crimes, disobey rules, and threaten violence often are victims of abuse, are depressed, or are mentally ill. As such, children most likely to be suspended or expelled are those most in need of adult supervision and professional help. . . . For students with major home-life stresses, academic suspension in turn provides yet another life stress that, when compounded with what is already occurring in their lives, may predispose them to even higher risks of behavioral problems.

Yet,

Despite high rates of depression and numerous life stresses that are associated with school-based problem behaviors, students are not routinely referred to a medical or mental-health provider on expulsion or suspension . . . and without a parent at home during the day, students with out-of-school suspensions and expulsions are far more likely to commit crimes. . . . Out-of-school adolescents are also more likely to smoke, use alcohol, marijuana, and cocaine. . . . The lack of professional assistance at the time of exclusion from school, a time when a student most needs it, increases the risk of permanent school drop-out.

These concerns might seem self-evident, but many schools routinely ignore them, and did so increasingly after the mid-1990s. Shortly before I began the research for this book, a seventeen-year-old Colorado boy and one of his friends shot and killed several people, including four of their friends and one parent. The seventeen-year-old then shot his accomplice to death as well. One of the shooters had recently been expelled from his school system altogether, and newspaper accounts of the school authorities' response to the incident are revealing. Questioned about the wisdom of first kicking the boy out of regular high school to a continuation school and then in short order kicking him out of *that* school, a spokesperson for the district said that the schools had acted quite appropriately, in her view. The high school authorities, she declared, "detected a problem and took care of it." Likewise, the continuation school, later, also "detected a problem and took care of it." There was absolutely no inkling that "taking care of" the problem in this fashion might have created new and worse problems, nor any sense that there might be a responsibility lodged somewhere in the community to engage this young man in some other way than simply putting him out on the street, with the issues that had gotten him in trouble at school still unaddressed.

This attitude seems so patently self-defeating that it is difficult to understand how anyone—especially anyone who deals regularly with adolescents—could adopt it. As is true in many families, however, fundamentally punitive cultural values trump more practical considerations—considerations of both developmental appropriateness and cost. It does not require great sophistication, as the Academy of Pediatrics makes clear, to understand that these practices are bad for teenagers, and they are almost certainly extremely costly in the long run because picking up the pieces after great damage has been done is always more expensive than working to prevent the damage in the first place. Yet the practices persist and are widely accepted: opinion polls suggest that most Americans support—at least in theory—zero-tolerance approaches to school discipline.

The patterns noted by the Academy of Pediatrics appeared routinely among my interviewees. The schools typically noticed problems but, instead of seeing them as a signal that some kind of supportive intervention was called for, viewed them through the lens of a passive but punitive individualism. Children's problems at school—especially if they involved a challenge to the authority of teachers or principals—were regarded as evidence of fundamental flaws of character, which called not for assistance but for exclusion. Youths with behavior problems were seen less as children in need than as enemies to be put outside the gates, and what happened to them then was not of great moment. Hence, the expression of problems at school brought heightened surveillance and monitoring but little corresponding effort to get to the bottom of them. The pattern tended to be self-fulfilling: troubled youth who came to school angry or depressed were likely to be labeled as bad kids and, accordingly, to be scrutinized—and sometimes bullied—by teachers and principals. In response, they frequently acted up worse than before—and even if they didn't, any mistake or transgression was more likely to be noticed because of the increased attention. The schools seemed determined to ferret out trouble among them, and they often found it. Many of my informants, indeed, felt that school authorities were lying in wait for them, ready to pounce at the slightest infraction—or even, in some cases, to "get in their face" without provocation. There are doubtless teenagers who accept this treatment or are "whipped into shape" by it, but that was not true of any of those I interviewed. Those who got this oppositional treatment at school either responded in kind or left school altogether in anger or humiliation. It almost goes without saying that this accelerated their journey along the road to whatever, stoking their anger, undercutting their sense of worth, and intensifying their sense of being outsiders—an understandable response, since the whole thrust of the schools' policy was precisely to put them on the outside.

"They Make You into the Bad"

Zack is lean, with spiky blond hair. Though he grew up in a series of comfortable suburbs, he carries himself and talks with a slightly menacing "ghetto" attitude. In elementary school this had not been much of a problem, but when he was in seventh grade he moved to a new school where his style was distinctly out of place. He got in a couple of fights and "flashed" on his teachers once or twice, and from then on everything went downhill. "I just started doing bad," he says.

> They put me in a class for not necessarily stupid kids but for bad kids. That was when it started, like, everything's on me. Know what I'm saying?

Here's someone you could blame it on. I got in trouble for half the *other* people's stuff that I didn't even do. It's just like, I guess, I got a sign on me saying blame it on me or something. I don't know.

And the worst part is, in schools teachers all associate. And they all tell war stories about how bad their kids are and other things. And by the end of the first quarter in seventh grade they put me in this class. That's pretty fast.

Once he was assigned to the class that was not for stupid kids but for bad kids, his own attitude deteriorated. By the time he got to freshman year in high school he was, like Terry, thoroughly alienated from school. He admits that he started off on the wrong foot:

When I got to Ravencrest High that was like probably the highest point of my drug use. And I was the most fucked up. And I got there like, "Fuck this place." Didn't even show up like the first few days of school. And me, I've always had a—this is my religion, you don't *ever* show up for the first day of school.

No one, least of all Zack himself, would suggest that he was an easy kid to deal with. But his hard-ass, oppositional style was quickly matched by the confrontational attitude of many of the adults at his high school. His freshman year became a sort of shoving contest in which both sides regularly provoked each other, with the school no less "in your face" than Zack himself. But it was, of course, Zack who wound up taking the fall:

At Ravencrest High our teachers treat you with no respect. And they tell you to shut up and shit like that. They get in your face. And the only time I'll ever respect a person like that is it's my mom. And I might not even respect *her*. She tells me to shut up, I probably won't even shut up. . . . How *you* gonna tell me to shut up? You don't even know me. You just some teacher! You don't mean shit to me. I made that point clear to all of them. And then I got kicked out.

In fact, like Terry, Zack got kicked out regularly; though he was not expelled permanently, he was suspended again and again:

> I'd go to class and talk shit to the teacher and she's like, "Suspended." And I walk out and I go, "Thank you for my vacation." Know what I'm saying? 'Cause I didn't give a fuck. That was just more time for me to kick it and get high.

In his second year he was determined to turn over a new leaf. A natural athlete, he wanted to get on the basketball team, and he was ready, more generally, to straighten out his life. This was the first of several times in his adolescence when Zack tried to catch himself in middescent. He knew he'd been no prize from the school's point of view and that he hadn't been doing his work, but now he was committed to changing his ways: "I came back and I had all new teachers and I thought, this is gonna be a good year." But it was not to be. His reputation had preceded him, new teachers or not:

> I walked in, and they go, "Oh, so it's Zack, huh? Sit down in the corner." Front seat. Front row. It's like, I don't know. They don't even give you a chance to be good. Off the bat, they just label you. "Zack. Watch out for this kid."
>
> They go, "I got this kid in my class, he was bad." And I was showing up! Like, "I'm gonna do all my work. I'm gonna be good this year. I'm gonna try." And I—I really—I *was* gonna start trying. And I started trying for a *second* and they just kept nailing me for the dumbest things. I can drop my pencil and get nailed for it, know what I'm saying?
>
> And it's just like, "Naw, man, *fuck* this." And I just stopped going to school.

On his own, Zack decided to leave regular high school, where things were clearly not working, and try making up his credits at Riley, a continuation school. I asked if the school had been cool with that decision; he said, "They were more than cool. They were ecstatic." He was convinced, in fact, that the school wanted to get rid of kids like him in order to appear more effective. "What they do," he told me, "is get rid of you as quick as they can so they can make statistics." Ravencrest High, he said, liked to boast that 98 percent of its graduates were later successful, "were gonna go on somewhere in life," but that was true only because "all the other kids that should be in the percentage get kicked out!"

> What happens is before they take the statistics, they went through the whole school and wiped the troublemakers out and sent them to Riley. And then they take the statistics. So Ravencrest High gets more money and more market value and gets a higher graduation rate. . . . So it's like, they get the kids out of there that are fucking up and they get the good kids in there. . . . So that's just how they work. It's all politics.

Zack wasn't surprised, therefore, that when he went to Riley not much happened on the educational front: "I don't even have to show up! Know what I'm saying? That school's hella easy. I can do it sleepin'. That's a waste of my time. Sit there and sleep all day long. Might as well sleep at the house."

To Zack, the simultaneously judgmental and passive character of the schools was familiar: his parents, he told me, had usually responded to him in the same way. When I interviewed Zack for the third time, he was languishing in the juvenile hall where he'd been sent after being kicked out of a drug rehab. By this point he had been locked in some sort of official custody for over a year and a half, and he was once again trying to get himself together and think about his future. He had concluded that he really wanted to go to college after he got out—he would try to get his GED and go straight to a community college. I asked if his parents were supportive of this idea; he said that they were in the abstract but that "they don't want to do nothing to help me." They thought he should get an education, but they didn't exert themselves, financially or otherwise, to help him get it. Zack said that this had always been their approach to him:

My whole life growing up, my mom and dad just sat there and *watched*. Watched me fuck up in school, and they said, "Why can't you do good? You're hella smart, why don't you finish your homework?" Teachers always said to my parents—they used to let me know that I had great potential, but I wouldn't do it because I never liked school. But they always sat there and bitched and moaned, "You're not going to school," and yet when I was home they'd never help with my homework.

Both his school and his parents "watched" him slide into alienation, drugs, and failure rather than intervene to help him find a different path. "They just sat there and watched," indeed, well describes the schools' approach to most of the adolescents in this book. With few exceptions, the schools' role was less an active, nurturing, capacity-building one than a passively monitoring one, a sorting of students into appropriate piles rather than a concerted effort to bring all of them up to their best potential. And this conception of the schools' role fits seamlessly into the larger culture of passive individualism in which the schools were embedded. If it is seen as being up to the individual, even as a child, to rise or fall on his or her own, then the responsibility of the school is less to help children rise than simply to measure how far they go—to classify them according to how well they meet, or how dismally they fail to meet, conventional standards of social and intellectual performance and to declare them officially out of the race if they fail badly enough.

Some of the adolescents in this book were fortunate enough to have had parents who did not accept this systemic passivity on the schools' part and who pushed the schools to pay attention to their children's needs. If, as in Zack's case, the parents took the same passively judgmental approach as the schools did, the child's passage through the school system was likely to be both painful and, in the end, a colossal waste.

It could be objected that someone like Zack, in the throes of his crisis at home and at school and deeply angry about the way he was treated, is not the most objective observer of how his school dealt with troubled students. But Zack's experience is echoed by many of my college informants, who had put considerable distance between them and high school, both chronologically and emotionally. Despite the passage of time and their current academic success, they still felt hurt by their treatment in high school. With very few exceptions, these extraordinarily capable young people found high school a horrible experience—"sheer hell," as one put it. "The educational environment was more like prison to me," says Lacey. "It was big gates, people monitoring the gates, trying to get out to do what you wanted to do, or trying to just find *something* that interests you. High school was horrifying." Sean, who had experience of both institutions, said much the same thing: school was "rather like the prison system."

Many of these students, for reasons they usually couldn't fathom, routinely elicited the hostility of school personnel. This was most likely to have happened, not surprisingly, if they had begun to act in oppositional ways themselves: they often reported that at the first sign of troublesomeness or defiance on their part, the school authorities would take a similar stance. But many felt that the schools' response to their fairly minor early acts of defiance or acting up was "over the top," disproportionate to the amount of real trouble they had caused. The school did not usually cause their initial problems: they often came to school with unresolved issues, mostly ones involving trouble at home. But the schools amplified the problems and, in doing so, accelerated these teenagers' downward spiral.

Like Zack, some had acquired a reputation for trouble before they arrived at high school and immediately found themselves under the extra-watchful eye of authorities once they got there. Sean, for example, had been self-consciously rebellious in junior high but had never been in serious trouble before high school. Yet he found himself typed as a "kid to watch out for" because of his dress and his punk style, and he started high school with a label attached:

There was a continuation school there, where the real screwups were, and that was pretty much what I was viewed as, and that was it. . . . The first kind of intervention I got was my first day at that school, where I was walking from gym class to homeroom, I think. I was still trying to figure out where everything was. And the dean comes up and calls me by my name, and I'd never seen this guy before, and he tells me he's *heard* about me, and he takes my notebook away to look at it for gang-related graffiti or something like that and makes me empty my pockets, tells me he's going to be watching me and this whole thing. . . . That was my first—that was the extent of their caring and intervention.

Trey had a similar experience. He grew up in a somewhat seedy midwestern suburb that had once been solidly middle class but, after a series of economic blows, began to deteriorate around the time he started high school. His own family's economic circumstances declined, and his parents fought a lot. He fell into a period of alienation and mild depression and spent a great deal of time on the street, getting involved in the local punk/anarchist youth culture and dressing the part: he wore big combat boots and provocative haircuts and hung out with a group of other kids who looked the same. His appearance made him a target of put-downs by his teachers and frequent bullying by the school principal. Once, when he went to school wearing his Doc Martens boots, the principal confronted him in the hallway and threatened to take the boots off by force.

These incidents accumulated, and the school's antagonistic attitude intensified the estrangement he and his friends were already feeling. By senior year, their sense of being on the outside of conventional institutions had reached a dangerous point. They began to think about attacking the symbols of authority, both at school and elsewhere: "There was this escalation. We were flirting with information on Molotov cocktails and what we could do with them, and how much would actually be accomplished. Things were getting a little out of hand, I've got to admit." They spray-painted graffiti on the walls of the school and "did some other things" to express their anger. The group did a lot of drugs, but it wasn't, Trey says, the drugs that drove their increasingly "out of hand" behavior:

> Maybe they had a significant effect, but we just had some outlandish ideas. And it was a different kind of high. It was doing these wrong things. . . . The same high you get from smashing a window. A kind of rush. And it was fun. For us. And we weren't really too—we didn't care too much about the expense of others that we were usurping, I guess.

Ultimately he decided to write a letter threatening the principal's life:

> I remember sitting down thinking like, hey, this is going to be funny. This is going to be just, you know, something that's really going to cause havoc, something that's going to disrupt the order, something that's going to be—makes a sort of wave. And for some reason, it didn't matter. . . . I was so disillusioned with high school and with the people there, and then problems with myself too. So I wrote him a letter, a threatening letter, and it did threaten his life, and it did say some bad things about him.

Because of what he calls his "inadequate terrorist abilities," he made a number of mistakes that eventually got him found out and arrested, and he spent more than a year in prison as a result.

As Trey puts it, he and his friends "didn't just wake up convicted felons." The escalation from generic teenage rebellion to a mindset of profound alienation and defiance was fueled by the schools' routine definition of them as outside the legitimate order, and the confrontational attitude of the school staff rubbed raw the already bruised feelings they had brought with them from their homes. Although few of my other college informants reacted in such spectacular ways, most of them reported similar feelings. Most often, it was a general climate of derogation and opposition rather than a particular incident that wore away at their self-confidence and bred a sense of injustice.

Lacey was a straight-A student through seventh grade. But in eighth grade, she hooked up with a clique of kids who wore trench coats and sometimes cut class:

> I started hanging around with the wrong crowd. I'd ditch class. I wouldn't go. I had a real sort of like *wall* around me that I constructed on some levels. . . . I wasn't aggressive, I wasn't mean, I wasn't loud. I wasn't—I wasn't a bad kid. I didn't hurt others.

Despite not being a "bad kid," she found herself treated as if she were. She had only one teacher who was consistently respectful and attentive, "who took the time to talk to me" and "didn't judge." But her relationship with most of her teachers was very different: "The other teachers would make you into the bad, the problem, the thing that needed to be corrected." She felt in retrospect that it would not have been hard to pull her back on track in high school if someone had just sat down with her to get to the bottom of why she was having trouble fitting in. But, she says, "that never happened to me. Never, never, never." She was recurrently in trouble in junior high school, often getting "slammed" by teachers for what seemed to be quite innocuous things.

> I was in yearbook. I was very popular, so I was voted into a lot of things. So I got picked for doing yearbook or something, . . . which is like the big thing for the ninth graders. Do yearbook, you're like the coolest of the cool. I pulled up my shirt in class. I had a bathing suit on. But the teacher suspended me for it. I was being obnoxious, clearly. But . . .

The students who didn't "fit" at her school endured a steady barrage of slights and snide comments that, while individually hardly devastating, added up over time and left them feeling both resentful and cowed:

> One teacher made fun of me because I read the CliffsNotes. And I was *trying*. I didn't know what to do. I didn't understand *Lord of the Flies*. You

know, I was struggling with this. I read the CliffsNotes, and then she made a comment, you know, "Thank you, Mr. Cliff." These really mean comments to me in class, and that really just shut me up in class. I mean, *I don't know.* OK?

Shutting up in class was a common response among my informants, and it meant that in a real sense they lost a good part of their high school years because they didn't feel able to participate. Ultimately, they retrieved their sense of intellectual and creative engagement, but the loss of it in high school increased their apathy, sense of disconnection, and feelings of care-lessness. Part of what my informants meant when they said they didn't care about anything was that nothing really interested them, nothing "grabbed" them, with the possible exception of drugs and danger. This made it much easier for them to drift—and indeed, there are few people who feel more adrift than bright and creative adolescents with no legitimate ways to express those qualities.

Most, like Lacey, were genuinely bewildered by the routine hostility of school personnel and remained so even years afterward:

There was a couple other teachers who really didn't like me and that whenever they saw me, they went out of their way to try to say comments to me, and I don't remember why. I don't know. I really honestly don't know why. I don't think it was my personality. I think it was more just—I don't know. . . . It baffled me for a long—I *still* don't understand.

I rubbed them the wrong way, perhaps. I'm sure I did. And sometimes I don't know why. Sometimes they were just *mean*, just downright mean. Sick of seeing kids. . . . Sick of seeing kids that come in tardy, sick of seeing kids that are having problems. They're tired, they're worn out, they're underpaid. I mean that's all stuff I understand now. But to me then they were just adults who were symbolic of structure and power, you know, who could make decisions about my life and I couldn't. So *I* was going to make some decisions about my life!

The school's oppositional attitude intensified her tendency to withdraw into the stance of alienated self-reliance that was so characteristic of many of the teenagers I spoke with. She had always found it difficult to ask people for help, and the climate of hostility fostered by her teachers made it even harder: "I'm extremely stoic. . . . People will say, 'You never ask for anything. You never ask for help.' And I'm like, 'I *can?*'" When she began having troubles in junior high, she didn't feel that she could confide in anyone there: "I was scared, because what would I say? Would it get me in trouble? There was not a lot of flexibility and openness about what was going on in the school's environment. There was always penalizing for things." The gratuitous hostility also pushed her into what she describes as "massive resistance," a stance that she adopted throughout high school and that predictably got her into deeper trouble.

The inability of these students to figure out why their schools were so quick to label and challenge them led many of them to regard the schools' behavior as both gratuitous and unjust. Thus it simultaneously fed their already corrosive tendency toward self-doubt and their growing sense that their schools, like other adult institutions, were neither legitimate nor on their side. If their schools did not respect them, they could certainly not respect their schools.

It would be difficult to overstate the level of estrangement these extraordinarily bright and capable young people felt. They often entered high school with high expectations, a good deal of enthusiasm, and unusually strong abilities, but they soon discovered that those strengths were ignored or even undercut by teachers, while any acts of deviance or rebelliousness, however trivial, were magnified. Indeed, in this kind of school climate, these acts of deviance tended to "become" the adolescent; their working identity in the eyes of school authorities was based not on their schoolwork, which was sometimes excellent, but on being the one who made faces in the classroom, mouthed off at a teacher, or wore combat boots. Rick puts it this way:

High school was a strange time. I mean actually this is kind of interesting. In my high school I was always in all AP [Advanced Placement] classes. Any of my teachers knew that I was at the top of every class . . . so I could have been identified as one of the smarter—you know, I could have been put in that sense. Instead I was identified as one of the kids that was obviously drinking and doing drugs.

The redefinition began after Rick got caught drinking during a school outing. Doing that was "really stupid," he acknowledges, but he'd never been in trouble at school before. Though his teachers made no move to help him tackle his drinking problem, they "looked at me very differently" from then on. He had an especially hard time with one teacher who made a practice of taunting and shaming students in the classroom:

One of my friends was Middle Eastern, and he would call him, you know, "the bomber," and say stuff that *here* [in college] would get you, you know, boycotted. . . . And he'd pick on people, and I was an extremely easy target because, you know, I was rebelling a *little* ways, so it was really easy to pick on me.

The fact that he had already been "rebelling a little ways" meant that, like Sean's and Zack's, his teachers had already "heard about" him, and so when he arrived in his high school physics classroom, the physics teacher was waiting for him:

He'd heard about me and knew me coming in, and it just went horrible. I remember one time . . . between drinking all the time and just being bored in high school—'cause the high school did not do anything for me—I slept a lot in class. And in the physics class I just stopped paying attention, just 'cause, I mean, the guy was a jerk. I remember he called on me one time, and I had been pretty much not paying attention for the last three weeks. I hadn't realized we switched units. We were talking about relativity, and we switched from, I think, electricity or something. So he asked me, you know, "All right, Rick, so what's C stand for?" And I was like, "Capacity," or said something that had to do with electricity. And he just stopped, and he's like, "It's the *speed of light*," and he just—he just went off on me in the middle of class. "And how did you not remember that? Have you been doing drugs this weekend?" He just basically tore into me in front of the class. . . .

So this is some of the stuff I had to deal with. And it just doesn't do any good at all, and it just makes you feel more isolated. I'm sure I went home that night and just like, you know, "I'm drinking *twice* as much tonight."

This went on even though both his grades and his extracurricular achievements continued to be outstanding:

Meanwhile, I had probably one of the highest GPAs in the school. I was winning all these awards and stuff . . . 'cause you had to do mandatory community service hours. I won the award because you had to do a mandatory of eighty. I had done a hundred already. . . . I had worked as a camp counselor during the summer. I won awards for GPAs. And the teachers that I was able to connect with knew that I wasn't—that I was a good student. . . . But I think it's really interesting that they grouped me in with, like, the bad crowd rather than, like, the intelligent crowd. I mean they could have put me in either one.

He was puzzled that the school authorities chose not to focus on his contributions or his strengths:

I mean, this is a school that loves to brag about how well their students do. You know, whenever anything good academically happens, they're posting it everywhere. Their sports teams have to be number one all the time. Their academics have to be number one all the time. So you'd think they'd be like—they could pretty much use me as an example. I just think it probably would have helped a little bit if somebody could have seen that this is someone who at least has potential.

The sense that their schools were willing to overlook their potential while relentlessly focusing on their weaknesses appears again and again in my conversations with formerly troubled college students. What comes through in Rick's account, as in Lacey's, is that the schools were only partly concerned with their students' intellectual abilities or academic performance. There was something else going on, even though it was unlikely to have been clearly articulated. The schools wanted something else from them—something that was more or less unspoken, that had to do with toeing the line, with not challenging the schools' inner culture. It was certainly not enough to be good at your schoolwork, to be intellectually capable—in fact, many of my students felt that being *too* capable might not have been a positive thing for them in high school. Indeed, the schools seemed willing to sacrifice a child's intellectual potential in the name of enforcing that inner culture. Lacey went so far as to return to her high school after she'd graduated from college to confront her old teachers on this score:

> I've gone back to my high school and left a couple of notes for those teachers who treated me poorly, like about five years ago, saying "You know, you really treated me poorly." I just told them the story of what happened between us, and then, you know, "I've gone to college, I've done all these things," and how I actually love learning. "You didn't encourage me to learn," and left it in their box. And signed my name. Well, because I want them to know that what they did was a disservice. You know, I had potential. Maybe I didn't show it completely.

TURNING IT AROUND

There is a kind of fatalism in the public discussion of adolescent problems. It's often assumed that by the time children reach their teens it is already too late to do much for them: their trajectory has been set in the first few years of life—if not before they are born. But a growing body of research now challenges these assumptions. We are learning that, far from being doomed to delinquency and despair, most people who endure serious problems in childhood or adolescence manage, at some point, to turn their lives around.

So it was with many of the adolescents in this book. Despite what were often truly dire experiences, feelings of hopelessness and self-loathing, and close brushes with death, they got back on their feet. They stopped doing hard drugs, stopped drinking themselves into unconsciousness, stopped hanging around with dangerous people, stopped having careless sex. What's more, some of them did so very quickly: they changed "just like that," turning on a dime. Many of them, moreover, emerged from their time of crisis not only "all right" but better than all right, stronger and with a clearer sense of who they were and what they wanted to do in life. As William Faulkner might have put it, they not only endured, they prevailed.

How they did, as I've said, was one of the questions that inspired this book. And just as there were common paths that led them into trouble, there were striking similarities in the ways they got *out* of trouble, some of which parallel what others have found in studying the sources of "resilience" among troubled or disadvantaged youth. The specifics of this transformation were as varied as their lives, but some underlying principles appeared again and again.

Two of those principles are particularly important. First, for these life-altering shifts to happen, adolescents had to begin thinking about themselves in a different way than they had before, and second, they had to have some mechanism available in the outside world to put their changed self-definition into practice. These did not have to occur in any particular order: sometimes it was a new opportunity, in school or work, that catalyzed the change in their self-conception; sometimes the change in their view of themselves and their potential moved them to seek out new possibilities in the world around them. But both principles had to be in place for the change to be enduring. I want to look closely at them for a moment because they offer clues about how we might help others in the same situation.

"It's Not Just Me": The Role of Redefinition

Since adolescents so often drifted into trouble because they had come to care so little about what happened to them, turning their lives around for the better required that they learn, or relearn, how to care about themselves—to regard themselves as people who mattered. Some had to overcome deeply painful perceptions of themselves as losers, failures, incorrigible delinquents. Others had never reached that level of self-deprecation: they had tried, with some success, to stick up for themselves as teenagers—to hold on to a basic conviction that they were not such bad people after all. But even for them, achieving a new sense of purpose and direction required that they reassess their value and potential, reject the pejorative definitions of their character imposed on them by parents, teachers, and other authorities, and decide that they had strengths worth building on and contributions to make. Given how deeply the negative views had penetrated, this was never easy, and for some the struggle to achieve a more positive sense of themselves was ongoing, even though it may have been years since they had been in serious trouble.

Crucial to this shift in self-conception was the ability to recognize that, though they might have done some "screwed-up" things, the problem wasn't only, or even mainly, *within them*. To put this slightly differently, they came to make a crucial distinction between having done screwed-up things and being a screwed-up person. Both parts of this understanding were necessary for the turnaround to take place. They had to recognize that they were on the wrong track, that they were doing things that could hurt them and that were unworthy of them, but at the same time they had to affirm that they were, at bottom, sufficiently valuable that making an effort to change their ways was worth the trouble and sufficiently "together" that they could pull off that change.

To get to that point, they had to be able to challenge the tendency for influential adults around them to "put it all on them"—to blame their troubles on their flawed characters and personal deficiencies. Most of them were more than willing to acknowledge their mistakes of judgment (indeed, while they were teenagers, they were typically altogether too willing). But over time some had managed to frame these problems in a way that was less self-critical and undermining. They came, as several put it, to understand that they were not the problem—or at least, not all the problem. They began to realize the contribution made to their situation by others, especially their parents, and to reject the self-serving rhetoric of nonresponsibility that many adults around them had adopted. This shift was always difficult to make: as middle-class teenagers, they had grown up in a culture in which the tendency to internalize blame and individualize responsibility was pervasive. But rejecting or at least softening those harsh cultural imperatives was an essential step toward developing a strong enough sense of their own value that they could start to care more consistently about what happened to them.

For some, the rejection of the label of loser or screwup was stimulated by an outside source—a friend, a supportive counselor or therapist, a concerned teacher, even a college course in sociology—that provided a reframing lens that allowed them to see themselves and their situation differently. Anna, for example, says that a "light bulb" went on in her head after she began seeing a new therapist at nineteen:

> It wasn't until I started going to a therapist that I finally started regaining my confidence, because she helped convince me that *it wasn't my fault*. And that was like such a landmark event, finally realizing it wasn't my fault. . . . I don't want to evade any sort of responsibility. But under the circumstances, how I was raised, I wasn't trying to do it to be mean or hurtful. I just didn't know any better. And when I finally realized that it wasn't my fault that I was abused, it wasn't my fault that I was mistreated, then that's when I finally started restoring my confidence, because I didn't feel guilty anymore.

Lacey had a similar encounter. Most of her experiences with professional counselors had been unhelpful at best and had served, at worst, to further undermine her already shaky confidence. But at nineteen she landed with a new therapist who helped her see that the problems she was having were not simply the result of some inner flaw:

> That was, I think, the main way I always felt with my mother. Like something was always wrong with me. And what was the most mind-blowing experience is when my therapist said, "You know, you have to realize it's her, too." And really set it in our relationship rather than in me.
>
> And I think that was profoundly important for me to realize. Because I was always the problem, versus—I mean, I started realizing that

my mom also had major behavior problems. . . . So it was good to hear that *she* had problems, too. And to bring her to the mat.

Similarly, one reason Rick was able to quit drinking during his first year of college was that he had become aware that he wasn't nearly as bad a kid as his parents regularly told him he was. By the time he got to college he had already begun to feel that there was something "a little weird" about their overreaction to his minor lapses at school and their inability to appreciate his intellectual strengths. In his case, this insight didn't come from a therapist. He had been to several during high school, but though he believed that most of them meant well, they had not shed much light on the running conflict with his parents and his school. It was his friends who provided a "different point of view":

> I think it helped that my roommate in freshman year met my parents a few times. He would just kind of be like, "Your family's really strange," you know? Bring these things out. . . . He's saying "They're really strange," and I'd be like, "What? It's kind of normal!" And we'd talk about it. I'd realize [it was] really unusual. . . . I think that might have been part of why I was finally able to figure it out on my own.

This external jolting of vision can be crucial because adolescents are often trapped within a small circle of people who have a great deal of authority over them, and thus they can easily be confused and overwhelmed by the negative definitions that adults tag them with. Unless something interferes to crack that isolation, they may simply internalize the picture of themselves that those adults are offering. They may sense that something is wrong with that picture, that it is not only upsetting and frustrating but also inaccurate, unjust, even "off the wall." But without an alternative angle of vision, it is hard for them even to find the words to express exactly what it is they think is not right, much less to come up with a less corrosive understanding of themselves.

Nevertheless, many adolescents manage to reframe their experience largely, if not wholly, on their own. They will say that no one in particular helped them put their family troubles in perspective, that they arrived independently at the conclusion that whatever was wrong at home wasn't just about them but about their parents as well. Some arrive at that awareness when they are still very young, and it can keep them from falling completely into care-lessness and despair. Armed early on with the understanding that their families' troubles are a two-way street, they are protected against the most crippling kinds of self-derogation. Jenny, for example, began to think of her mother's behavior as fundamentally inappropriate early on and by age ten had concluded that she would have to break away from her to survive emotionally:

> When my mom tried to kill herself, for a month or two beforehand she had sent me to live with neighbors. You know, I was sleeping on a cot. I mean, these people were wonderful, but essentially I didn't *have* parents for probably six months of my life because she was hospitalized for quite a long time because she was such a high risk. . . . I was more sort of of-fended that she wanted back in my life after she tried to do something like that. It was like, "You want to kill yourself so bad, and you've tried to kill *me* with you, what do you think you're gonna offer me?" Probably if it had not been state-mandated that I stayed with her, I definitely wouldn't have, at that point in my life, because she was not offering me anything.

Carly, similarly, concluded quite young that her parents were "pretty fucked up" and "dumped" them emotionally well before she left home for good at sixteen:

> So by the time we're in [the suburbs], I'm already feeling like my family's just not *right*, you know? Which I think is different, 'cause I think a lot of kids don't stop to say, "Wait a minute." They either start internal-izing, blaming themselves, or accepting what's going on as, "This is nor-mal." But I always was like, "This just isn't right. This is not how it's

supposed to be." And I don't know where that came from or what that was about, but I think I always had that going on, and I think that that played a big part in things that happened later on in my life.

For as long as she could remember, she had recognized that living a "normal" life would mean giving up on her parents in a fundamental sense:

> I don't really remember when it started, but I know I pretty much hated my family and just wanted to be gone. 'Cause I didn't think there was anything wrong with me. I thought I was just fine, you know? And I still think I'm just fine today. I'm not perfect, by any standards, but I don't think there's anything wrong with me. And I don't think there's anything wrong with *them*. I just think that I was probably not what they wanted. I didn't behave the way they wanted. I didn't have the . . . dreams the way they wanted. I wasn't shapeable by them as far as what I wanted. I was pretty well influenced by what *I* wanted to be influenced by, which was not them, because I didn't want to have all the same problems that they were having. . . .
>
> I didn't think it was normal to move around like that. I didn't think it was normal to have the fights in the house the way they were having. I didn't think it was normal to have all the drugs and stuff in the house. And I just wanted to have friends, go to school, do activities. I wanted to do things like go to dance class when I was a kid. You know, I never got given those things or even given the opportunity to do those things. And so I was always looking for something that they weren't providing.

As Carly suggests, the fact that these adolescents rejected their parents' views and values did not necessarily mean that they now blamed them for all that had gone wrong in their lives. Sometimes they simply concluded that their parents were limited people—that they didn't have it in them to do much better. Some, in fact, still felt considerable loyalty to their parents, or to at least one of them, and many had maintained or re-created fairly good relationships with them. But almost all had gone through a process of critical reassessment of their families, and many, at the end, "fired" their parents (as one of my informants put it) and moved on. At the very least, they broke with parents emotionally; some also fired their parents in the more wrenching sense of leaving home very early to build a more tolerable and supportive life on their own, even if that involved great hardship and uncertainty. Jenny ultimately reconciled with her mother, for example, but was adamant in her conviction that breaking away was absolutely critical to her turnaround and that the inability to make that kind of break often trapped other adolescents in desperate and miserable lives:

> I think where people trip themselves up—because it's very common not to have parents that are normal. I think it's probably more common to have not normal families than it is to have normal ones. And some people can't separate that. They just didn't have whatever it is that makes you say, "OK, I don't have to need you. I mean, you're my parents, and I can *care* about you, but I don't have to need you, and if I had to do it, I could do these things on my own."

"I don't have to need you" captures very well the emotional place many of these adolescents had to reach to make this decisive change in their lives. Most did not cut off all contact with their parents, even if they now defined their parents as abusive or negligent or generally "fucked up." But they had made a conscious decision not to depend on them for either practical support or personal validation. And they believed that they could not have moved forward without making that decision. Still, many also believed that making the break had taken a lasting emotional toll on them. Jenny, for example, says that by the time she decided to cut all ties with her mother, she found it almost too easy:

> I just got used to being, in a way, very introverted, and it's almost at times been to a sort of scary level in that I can walk away from pretty

much anything or any relationship in my life at any point and have very few regrets, or at least be able to get over them quickly. And I think that's probably the only thing about my personality that does scare me. . . . It's not that I can't love people or have relationships, but. . . . It's just like, "All right, this isn't working for me, I'm gone, have a nice life, you know. I don't wish you ill, but really I just . . ." I've done that several times. I just totally remove myself from people.

I mean, there was no question in my mind that I was not going to talk to my mother again, at seventeen years old, and that would have basically left me without family, and I was fine with that . . . and I've just been able to move on like that because I can walk away and cut all ties. . . . I mean, it *is* sort of cold-blooded.

Like Jenny, many adolescents who grow up with that sense of having to deal with life on their own feel that they have been hardened by that experience. They are proud of their capacity for independence and confident in their competence to rely on themselves for most of what they need in life, but they cannot escape the feeling that these abilities have come at a cost.

Along with the rejection of negative definitions of themselves, a closely related change of heart and mind often helps adolescents begin taking themselves more seriously in ways that allow them to alter the direction of their lives. Many of my informants said that at a certain point they simply decided that they did not like the person they had become and that they didn't want to be that person anymore. They seemed to get outside themselves long enough to look at their lives from an external vantage point and to conclude that they were disappointed or even appalled. Mickey put it this way in describing how she came to feel that she wanted to stop doing heavy drugs and selling her body to pay for them.

Was there anything in particular that made you want to change?
Yeah. I think I just had a moment of realization, I guess. I just saw myself through somebody else's eyes, and I didn't like what I saw.

Similarly, Tracy decided to abandon the life of speed, crime, and risky sex that she'd begun at thirteen when she woke up one morning in a crank house and realized that she could not like or respect the "horrible person" she had become or the "gross" people she had surrounded herself with:

But what made me go back—that house got raided, you know? So I went and stayed at this other crank house, and *it* was about to get raided. And I didn't want to stay there. So much drama went on. Cops were there all the time. . . . I fell asleep, and I woke up the next day, and I was just like, "Shit, where do I *go*? What am I gonna *do*?" I just didn't feel like smoking crank anymore. "I don't feel like smoking crank. I don't feel like drinking beer. I don't feel like using." I was just like, "Damn! I want to go home!"

Sticking with that decision wasn't easy, in part because handling normal life was very difficult for her. She was unsure of her ability to cope with even the most mundane things, once she was away from the peculiarly supportive and forgiving drug subculture in which she'd been immersed for most of her adolescence. She didn't know or remember how to "have fun" outside the drug world, and having been seriously addicted to methamphetamine, she found staying away from it a constant struggle:

When I go to work and stuff . . . it's like I don't think I'm gonna make it through the day. Through normal days. And it's weird. I *always* made it out there [in the drug life], and I knew I was always gonna make it. But today it's like—I've got the whole day ahead of me. Am I gonna make it? You know? And it's hard. It's so hard.

She was determined to learn how to deal with the pressures of a "normal, respectable" life and to distance herself from the person she could no longer tolerate being. Her aims at this point were both hazy and mundane:

I don't have no idea what I want to do. But I'm just setting goals. In a few years, you know, I want to be able to have a credit card and checks and not overdo it. I want to get a new car one day. I want a family. I don't know. I just—I want to be OK with myself, is the main thing. I want to like myself . . . I want to, I don't know, I just want to be OK.

For many, the decision to change often involved not only the realization that they no longer liked who they were but that they were no longer able to do things they cared about—things that they had been able to do before they went so badly off track. They had become incapable in their own eyes, in significant ways, and their incapacity troubled them deeply. This was not the global criticism of their character that parents and others often laid on them but a pragmatic and clear-eyed understanding that they had lost abilities or relationships that mattered to them. "At one point," Anna says,

my mind was so foggy from doing so many drugs that I was trying to add something, and I couldn't even do simple math. Something that I used to do really well I couldn't do. And so that was one sign of, oh, my God, what am I doing to myself? And also I just got really, really skinny, and I'm so unhealthy, and I'm sick constantly, and so, yeah, that was one aspect—that I did not care until it got really bad. And finally there were enough warning signs that I decided to stop.

Sick, skinny, unable even to think clearly, she felt that she was "basically decaying."

I just remember feeling so bad about myself. And so devoid of anything, so unfulfilled. And actually I—this is a funny story—but what really showed me that I needed to make changes was [that] my cat, who loved me so much at one point, was afraid of me! She didn't like to be around me. Like, when I was on drugs, she would not come near me. One day I just remember looking at her, and she was so scared of me, so petrified. And I guess in a sense I saw myself in her, like that scared, petrified person who was reaching out to drugs to try to in a sense liberate myself and validate myself. . . . I saw in her that I wasn't validating myself. I was basically decaying and becoming even more fearful and scared and negative and bitter. And so, yeah, actually that experience showed me—her response to me showed me that I needed to stop.

Rick had a similar revelation about his drinking. Just as he was beginning to understand that his family's treatment of him was "pretty strange," he was also becoming aware that drinking himself into a stupor on most nights was wrecking his life and keeping him from doing other things that had really mattered to him. The defining moment came after an incident in which he had gotten blind drunk and smashed some of the furniture in his apartment:

> You know, I saw this. I think then it hit me really hard: this is a direct result of what I did when I was drinking. And I had already come to the conclusion that, yeah, I'm really not able to *do* anything. I'm really not able to hang out with my friends anymore. I'm really not able to function fully in school. And so then I pretty much quit cold turkey.

Quitting was no picnic. For several days after he stopped drinking he couldn't sleep and had severe withdrawal symptoms, at one point suffering a seizure in bed and hallucinating. Determined to stay sober, he threw himself into playing in a rock band. Music, which had been a passion since he was a child, had been mostly abandoned after he began drinking heavily; now he found that regaining his ability to play gave him back a lost sense of competence and helped keep him away from alcohol.

On the surface, this feeling of not liking what they saw may seem similar to the feelings of self-abnegation that often underlie adolescents' drift into heedlessness. But it actually represents something very different—and far more positive. This kind of self-criticism was productive and empowering: it was always based on a sense,

even if an inarticulate one, that they were people with more potential than they were demonstrating, that what they were into was not
really worthy of them.

Stephanie arrived at precisely this position when I last spoke with
her. It was an enormous change. When I first met her, a little more
than a year before, she had just been released from emergency hospital care after a near-fatal overdose that had left her confused and,
for some weeks, unable to speak clearly. She was deeply angry at her
parents and the various treatment programs she'd been involved in;
she had no idea what she wanted to do with her life other than to do
more drugs and within days of being released from treatment was
back on the street. Over the next several months she had a long run
of both heroin and speed, often going for days with little food or
sleep; she was arrested at least once and raped twice. But shortly before her eighteenth birthday she decided to get out of that life completely, and when we last talked she had been clean for several
months, was working, and planned to go back to school.

She looked and talked like a different person. When I remarked
on how changed she seemed and on how hard it must have been to
come so far so quickly, she said that it hadn't really been difficult.
She certainly had moments of wanting to get high again, and the
appeal of the street hadn't entirely disappeared. But she was now
looking toward the future, for the first time since she could remember: "I just have to think about what I want long term. . . . And I
know that if I go out there and use again I'm going to be screwing
myself over. It's most definitely not going to be just like one last
shot or one last drink." I asked what had made her able to stick to
the long-term view when she had never been able to in the past:

> I just remember where I came from. . . . I remember being out there on
> the streets and using to the point where I didn't want to be doing it but I
> felt like I had to. . . . All the problems that I had, as far as I'm concerned,
> were related to my using. . . . Having friends who were out there on the
> streets since they were about eighteen or nineteen and they're like in

their midthirties, still sitting there getting sick and complaining about how they need to get more stuff. . . . And realizing that's really not what I want to do with my life. I can do a lot of other things and I can have something to be proud of. I don't have to waste away using.

The recognition that she could be doing "a lot of other things," then, was the flip side of the realization that she was becoming like the thirty-something street addicts that she pitied and could not respect. She realized that she was squandering the possibility of doing something with her life that she knew she was capable of doing; she was increasingly troubled by a sense that she was "wasting herself ":

Just being out there and sitting on [the street] panhandling, when it made me feel really shitty to be asking people for money when I knew I was totally capable of working and that if I had a job that'd be something I would be proud of. Knowing that I could have been in school and, you know, been a freshman in college or something, but instead I'm sitting out there on the sidewalk trying to find ways to collect money so I could get another shot.

From her new vantage, many of the things she'd done while she was on the street seemed bizarre and beneath her:

I was in a relationship with someone I really liked, and we would fight over drug-related stuff. I got in an argument with this person over, like, that he had two units more of speed on his rig than I had on mine! And we fought over that for an hour practically, because we were so spun.

And she saw others around her sinking into ever more profound danger and personal disintegration:

Seeing friends of mine die, seeing people I cared about getting really close to death and, like, having to save them. . . . And also someone who

I was really close to for a period of time completely lost their mind to using because they stayed up for a few too many days too long and started to hallucinate and not know what was reality and what wasn't, and that was really upsetting to me.

Often such glimmers of recognition are reinforced for adolescents by something external—the discovery, for example, that they enjoy learning, that they want to change something about the world in which they live, that they can be in a strong and mutually enriching relationship. But the first step is simply the realization that they can be something different if they try hard enough. Where the belief in alternative possibilities comes from is difficult to say. For some of my informants, like Lacey, it seemed to flow naturally from the sense of intrinsic worth I've described before. Though their relationships with their parents may have been rocky, they still came away feeling, as Lacey put it, that their lives "had some value." Even those who had gotten a much more negative take on themselves from their parents often noted, in retrospect, that the overall message they had absorbed in childhood had been a mixed one that left open the possibility that they had potentials worth fulfilling. Carly's parents, for example, put her down in private, told her repeatedly that she was worthless, and on several occasions said that they wished she'd been aborted. But at the same time, they would publicly boast about her accomplishments and abilities. Looking back from a few years' distance, she felt that this mixed signal, though painful at the time, may have provided a reservoir of more positive definitions that she could draw on later in deciding to make the move out of a risky and self-destructive life:

> I probably held on to some of the "OK, I am OK" rather than hold on to the "I'm worthless, I'm this, I'm that." Because I don't really remember ever feeling completely worthless or not good enough. . . . I always remember thinking they're pretty fucked up.

Sometimes the kids' sense of possibility came from sources outside their families. A teacher may have told them they were smart, even though their parents had told them for years that they were stupid. That was true for Carly, who, unlike most of my other interviewees, loved school and blossomed in her early years before her parents pulled her out. For those whose experiences with school were mostly negative, the sense of possibility often came from the imagination, particularly from reading. Many who were unhappy in their experience of the real world of school and family found solace and inspiration through immersion in books. Their passion for reading usually developed outside of school or even in opposition to it. But it served them well in two related ways: it provided them with a tangible skill—a form of what some social scientists call "cultural capital"—that would later help them make it into college and do well once they got there, and it offered different angles on the world and on themselves. Books not only allowed them to envision alternative ways to live, alternative ways of relating to others, but also to see that they were not so peculiar after all, that there were other people who thought and acted the way they did. Jenny says that though, as a child, she never got much support or guidance from her parents, what she had was books:

I read a lot, and I could always be the smartest one in my class sort of thing. And everything else was like secondary, or it wasn't as for sure as those things were. So I just started reading a lot. . . . You can imagine things.

Part of my youth was definitely spent imagining a different life. . . . For a while I wanted to have a different name. I think I wanted to be called Heather or something. . . . I would spend hours on end by myself drawing pictures of, like, house layouts. I was always into architecture and design, so it was house layouts and, you know, just people and different situations, and I would have these stories going on for the picture and no matter what was going on around me, I could sort of fade back into that and pretend that my life was different than it was, that things were just different.

Books gave Jenny both a glimpse of a broader and richer world beyond the confines of her family and confidence that she could do well in that world because she was smart. Much the same was true for Lacey, even though she discovered her love of reading much later, after she had left high school. In school she'd always had trouble reading and had concluded that she wasn't good at it. Her teachers didn't help:

> I found that any attempt to try to read would be made fun of. Like I didn't do it right, or I didn't punctuate, I didn't spell right. . . . I was constantly ridiculed for stuff like that, not told how to do it right but just like, "Why didn't you?" You know, just hostile. So there was very little help to make my skills any way better, which I think is horrifying. I mean, that's the worst thing you can do, because then you can't *do* anything. I mean, the kids have *nothing* when they leave the school.

She, too, left school feeling that she "had nothing," but once out, she began reading voraciously on her own: "I just started pulling books off the self-help section, like *The Road Less Traveled.* You know, just reading stuff that would make me think about what I'm doing. And then I realized I loved reading, and I'd never really known that before." She also traveled widely while still a teenager, spending several weeks on her own in Europe, where she made the "mind-blowing" discovery that "the world is really large . . . and there's a lot of ways of being, a lot of ways of seeing, a lot of ways of perceiving." Being taken out of her normal milieu made her realize that she "didn't know diddly about the world," and she resolved to learn more. Ultimately, her resolution led her all the way to graduate school.

Wherever their sense of potential came from, most of my informants were adamant that the strength to act on it came mainly from within themselves. "That was all just me," Jenny told me, "and no one else had anything to do with it." Apart from the help of a few friends, Rick said, it was "basically all me." It is striking how frequently adolescents who have managed to turn troubled lives around say something like this, that it was something inside *them* that made it possible to take hold of their lives. A few, as we've seen, felt that professional help had facilitated their decision, but most did not, and even those who did believed that the outside help was only ancillary to their own independent choice, their own will to take charge of themselves. Stephanie says, for example, that she "pretty much went through hell" until, at a certain point,

> I just said to myself, I don't want to be doing this anymore. And decided *on my own* that I was the one that wanted to get sober and made it through that before I even got sent to a program. It's not like I had someone else, like a probation officer or a parent, who said, "Well, we feel that, like, you've gotten too many dirty UAs [urinalyses] when we pee test you" or "You know, you're coming home really late and you're not getting good grades in school and you're cutting a lot and you ran away two times in the past six months, so we're going to send you here."
>
> It's like, no, *I'm* the one who wanted to get sober, *I* put myself through hell, *I* thought it was fun at first and it ended up being not so much fun after I lived that way for a while, and *I* decided I don't want to do this anymore.

Like Stephanie, many other adolescents attribute their triumph over drugs, drink, or despair to a sense of efficacy, an independence of mind—and that belief tallies with findings from a number of studies of troubled or disadvantaged youth's paths to success. What some social scientists have called an "inner locus of control" often distinguishes those who prevail in spite of unfavorable beginnings from those who don't. Where that capacity to give themselves both a sense of direction and the will to follow it through comes from is not always easy to say. But one paradoxical explanation appeared often among my informants: that it was precisely the self-reliance forced on them by the abdication of their parents that made it possible for them to forge a new life out of deep crisis. Looking back, they believed that the experience of having to take care of themselves that had caused them so much pain and difficulty at the time had also schooled them to handle the vicissitudes of life on their own. Enforced independence had given them a rocky childhood and a perilous adolescence, but it had left them with an inner strength and a capacity for independent thought and action. If that experience of systematic neglect didn't destroy you altogether, as some put it, it was likely to make you stronger.

That was Jenny's view. On the one hand, the absence of competent adults in her life had robbed her of anything resembling a real childhood:

> I think the hardest part for me was ever trying to be a *kid*, because childhood is supposed to be this time of sort of innocence and not having to worry about any of the real-world things. . . . You know, you're supposed to be oblivious to all this stuff. And I just never really was. You're not supposed to know to call 911 if your mother screams too loud during a fight with her husband, or know what people are like when they're passed out, or know *any* of the things that I knew.

On the other hand, having to learn to manage for herself at an early age and to make adultlike decisions about the most basic aspects of life bred a sense of determination and a certain confidence that served her well later on:

> I don't see and I never have seen limits to what I can do, and this is since I was a child. If I want to do something, I see no reason why I can't do it if I work at it. And I think really what that comes down to is being very, very young and not having stable people surrounding you. 'Cause I was an only child, and my dad was gone when I was two, and my mother was very strung out for the majority of my early childhood, and I was alone a lot.

Think about it—if you've got a parent that's passed out and you've got to feed yourself, you're *gonna* figure it out. And you're gonna make mistakes, but you've got to do that.

I mean, that's really it, because I was so young and so many people weren't around and part of me blamed me, but I think most of it was more just like, no, people aren't stable, so I have to be what's there for me.

The self-reliance born of having "to be what's there for me," as we've seen, made it hard for Jenny and many others to avoid bad situations, but it also allowed them to pull themselves out of those situations, to skirt the edge of destruction and emerge intact. Jenny did a lot of drugs and drank far too much but quit on her own, without the intervention of therapists or programs. She drifted into an abusive marriage as a teenager but found the strength to leave it before she was twenty:

I'm that way by nature. It's not anything anyone's ever done for me, because no one ever put a lot of demands on me. The only person there who ever put demands on me was myself, and so I think that's why I was able to not do some things or not fall into the traps. I mean, I could do them, and then I could come out of them.

Lacey, too, felt from childhood that she could do practically anything she set her mind to:

I moved to Italy when I was like eighteen and a half. All by myself with forty dollars in my pocket. Well, I mean, you've got to have courage to take on things that are completely new. I think that's one of the things that benefited me, was that I just sort of would go and *do* it. There wouldn't be a question "Can I?" It would be like, "I will."

She thought that her capacity to just "go and do it" was nurtured during her years of being bounced from one foster placement to another:

Having to negotiate new cultural, family, social environments consistently helped me learn to navigate highly new situations and learn to adapt. I guess when you grow up in a situation like I did. . . . you don't have the rigid structures that a family provides—and the rigid fears that they provide. . . . You don't have the same limitations on yourself. You have different limitations, but you don't have the same ones that add to people's repeating patterns. . . . Even though you may have been abused, if you move out of it, it sort of breaks some of that.

Like Jenny, she felt that being able to survive a rough childhood intact had made her more autonomous and better able to weather difficult situations:

The therapist I worked with from the time I was thirteen to eighteen, she's like, "The one thing I've always been amazed by you is resilience. You were able to always pick yourself up and keep going. After everything is shattered and broken." I didn't realize that was resilience. I thought that was life.

The harrowing times many had endured on the street after running away or being ejected from their parents' homes had a similar effect. Tori, having survived years of street life and addiction, felt that practically anything she encountered thereafter, including going to a highly demanding university with very little academic preparation, was relatively easy: "I think in a way that I wouldn't be at [the university] if I didn't go through all that. If I didn't do all those drugs and live that miserable life, I don't think I would be able to be here," she says.

If I could do that and survive, then this should be nothing. I don't think that during *midterms* or finals! But for the most part this is *cake* compared to trying to live while you're doing drugs and trying to not get murdered or raped or—or whatever—all those horrible things that can

happen to you when you're in the element. This should be nothing. . . .
This is stressful. I mean, it's hard. It's hard work. But not as hard as
other things.

The years on the street also gave Tori a sense of purpose. Like
many once-troubled adolescents, she had learned what were essentially political lessons from her time of crisis—lessons that made
her want to devote herself to attacking the problems that she had
experienced up close. She'd been involved with a drop-in program
for runaway and homeless youth when she was using on the street
and began to volunteer as a worker in a similar program while she
was in college and sober. After graduation, she was offered a paying
job doing similar work and took it on without hesitation. "I don't
think I could do that kind of work if I didn't live through it," she
observes. "So it kinda gave me a direction. . . . It's one of the few
things that I really strongly, strongly believe in. . . . I can, like, *want*
to go to work every day."

Along with the belated recognition that their troubles were not
just "their fault," many began to understand that those troubles reflected larger injustices and deficits in the society around them, and
were drawn to use the insights they had gained through painful experience to help others in the same situations or to become advo-
cates for change. Stephanie, who got off the street and cleaned up
on her own at eighteen, looked forward to mundane and practical
things like having some money of her own without having to demean herself to get it, but she also wanted to go to college so that
she could learn to do something that would help people like her.
Sean wanted to go back to youth prison to speak to other kids behind bars and provide a model for a different future. Carly worked
as a volunteer with addicted women, and Trey looked forward to a
career in community activism. Studies of how troubled children
and adolescents fare in later life have also found this desire to
transform personal troubles into social action—to confront on a
larger scale the issues that nearly engulfed them earlier in their

lives, to offer help to the vulnerable, and to challenge social injustice. Emmy Werner, for example, saw it among teenaged mothers in Hawaii who had successfully stabilized their lives by their midthirties.

These young people, in short, did not simply become conventional adults once they put their years of crisis behind them, did not become compliant conformists after extricating themselves from drugs, alcohol, or the life of the street. Instead, they often turned into thoughtful critics of the society around them, and some became committed to changing it. Even those who did not involve themselves in this kind of activism or social concern almost always chose new lives outside conventional lines, centered on music, scholarship, and other creative endeavors. They survived and flourished not by adjusting to the world they had had so much trouble fitting into earlier but by challenging or transcending it. They rarely wanted to change *everything* about themselves; even though they knew that it was necessary to move on from the lives they had been leading, they did not renounce what they took to be their core—or even, for that matter, all the "bad stuff" they had done. They believed that their mistakes had helped them become the people they now were—and they were generally happy with themselves. They didn't wish that everything had been different, that they had never gotten off track, that they had been wholly normal kids. What they had learned from being close to the raw edge, they thought, had been a vital part of forging their characters. "You know," Anna says,

I honestly don't look back on any of those experiences and wish they never happened. I'm *so happy* that they happened because I've realized that if I ever were to deny those experiences, I would be denying myself. And I feel like I'm really happy with who I am today. And those experiences made me who I am.

Jenny puts it more acerbically:

I would not want to be any other way even if that does mean I had to grow up this way and go through those things. That's fine with me. I *like* who I am now and I know where my strengths lie and where my weaknesses are, and that's a good thing, and I would much rather be in this place now and know these things than to have had a college fund and a trust fund and a car when I was sixteen and be this sort of bumbling moron.

Some felt that the experience of being an outsider during their teenage years—by choice or otherwise—gave them an embryonic social and political awareness that they were later able to hone into a more focused and sophisticated critical vision. Trey, for example, was aware that he had lost a good deal that had been important to him when he plunged head-on into a volatile punk rock culture in his high school years. He'd given up sports, which he'd loved when he was younger. He knew that he had done crazy things during that period, including many that he was not proud of, and he had spent a significant part of his adolescence in prison. But he was convinced, in his mid-twenties, that his years on the outside had also provided insights that he would not have had otherwise and that helped him forge a critical, activist outlook at college: "Turning to the punk rock thing when I did so, it also opened up some new ways of thinking about things that are still with me today— that I wouldn't have done had I stayed maybe the nice, good kid, as bad as—as weird as that is to say." For a while he and his friends had been into a racist white power scene; he regretted that phase and felt embarrassed about it. But though there had been a great deal of what he now called "misdirected energy," he had still "learned a lot" during that time, and his early critical impulses stayed with him. He threw himself into studying political economy in college and looked forward to becoming an advocate for the poor.

Crucial to the ability to take on a new identity, in short, was the capacity to appreciate the people they had been before, even while rejecting the self-destructive or wrongheaded things they had done, the capacity to find a sense of identification, even kinship, with that struggling younger version of themselves. Many also retained considerable affection and respect for their friends from "that time," and some kept up the connections into adulthood. "I didn't feel at ease with, I guess, the mainstream of people," Trey says, "and I clicked with—I hate to use those clichés, clicking with this 'bad crowd,' because a lot of those 'bad' people are still my friends today."

"I Found Out I Could Actually Do Something": The Role of Pragmatic Help

To make the decisive shift away from care-lessness to a new kind of seriousness and a sense of value and purpose, then, required a profound and complex change in self-perception. These adolescents had to stop regarding themselves as the problem but also had to acknowledge that they needed to change their ways, and they needed to believe that they had it in them to do so. But there also had to be an institutional mechanism available to help them make the change once they had decided to make it. Their successful turnaround, in short, usually involved a fortuitous combination of internal shifts and external opportunities.

For my informants, the external opportunity came most often from the educational system, not from the regular high school, which had usually been part of the problem, but from more attentive, pragmatic, and forgiving institutions—alternative high schools, public community colleges—that provided an educational experience that was the virtual opposite of what they had encountered before. These institutions served as ladders out of stuck and desperate lives precisely because their inner culture was so different from that of the typical high school. They often took note of the potential of even the most marginal or troubled young people, where the regular high school had generally focused on those students' failings;

they were frequently willing to roll up their sleeves and tackle a youth's problems, where the regular high school or middle school had been neglectful or rigidly punitive. Often these institutions succeeded simply because they were relatively neutral places, where the conventional high school had typically been intrusive and moralistic—places where talents and interests could be explored, and credentials gained, without the atmosphere of surveillance, disparagement, and confrontation that so often marred the regular schools.

Anna had a dreadful time in school in her hometown, dropped out when she was thirteen, and then put herself back into school full time on her own at sixteen, after she had left her mother's home for good. She began in a public high school she describes as "just awful" but soon moved to an experimental alternative high school, where for the first time someone in authority paid serious attention to her. She started off well, but she was still deeply depressed and heavily into methamphetamine; her grades began to fall.

> And I remember all of my teachers getting together with my sister and myself, which is good that they had me present, and all of us talking about why my grades had fallen. And although I couldn't really tell them, well, *all* of it, just from them making that effort did help me because then I realized, oh no, I really need to make an effort or this could be really bad news. I definitely didn't want to be expelled from the school because it was such a nice environment compared to the other school I was going to. And so that gave me a push in the right direction.

Unlike the teachers in the other schools she'd attended, the staff were willing to sit down with her and "troubleshoot"—to "track me and see what was going on." Fortuitously, she had already decided that she wanted to get off the path she was on, wanted to stop doing drugs, stealing, and generally feeling terrible about herself:

If they had done that when I was in a different frame of mind, it probably wouldn't have mattered. I would have still done what I needed to do to feel good about myself. But I was finally realizing that drugs weren't making me feel good about myself. I was ready to try something new. . . . It was perfect timing.

Anna's grades went up quickly and dramatically after the series of troubleshooting meetings; soon she began to feel what she describes as "a new identity, a new persona, a new sense of myself." What is remarkable is how quickly this shift happened once the school intervened with serious help—especially given her long history of family trauma, institutionalization, and drug abuse and the rock-bottom sense of failure and "incrimination" that history had produced. Having made the decision to stop doing crystal meth, Anna quit immediately:

> I stopped going out. I no longer hung around this girlfriend of mine, who was also heavily involved in drugs and that whole scene. It was actually so easy to just stop. I just had enough, and my body was tired. My mind was tired. I was sick of never getting any sleep, of just having this very chaotic life. And that's when I started getting really involved in school again and just directing all my energy into that. And as a result I began feeling validated again through school. And my grades started rising. I remember at the end of my experience at that school feeling really fulfilled, just because I had gone through so much, and just seeing it all pay off. . . . It was very simple for me to make that transition. For some reason, it was so easy.

Trey was sent to an unusually supportive public continuation school while awaiting sentencing on a charge of having threatened his high school principal. "I loved that school," he says. "Six months I went there, and I loved it. I loved every single day." No one got in his face about his clothes or his haircut; the teachers offered intensive individual attention. He especially loved the principal, who was respectful, encouraging, and attentive: "She was great. I told her, 'I will never write *you* a threatening letter.' She said, 'Oh, thank you.' She was actually touched by it." In a fateful move, the local school district, which was weighing whether to expel him permanently, decided to keep him in the system. This was the first time he had ever felt that a school actually wanted him around, and the decision forged a bond with school he had never felt before: "I've gotta stay. I *want* to stay. Oh, my God, I want to stay in school. For the first time in my entire life . . . I'm finally happy. I've gotta stay." He didn't actually get to stay long, because his schooling was interrupted by nearly a year in prison. But the newfound experience of being welcomed in school stayed with him, and he credits it with helping him move from prison to a community college and then on to a major university.

Often such moves were facilitated by not just one but a series of supportive institutions that picked up adolescents at the point when they were primed to change and ushered them into progressively more secure and responsible situations. The help these institutions provided was generally very basic. But it often turned out to be all they needed. Carly was seventeen, for example, when she decided simultaneously to stop using hard drugs and to leave her abusive husband for good. She had called the police on him for the fourth or fifth time, but when they arrived, they took her to the police station instead because her husband was bleeding from a scratch she had inflicted. When she left the station she crashed for a few weeks in the back of the restaurant where she worked and then one day decided to look for help. Thumbing through the telephone book, she stumbled on a feminist community organization that took her on for free. The group provided drug counseling, put her to work answering the phones, and connected her with what she describes as "real basic information"—how to get food, how to sign up for the health insurance she had never had, how to get a restraining order to keep her husband at bay. She showed so much initiative and ability as a volunteer that the staff urged her to go on to college; embarrassed, she finally admitted that she had never gotten past the fourth grade. So they persuaded the local public "adult school" to allow her to work toward a high school diploma, even though she hadn't made it out of elementary school. The adult school in turn connected her with a (short-lived) state-funded program that trained students in child care work while offering day care to their children and paid for most of her school expenses. She went on to the local community college, where she got good enough grades to gain admittance to a major university. Once there, she was eased into its intensely competitive atmosphere with the help of a reentry program for students who had been out of school for some time.

Certain elements appear again and again when young people describe the institutions that helped them sustain their decision to turn around troubled and aimless lives. Those institutions were willing to take even very problematic people under their wing. They were often unusually flexible, willing to bend the rules in the service of providing the right help at the right time. They saw themselves as in the business of opening gates for struggling young people, where so many of the institutions those teenagers had encountered in the past were essentially in the business of closing them—of sifting and ranking rather than building capacities. In all these ways, they countered the Darwinian drift of the surrounding culture. They did not simply measure who was successful in the race for achievement and who was not; instead, they actively nurtured abilities and confronted obstacles to success. They went out of their way for young people, and they rarely allowed anyone to fall through the cracks.

Public community colleges played a particularly important role in the transformation of many of the students in this book, and they are prominent in other studies of resilience among the young as well. Emmy Werner found that attendance at community college was an important predictor of success in later life among

delinquent youth and teenaged mothers in Hawaii. Public postsecondary education or training under the GI Bill was a crucial av-
enue toward success among children of disadvantaged Depression
era families studied by the sociologist Glen Elder and among children from "multi-problem" Boston families studied by the Harvard
psychiatrist George Vaillant. These studies often suggest that community college or vocational education after high school work
mainly for economic reasons—by providing skills and credentials
that enable young people from less than promising backgrounds
to get better jobs later in life, which in turn provide the economic
base for them to marry and raise families. But for the middle-class
youth in this book, community college offered other benefits as
well.

Perhaps most crucially, it provided a setting in which intellectual and creative interests could be explored without the hindrance
of having to conform to the often unspoken cultural and moral
code of the conventional high school. The community college did
not care if students arrived on campus with green hair or Doc
Martens combat boots or if they wore too much hair gel. It did not
care about its students' reputations with their previous teachers or
whom they spent their leisure time with. It was open to all comers
who could do the work. The extraneous elements of high school,
in other words, were largely trimmed away, leaving only the
genuinely educational functions. And though the education was
decidedly uneven in quality, it opened new vistas to these adolescents. That community college was inexpensive also helped: students could pay out of their own pockets and were therefore not
dependent on their parents' money or approval. Some, accordingly, went straight from the street to community college class-
rooms; often, like Lacey, they just "wandered in"—no one
referred them, no one sat down with them to plan their educational futures.

In some states it was possible to enroll in community college
even without a high school diploma and, if you did well enough

academically, to move after two years into the state university system. You could, moreover, have a false start at community college, or even several, and still come back later. The public community college has sometimes been called a second-chance institution, but for many of these young people it was a multiple-chance institution. And it could be a lifesaving one. In the nonjudgmental atmosphere of the community college, adolescents could discover, or rediscover, that they were capable people who were good at things and who could be turned on by something other than drugs and danger. Tori, for example, "walked right off the street" into a community college and quickly discovered that she was not the "burnout" she'd been told she was in high school. "I was doing well, and I wasn't even trying that hard," she says. The revelation that she could succeed at something "kinda started this weird ball rolling":

> The place was a joke basically. I mean, you don't have to do anything, except in Calculus. But I guess that was good because it got me kinda excited about school. And I started to feel smart . . . and that semester, I had like a 4.0, and I was just like, wow, you know? It blew me away, because I didn't ever expect to have a 4.0. Until I took Calculus, and then I lost my 4.0, but . . . the fact that I was doing well, it got me excited about that I could *actually do something*.

In high school, her teachers had repeatedly told her that she wasn't college material and shunted her into vocational school, where the main offering for girls was cosmetology. Like Lacey, she felt that "high school didn't seem to prepare me for *anything*. I got to community college, and I didn't know how to write an essay, a decent, coherent, well-structured essay. I had no idea. I didn't know how to use a comma."

Discovering that they "could actually do something" nourished these adolescents' emerging sense that they could also *stop* doing things that they had believed to be out of their control. It heightened their sense of themselves as subjects who were capable of giving direction and meaning to their lives. This was a lesson many, like Tori, wanted to convey to others:

> In a month exactly from today I'm going to be walking across the stage, and they're going to be handing me that little fake diploma. I can't even believe it. You know? And my friends that are still back home that are still using or stuff are just amazed. I was kind of hoping that it would be an example. Not even so much for them to go to college or whatever, but just like, You don't have to stay on drugs forever. That it's possible to stop. Not necessarily going through twelve-step or whatever, not like any of that, but just that . . . you can stop and have a life.

For Sean, the same revelatory experience was provided by a program offered behind prison walls. After his sentencing for the near-fatal shooting, he went through a period in which he was convinced that he had destroyed his life and ruined any possibility of a normal future; he was resigned to being "just a total loser and a hard case for the rest of my life." But he drifted into a two-year college program operated in the prison, one of the few such programs for imprisoned youth at the time. (There are fewer today, after Congress in the 1990s eliminated federal Pell grant funding for low-income students behind bars.)

What's remarkable in these stories is how little it took to help even extremely troubled and wounded adolescents make enduring changes in their lives. They rarely embarked on those changes as a result of formal therapy; indeed, professional therapy was among the least significant sources of change for them. Their experience tallies with what Werner and Smith found in studying adults who had turned their lives around after a troubled adolescence:

> Fewer than 10 percent of the individuals who had been troubled teenagers rated mental health professionals of any kind (psychologists,

psychiatrists, social workers) as helpful in times of crisis or stress. . . . Mental health professionals were ranked twelfth among fourteen sources of support, far behind spouses and friends, parents, siblings, members of the extended family, coworkers, teachers, mentors, ministers, and faith and prayer.

The help that mattered most to these young people was usually pragmatic rather than therapeutic. It was designed not to change them but to facilitate changes they had chosen to make. I'm not suggesting that none of them needed a deeper kind of help; some surely did. And as we've seen, some benefited from one kind of therapeutic intervention in particular, the "lens-changing" experience in which a particularly empathic therapist helped them learn to stop taking all the blame for their troubles. But by far the most significant help came from institutions that asked few questions about their character, made no global demands that they become a certain kind of person or conform to extraneous rules, but offered either a new opportunity or practical assistance that could help them get their lives in order. The most useful assistance, indeed, was often the most basic. If they were living on the street, they needed a stable roof over their heads. If they had dropped out of school and had no legitimate skills, they needed a place to get them. Those who had never been motivated to use their intellectual capacities, or never knew they *had* intellectual capacities, needed the opportunity to flex them. Teenage girls who had borne children needed child care and employment skills. When young people got these things, even in relatively small doses, their lives could, and often did, shift quickly and dramatically.

None of these adolescents mentioned fear of formal punishment as a catalyst for that shift. What criminologists call "deterrence" had little or no influence. Most, after all, had experienced conditions that were far worse than anything the criminal justice system could throw at them. Those who had been in "the system" uniformly believed that the experience had been at best irrelevant, at worst massively counterproductive. It was, if anything, one more push down the road to "whatever," because it simultaneously contributed to their growing alienation from the "normal" world and stiffened their identification of themselves as bad kids, fit only to associate with other bad kids. Once they had been in jail, juvenile hall, or prison, moreover, most came out firmly convinced that they could handle that situation perfectly well if they were threatened with it again—just as they could handle nearly anything else. Most had already endured a steady diet of punishment and disapproval; more of the same was unlikely either to faze them very much or to contribute to a constructive change in the way they thought about themselves. In their view, positive change had come from being treated better, not worse—from having had opportunities to demonstrate that they could do something well and from being acknowledged when they did.

Tom had drifted through most of his high school years, ultimately dropping out of school and "pretty much doing nothing" for several months. During this time his main interest was in racing souped-up cars on the local freeways and country roads. Sometimes he and his friends would race one another two abreast up dark two-lane canyon roads with the headlights off. Like Terry and Dale, he didn't feel, in retrospect, that he was actually trying to kill or injure himself; he just didn't think much about what he was doing one way or another. He felt that in general he was not able to take himself seriously in anything that he did—certainly not enough to rein in his reckless driving or think about his future. At one point he threatened another youth with a gun during a trivial argument and was sent to juvenile hall. The experience left him feeling no less aimless and even more angry than before. He went back to the life of racing cars and sleeping until noon until, like Lacey and Tori, he drifted into the local community college. Once there he quickly began to accumulate the stellar grades that got him accepted into a major university. Most importantly, he discovered that "people actually gave a damn that I was doing well":

And it had been so long since I felt like someone's really *happy* with me. I loved it. I loved the fact that, hey, not only am I doing something with my life, but I'm making these people that I really care about very happy by doing it.

See, some people say that human beings do things to avoid bad situations. Other people argue that human beings do certain things to achieve good situations. . . . I didn't give a damn about the bad situations. I'd been in jail. You want bad? I've got a roof over my head. I can walk outside whenever the hell I want. Bad? No. But the good situations—I love them.

He still had moments when his new sense of purpose and motivation felt fragile, when he thought he could easily slip into the old feeling of "not giving a shit":

It's still with me at times. Once someone's dropped out of high school, stopped going, stopped caring, it is amazingly easy to slide right back into that. . . . Just like that, I could go down that path again. For the most part I'm safe, but . . . every once in a while, I don't give a damn.

He also hadn't entirely lost his appetite for risk. Although he had given up the late-night road racing, he took pride in his ability to weave in and out of freeway traffic at breakneck speed. But something had changed:

I'm not trying to brag, but I was actually pretty good at it. When I saw a pocket of traffic, I'd find a way, even at a hundred miles an hour, to weave through it rather well. But there'd be some close calls. And now I just—if there's a straight stretch with a couple cars, I'll do it. To this day, I still, hypothetically, will crack 120 on the freeway every once in a while for the fun of it. But that's purely for the fun of it.

And part of that's probably just getting older and calming down a little bit. But a lot of that's because I feel like there's a lot more—I have a lot more *to* me now.

. . .

The feeling of having "a lot more to me" represents the opposite of the sense of worthlessness and emptiness that afflicts so many American adolescents, and getting to that emotional place is a crucial step in their journey to a more mindful and productive life. As these stories suggest, fostering that new and life-affirming feeling of substance is often hardly a difficult proposition. A few successful courses at community college, a reasonably responsible job or volunteer position that they can do well, a little nonjudgmental and supportive guidance—these are often all it takes to catalyze an upward spiral in the lives of troubled adolescents. Yet in America today even this modest help is rare. Too many of the institutions adolescents encounter seem designed to convince them that there is less to them than they might think, not more. Carly put her finger on the problem in reflecting on her own successful turn-around:

> I don't think I'm the exception. I think I'm more like the rule with people because, you know, people are motivated. If you give them an opportunity to say, "Well, this is what I would like to do," they're going to go after it. And maybe they'll fall a little bit here or there, but if you just help them back up, they're going to keep going. But we'd rather just keep keeping them down.

And Carly is surely right. All the evidence suggests that it is indeed true that "if you just help them back up, they're going to keep going." It is not fated, by biology or personality, that adolescents remain stuck in a pattern of heedless and destructive behavior. But their stories also show that breaking out of that pattern is too often almost a random process—sometimes not much more than luck, a matter of being in the right place at the right time. Helping people up in a systematic way does not come naturally in American culture: often these young people escaped from apathy or desperation only because they stumbled on one of the relatively few institutions that were able and willing to do it.

If we want to do a better job of saving adolescent lives and spirits, we will need to provide that kind of critical assistance more systematically and less grudgingly. In the next chapter, I want to suggest some ways in which we might do that.

TOWARD A CULTURE OF SUPPORT

The new middle-class world in which many American adolescents grow up is one that combines harshness and heedlessness in equal measure. It is a world that is quick to punish and slow to help, a world paradoxically both deeply moralistic and profoundly neglectful. Hence it is hardly surprising that so many mainstream teenagers are in trouble, for that world makes it very hard to grow up. It makes it all too difficult to achieve a strong and abiding sense of worth and all too easy to feel like a failure and a loser. It makes it all too easy to feel like an outsider, all too difficult to feel appreciated or respected for being who you are. It is a world in which it is treacherously easy for adolescents to trip up and break the rules but in which no one can be bothered to help them avoid tripping up in the first place. In that context the troubling behavior of mainstream adolescents—their care-lessness, their self-destructiveness, their occasional rage—becomes less mysterious. Adolescence is rarely an easy time. But it need not be as hard as it often is in America.

The central point in understanding the care-lessness among mainstream teenagers is that it mirrors the larger care-lessness of the society around them. For the adolescents in this book, the bottom line is that, too often, nobody cared enough to put in the sustained work that they needed to grow and thrive. That was especially true if something went wrong, if they started to flounder or lose their bearings. Over and over again, at that critical point, it turned out to be no one's job to help them get back on track. "I had to do it on my own," "It was all on me," "There's no help out there." This failing was not restricted to a handful of inadequate or incompetent adults: it was a reflection of the growth and spread in America of a broader culture that has turned what would once have been regarded as sheer negligence or irresponsibility into a virtue. Adolescents ran into this attitude like a wall, wherever they turned. They found it at home and in the schools; they found it if they were sent to a program or to juvenile hall. They grew up in a world in which the values of mutuality and reciprocity that were once an important part of middle-class culture had been overwhelmed by a shoulder-shrugging individualism that excused most adults, and indeed society as a whole, from what we normally think of as adult responsibilities of nurture and support, that put most of the burden of managing life on children themselves and was quick to discard them altogether if they became too much trouble.

I've described that culture as a kind of visceral social Darwinism, a largely unspoken worldview that drives the operation of most of the institutions adolescents must navigate on their way to adulthood. It is the working philosophy of many of the schools they attend (or do not attend) and of many of the helping agencies that they encounter when they get into trouble; perhaps most critically, it is the moral outlook that often shapes the inner life and culture of their families. This world is, of course, only one region of the American landscape. Many teenagers, fortunately, grow up in environments that are more nurturing, more forgiving, and more supportive. But many do not, and we cannot understand the crisis that engulfs them without understanding their world and the values that suffuse it.

I am not suggesting that those values are entirely new. There has been a hard and punitive edge to the American brand of individualism from the beginning. But today that punitive ethos has been fused with a new recklessness—an unwillingness to think about consequences or take on the responsibilities of mature and generative adulthood, to work out mindful plans for the collective future, whether the issue is the raising of children, the sustaining of communities, or the husbanding of the planet. The new Darwinism is not only tough but also distinctly uncaring and irresponsible; under its sway, we have become a society that is often self-righteously hard on children but simultaneously unwilling to accept the responsibility of actually bringing them up.

Comparisons with the past are risky, for there is always a danger of falling prey to nostalgia for a warmer and more supportive age that may have been more a longing than a reality. But I believe that the new Darwinism represents a significant departure from the moral vision that prevailed in much of middle-class America in the 1950s and 1960s. That earlier vision took for granted certain basic notions of inclusion and collective responsibility, embodied in the spread of public higher education, affordable health care, job protections, and other middle-class entitlements that blossomed in the years after World War II. It was the driving moral force behind white middle-class support for civil rights, humanitarian reforms in juvenile justice and the schools, and a kinder and more flexible approach to child rearing. In many ways, the harsh new individualism of the twenty-first century constitutes an attack on that more generous vision and the social policies that flowed from it.

But the contemporary Darwinism is not simply a throwback to the nineteenth century. The older brand of individualism that flourished in America after the Civil War included, at least in theory, a sense of mutual obligation, a limited but significant idea of reciprocity. The historian Richard Hofstadter, in his classic study of social Darwinism in American thought, lists the virtues preached by influential thinkers in that tradition, like Herbert Spencer and William Graham Sumner, as "personal providence, family loyalty and family responsibility, hard work, careful management, and proud self-sufficiency." These values, he argues, were not just platitudes disingenuously promoted by "greedy plutocrats" for their own purposes: they were widely accepted "middle-class virtues." But with the possible exception of "proud self-sufficiency," they are not values that figure prominently in the culture in which middle-class youth like Dale and Jenny, Stephanie and Alyssa grew up. Careful management and family responsibility, in particular, are hard to find in the stories of most of the young people in this book. A heedless attitude toward the management of life generally and the raising of children in particular, along with an often explicit rejection of responsibility for others' welfare, dominated the inner culture of these families, and versions of those attitudes also pervaded the culture of the schools they attended and most of the agencies set up to help them.

These attitudes were not confined to individual families and the institutions that served adolescents: a similar moral vision drove much of American social policy during the lives of these teenagers. This was the era of a bipartisan welfare "reform" that eliminated a sixty-year-old guarantee of basic income support in the name of "personal responsibility"; of a massive expansion of the prisons, supported by presidents and legislators of both political parties, that gave the United States far and away the highest rate of incarceration in the world; and of the slashing, even for the middle class, of social supports—notably health care—once taken for granted. It was the era in which, for the first time, middle-class Americans in large numbers refused to allow themselves to be taxed to preserve the traditional guarantee of a public school education for everyone. In all these realms, we witnessed the same absence of concern for consequences that permeated the behavior of parents, school authorities, and mental health workers toward the adolescents in this book. We know this culture by the questions it does not ask. What, for example, would happen to the mothers we threw off welfare in the name of enforcing personal responsibility—and to their children? What would happen when the masses of mostly young, angry, and unskilled inmates of our bursting prisons returned to the streets, in the

hundreds of thousands, year after year? And what would happen to
their children while they were out of sight and mind behind bars?
How would children learn to become capable citizens without competent teachers—or even textbooks? No one knew or seemed to
care. The question of what would happen down the road was simply
not an issue, just as it is not for the parent who doesn't ask what will
happen to the fifteen-year-old who is kicked out of the house or for
the school that doesn't ask what will happen to the troubled student
expelled to the multiple perils of the street.

Thus the broader social policies of the post-Reagan era—the era
in which all the young people in this book grew up—reflected most
of the themes I've said characterize the social and cultural surround
of these middle-class adolescents: the reflexively punitive and exclusive mentality, the readiness to wash our hands of people when
trouble arises, an unwillingness to tolerate deviance or failure, a
willingness to let those who cannot keep up or who have trouble
conforming to the rules of the struggle fall to the bottom of an increasingly unforgiving and depriving society, and above all, an indifference to the longer-term consequences of these ways of relating
to others. Put these themes together and you have, in the lifetimes
of the adolescents in this book, the rise and spread of a particularly
stark version of market society, in which the principles of mutuality,
of commitment to particular people, communities, or institutions,
and of collective responsibility have withered—in some places, to
the vanishing point—with profound and fateful effects on the lives
and spirits of American adolescents.

Explaining these shifts in middle-class culture necessarily involves
a good deal of speculation. My own feeling is that they reflect several
broader sea changes in our economy and society. One of them is the
shift from an economy based on production to one based on consumption—a shift that has resulted from our growing technological
capacity to produce what we need with less and less human labor.
That shift has, among other things, progressively weakened what
were once the central American middle-class values of competence,

responsibility, and a planful orientation to the future—all of which flourished in the context of a production-oriented world. As Hofstadter points out, the sturdy bourgeois attitude toward "training up" children was essential in developing a competent labor force for the emerging industrial economy, which demanded both technical skills and internal discipline. But the shift toward a consumption economy, already discerned by social critics in the fifties, has chipped away at the economic foundation of those values. In their place—much more so today than in the fifties—is a relative rise of the values of acquisition, comfort, and convenience, the core values that underpin a society in which growing numbers of people are "surplus" in relation to the need for their labor and in which the constant stimulation of consumption is imperative if the economy is to survive, let alone prosper. Those economic imperatives became urgent in the latter part of the twentieth century, and as they did so, the accompanying values moved from the economic realm of marketing and advertising to the world of social relations, shaping the way we deal with one another in the community, in the family, and in the larger polity. As the function of the middle class has changed, so have its values.

The shift from an individualism rooted in a context of production to one grounded in consumption has arguably given us the harshness of nineteenth-century Darwinism without the saving grace of its commitment to responsible husbanding of human resources. At the same time, the shrinking need for traditional middle-class skills has upped the ante in two related ways: it has made the competition for upper-level positions much more intense and it has rendered interchangeable the vast number of people who fail to make it in that competition. One reason some of today's middle-class adolescents feel enormous pressures to be "perfect" is that the less perfect may be consigned to lives that, if not exactly on the margins, are not ones that can reliably offer dignity, esteem, or personal fulfillment. And one reason we do not much care if some fail in that struggle or even drop out altogether is that within the parameters of the present economic order, we do not really need them anymore. Thus it is not accidental that so many adolescents today are so easily discarded, for they have become, in this sense, dispensable. That fate overtook the youth of the lower classes decades ago, and we are still suffering the consequences: it is now catching up with the children of the middle.

Add to this shift the related intensification of the pace and globalization of economic activity, which has not only helped shrink the economic base of traditional middle-class life but created a rootless society in which capital and resources, jobs and people are shifted with dizzying speed from place to place, city to city, country to country. Economic and social institutions are rapidly built and as rapidly abandoned; whole communities—and occupations—are quickly created and as quickly decimated. Indeed, the communities thus created are often little more than adjuncts to an economic process whose momentum is no longer really controlled by anyone. Like the shift away from the productive values of training and commitment, this change is surely evolutionary, not revolutionary: it was certainly evident in the mid-nineteenth century, when Karl Marx wrote that under the sway of industrial capitalism "all that is solid melts into air." But it has accelerated in the new global economy. Richard Sennett describes one aspect of the change in writing about the "corrosion of character" that, he argues, accompanies contemporary economic life. "The most tangible sign of that change," he says, "might be the motto 'No long term.'" People do not expect to have much continuity in the work that they do or the communities they live in, and consequently they feel little sense that they are able to plan for a reliable future. The problem this creates for human relationships is profound: "'No long term,'" Sennett writes, "is a principle which corrodes trust, loyalty, and mutual commitment. . . . Transposed to the family realm, 'no long term' means keep moving, don't commit yourself, and don't sacrifice." It is not hard to see the connection between that broader eclipse of the long term and the profound care-lessness that afflicted both the adolescents in this book and the adults around them.

This change has been compounded by the political triumph, in the last quarter of the twentieth century, of a particularly harsh version of the "free market" approach to social and economic development. The celebration of private gain and the denigration of the public sphere have always been prominent in American political culture, but they acquired unprecedented influence after the Reagan revolution of the 1980s. We often focus on what that revolution meant for the poor—cutbacks in welfare, a swollen prison system, the shrinking of public health care—but it also helped transform the lives of much of the middle class and indeed change what it *meant* to be middle class. The triumph of a market vision of American society—a vision in which intense competition for diminishing numbers of good jobs and steady incomes is carried on in the face of diminished social supports—has accelerated the erosion of many of the institutions that made the traditional middle class middle class: labor unions, affordable health care and housing, relatively stable employment. The erosion of those supportive institutions is both cause and consequence of the waning of the more generous and solidaristic values of the postwar middle class in the United States. The Darwinian values of the modern market ideology—the denial of mutual responsibility, the insistence that it is better not to offer too much assistance to the vulnerable, the injunction to make it on your own or fall to the bottom—tend to perpetuate themselves. The insecurity and harshness of ordinary life that result from the market's stripping of community and stability promote a lifeboat ethic that has replaced the more inclusive middle-class morality of the fifties.

It isn't wholly surprising that hard-pressed middle-class parents with too many jobs and too few sources of social support develop harsh attitudes toward their children's misbehavior—and simultaneously resist spending money to provide services and supports for other people's children. Nor is it surprising that harassed school officials or treatment providers operating with perennially pinched and threatened resources develop a triage mentality toward young people with problems. And the farther we spiral in this direction, the more these trends become self-fueling.

We need to stop that spiral for many reasons, including our self-interest. Adolescents who feel themselves to be marginalized, disrespected, punished, and discarded will not simply disappear, much as some might like them to. The damage that we inflict on them will come back to haunt us in one way or another. We shouldn't any longer need reminders of this, but it seems that we do. As I write, my newspaper reports that a Columbine-style plot to attack a high school and kill students and teachers was discovered, in the nick of time, by authorities in the small city where one of the teenagers who figures prominently in this book grew up. I don't think that we have even begun as a society to address the conditions that continue to breed that level of anger and desperation.

But more important, we need to confront those conditions because to do otherwise is simply unacceptable, particularly in a country with such extraordinary resources. That a society of unprecedented affluence cannot find ways to do better by its young people is not only tragic but scandalous. A society so driven by an ethos of neglect and exclusion not only breeds adolescent disasters with frustrating predictability but also fails to measure up to reasonable standards of what it means to be civilized.

In this concluding chapter I want to say something about what might be done to prevent this spiral. The trauma and self-destructiveness that consume so many mainstream adolescents today are neither tolerable nor inevitable. Most adolescents with serious problems are not fated to have them forever, not doomed by biology or some hard-wired disorder to lives of futility, danger, and failure. Most—like the ones described in this book—turn their lives around largely on their own, without much help from the outside. But many do not, and even those who manage often suffer needlessly first. We can do much better than this. We can do much more than sequester, punish, or medicate troubled kids, and stand back and wait to see if they make it on their own—and we owe it to them to try. The fact that their troubles are so often related to identifiable social and cultural forces means that it is within our power to alter them.

Offering a better deal for adolescents in America means challenging, in small ways and big ones, the culture of negligence and exclusion wherever it is found. It means creating settings for adolescent growth and development that are more attentive and more inclusive, more willing to accept responsibility for the vulnerable and less quick to punish. It means shifting the focus away from individual blame—and even individual treatment as it is conventionally practiced—to a more complex and empathic understanding of the dangers adolescents confront today and the limits of their capacity to get through these difficult years unaided. In a more subtle sense, it means providing a richer array of opportunities for succeeding in one's own eyes and those of the larger community, a broader variety of definitions of what it *means* to be successful—a facilitating rather than restricting individualism. It means adopting a less punitive conception of what we wish to mean by "help" and making sure that it is actually available to those who need it. And it means ending the self-defeatingly neglectful culture that still flourishes in too many of our public schools. Without claiming to offer a detailed blueprint, I want to suggest some steps we might take in these directions.

1. Places to Go

One of the most critical problems for troubled adolescents in America is that there are few places for them to go if they can no longer survive emotionally at home or are thrown out by angry or overwhelmed parents. As it stands, their choices are almost all bad ones. They can go to a relative's house for a while, but usually not for long, and since the relative often shares the same attitudes as the parents, the underlying crisis quickly reappears. They can "couch surf" at other people's houses, but that is only a temporary strategy, and a disruptive one. They can live on the street—and a startling number of them do. Depending on the nature of their trouble, they may find a place in a residential treatment agency, but they can rarely stay for long, especially given the tendency of managed care to find ways of pushing them out as quickly as possible. Moreover, only some need the sort of treatment that these institutions, even at their best, have to offer. Most need something simpler and more practical: a safe and supportive place to live while they get themselves back together and get on with their lives.

Most of the teenagers in this book experienced several of these temporary situations, often in rapid and disorienting succession. Not having a place to go that was stable, welcoming, secure, and nonjudgmental was a constant problem for them, and one that predictably generated others. It forced them into living situations that were often dangerous and that increased their exposure to harm and exploitation. It sometimes made them dependent on problematic relationships for sheer survival; this was especially true for girls, who, once out of the family home, often had to rely on volatile or predatory men for a place to stay and some protection from the even greater dangers of being alone on the street.

Simply hoping that families will improve isn't enough. We should certainly offer more—and better—help to troubled parents than we now do, to try to keep families from melting down to this point in the first place. But we also have to acknowledge how often and how badly middle-class adolescents are failed or endangered by their families and to be willing to provide alternative living arrangements for those who need them. These should be places where teenagers can live without there being something officially wrong with them, places run by competent and empathic adults that provide structure but are not punitive, that are supportive but not necessarily "therapeutic," that do not resemble the bleak and often dangerous homeless shelters that too often are all that is available for teenagers in need of shelter and respite. Some could be designed for short-term stays, some for the longer term, but they should always be understood as real places to live, where adolescents are offered reliable and steady support and where something is asked from them in return—some kind of work or other participation that allows them to feel that they are making a contribution. These residential environments might include inhouse schooling or simply provide housing for adolescents still attending regular school. They might provide varying levels of counseling, but with the understanding that these are not places where adolescents go to be "fixed" but places where they can live in dignity and security while they get on with whatever needs doing in their lives.

2. Things to Do

Not all adolescents in trouble need alternative housing, of course. But most need a richer array of opportunities in the community for meaningful work and creative endeavor, especially those who are deeply estranged from school or have dropped out or been kicked out. In most American communities the school is the center of institutional life for adolescents, and in some places it is virtually the only game in town—the only institution, other than their families, with which they have much contact. If they hate school or if their connection with it is severed, they often have nothing to do, at least nothing that is both legitimate and interesting. It is hard to describe the level of isolation and sheer desperate boredom that this situation can engender for the adolescent who lives in a community that, however rich in terms of per capita income, lacks alternative opportunities for engagement and creativity outside the schools.

Many adolescents grow up in what I've come to think of as "stripped" communities—stripped, that is, down to a handful of basic economic functions and depleted of much of the social infrastructure that could make life not only less stressful but also richer and more meaningful. This is another consequence of the larger heedlessness of the culture, a reflection of our willingness to move people rapidly from place to place in response to economic forces beyond their control, without regard for the human consequences. What is left in these unstable enclaves is often little more than the home, the school, and the shopping mall. For adolescents, this kind of stripped-down community can at least be bearable, if not fulfilling, as long as they remain connected to family and school; if they lose both connections, these communities can become places of devastating and demoralizing emptiness.

At that point, the things that could get youth in trouble or put them in danger almost inevitably move in to fill the void, taking on a central place in their lives. Zack put his finger on this problem in describing the modestly affluent but oddly barren suburb where he lived as "an adult town, not a kid town." What he meant was that adults at least had their work, which was done mainly in offices far from town; for kids, there was nothing to do except "homework, drugs, and mischief." Take away the homework, and all that's left is drugs and mischief. This was a sentiment I heard over and over again. The sense of narrowed options for meaningful things to do formed a backdrop for much else that went wrong in the teenagers' lives, an almost taken-for-granted context in which trouble was practically inevitable. Jake describes his sprawling suburban community this way:

> It's a big city and everything, but there's like—everything there is to do is kind of boring, like going to the movies, going to the mall. It's old. Doing drugs, that's even boring now. Yeah, you *sit* there. Like, "What are we gonna do? What are we gonna do today?" There is nothing to do. So you're just like—you know it's there, so you get it.

The problem is especially intense, as Mickey points out, because their parents' overwork so often adds to teenagers' isolation. "I just hate living in the suburbs," she told me. "There's nothing to do, especially for teenagers." But she quickly amended this: "There's stuff to do, but it's not exactly legal. . . . For somebody that has to take care of theirselves or rely on something else to keep them entertained while their parents are at work or they're not in school, there's nothing to do except get high."

One response to this deficit would be to create new ways for adolescents—whether they are in or out of school—to engage in challenging and useful work on important social issues in the communities around them: working with children, the elderly, or the homeless, tackling environmental problems, improving recreational opportunities, advocating for better schools. As we've seen, many adolescents who have known trouble have a strong desire to help others like them or to work to remedy the injustices that they see—often more clearly than others—around them. And they are frequently very good at this kind of work: they have "been there," and they "get it" in a way most people do not. Working with the vulnerable helped pull some of the teenagers in this book out of despair and aimlessness, including Tori, who went from street addict to program coordinator for the homeless, and Sean, who wanted to bring his story to other teenagers in prison as a message of hope. In discovering that they cared passionately about something outside themselves, they also learned that they cared about themselves as well. The same motivation to help or give back has turned up in other studies of the road out of delinquency or adversity. We need to think more systematically and creatively about how to mobilize this enthusiasm and native skill.

An example of what I have in mind is a program developed in twelve sites across the United States by the Innovation Center for Community and Youth Development, which engaged young people in "civic action" projects to "identify and address problems in their communities." In Washington, D.C., youth helped to craft new regulations governing group homes for adolescents; in Denver, they helped create a new school district policy on sexual harassment. These efforts were based on the premise that, as the center's president puts it, "teens alienated from the mainstream are not attracted to the typical after-school programs and clubs. They are interested in joining groups that work toward social change. They simply want to be actively involved in making life better." In the words of Joan Wynn of the University of Chicago's Chapin Hall Center for Children, what may appeal most to youth estranged from conventional settings are "hands-on activities focused on issues that matter for them, where they can make a contribution that ends in a product or performance or some way of demonstrating mastery," and that also have high expectations and offer "sustained support over time." This program, like most others designed to involve youth in grassroots community action, was aimed at disadvantaged teenagers. But nothing prevents us from offering similar opportunities for civic action to kids who are not poor but who may suffer equally, if not more, from a corrosive sense of disconnection, isolation, and meaninglessness. Such programs could offer the moral equivalent of the military experience that turns up in many studies as a critical turning point in the path to success for disadvantaged or troubled youth.

We don't have to wait for youth to get in trouble, of course, before providing these opportunities. Linking teenagers with organizations that can mobilize their energy, their craving for justice, and their empathy with the less fortunate ought to be something we do regularly and offer to anyone who is interested. We could do these things under the auspices of the schools, but I think it would be best to do many of them through nonprofit or public agencies outside the school systems; otherwise, we exclude those who are not in school and who may need these opportunities most, as well as those who are in school but inclined to reject anything connected with it.

3. Inclusive Schools

Reversing the downward spiral requires not only providing more constructive opportunities for adolescents but eliminating needless obstacles that we put in their way. Here, the culture of the public school is clearly the most important target. I am not suggesting that good and nurturing schools do not exist; there are many of them in America, with engaged and creative teachers. At their best, these schools are probably more effective and more supportive than anything that was available when I was an adolescent. But the ground truth is that too many schools really do, as my informants so often put it, "suck." This is hardly a new problem: it was exhaustively addressed as far back as the 1960s and 1970s by critics like Edgar Z. Friedenberg and Charles E. Silberman. What is remarkable is that the problems they saw in the schools decades ago not only have remained dismally similar but have in many ways gotten worse under the impact of the new American Darwinism. Thinking creatively about how to make schools less estranging and more appealing, especially to adolescents who are now routinely condemned to the educational margins, is crucial, and there is much to be learned by listening to their own take on what it is about the current schools that drives them crazy.

As a start, we need to reverse the trend toward reflexive punitiveness in school discipline policy, especially the knee-jerk zero-tolerance strategies through which inattentive and uninterested schools justify washing their hands of struggling students. It would be difficult to find a clearer example of our cultural indifference to the consequences of official actions than the widespread resort to simple exclusion from school as the default response to students who are having trouble. Again and again, however, that is what the adolescents in this book describe, and the statistics show that their experience is common. Adolescents are now routinely and repeatedly suspended for minor infractions and expelled from school districts altogether without anyone's bothering to ask what exactly they will do with themselves—and often without any discernible effort on the part of any agency to follow up on their welfare. Step one in changing this thoroughly self-defeating approach is to roll back the policies making suspension or expulsion easier or even mandatory—policies that spread like weeds through the school bureaucracies and state legislatures in the 1990s—and return our schools to a conception of inclusive discipline, in which the first priority is to understand why a student is having trouble and in which throwing kids out is the last resort, not the first.

To do that, of course, means that there must be something else in place—some clear mechanisms to respond early and attentively to signs of trouble in school. The flip side of the easy resort to exclusion is the absence, in many schools, of any strategies to prevent these problems in the first place. It is stunning how regularly teenagers say that, when they started skipping school or coming to class drunk or being so stoned that they fell asleep on their desks, no one in authority actually sat them down to talk about what was wrong.

It would not require rocket science or great amounts of money to fix this. Part of the problem is that, even in some affluent communities, the public schools don't have sufficient resources to hire enough staff to take on this job competently and compassionately. Here, too, short-term thinking prevails: even though the consequences of having so many children leave school are both grim and obvious, we are not willing to put up the money to avoid them—especially if the children are other people's. But there is surely more to it: many schools are less than eager to provide troubled students with the support they need. Even without large infusions of money, after all, we could think of a variety of ways to get those students the attention they so desperately need. We could, for example, place a cadre of retired people in the schools who are deeply concerned with children's welfare and who may be better able to put a student's troubles in larger perspective than the run-of-the-mill school counselor. Or we could make more use of volunteers from colleges or graduate schools, who, being closer in age to teenagers, might have greater credibility with them as well as greater empathy and who are certainly less likely to be afflicted with the cynicism and resentment that too many school personnel now bring to the job. We need to put people to work in the schools who are not mired in the culture of punitiveness and who can move beyond the passive and "watching" attitude that Zack and others describe, people who are capable of working actively with students so trouble doesn't happen—and empathically with them if it does. It is precisely that active engagement which helped many of the college students in this book turn their lives around. There is nothing in their stories, moreover, to suggest that this work need be complicated or arcane. Most often, it is the overarching attitude that counts, the willingness to roll up one's sleeves and work with children's problems—to "troubleshoot," as Anna put it—rather than ignore those problems or wait for kids to "mess up" and then punish them.

We could learn much in this respect from existing school-based programs for disadvantaged youth who are at risk of failing academically. Some of the most successful of those programs have adopted an approach that is diametrically opposed to the quick resort to exclusion that is so common in schools today: they make every effort to keep students under their wing at all costs, even when—or especially when—the students show signs of difficulty. The Quantum Opportunity Program, for example, developed initially as a dropout-prevention program for inner-city high school students under the auspices of the Opportunities Industrial Centers in Philadelphia, is an intensive, hands-on program that offers after-school mentoring, skills training, cultural outings, and round-the-clock counseling. Students, in groups of about twenty-five, remain together throughout their four years of high school. They "cannot be dropped from the group, even for non-attendance." Students who leave school for whatever reason can return to their group at any time; as one careful evaluation of the program puts it, "the promise of opportunity is never withdrawn." Given the difficult populations this program and others have worked with, their results are impressive: many students who would have failed in less engaged settings have succeeded in school, stayed away from delinquency, and gone on to productive lives. The specific content might be different if we applied similar principles to middle-class students at risk. But the principles represent a compelling alternative to the passive and excluding culture of too many public schools.

Thinking about school policies in terms of inclusion rather than exclusion means a commitment to viewing children in school as members of a community of learning. Students have many responsibilities to that community, to be sure, but the community also has responsibilities to them. The best schools and colleges in America, public or private, already think this way; the problem is that too many schools are not like the best. Once again, the obstacles are bureaucratic and cultural, not technical. It isn't hard to understand how to treat students with care and respect; we need to insist that schools act on that knowledge. That means rooting out the peculiar culture of opposition that pervades some schools (and that several of my interviewees describe) by, among other things, changing the way future teachers and principals are taught. I am not sure how much effort schools of education now invest in inculcating values of tolerance, mutuality, and respect for students as part of their curriculum; what's clear is that these values aren't sufficiently honored "on the ground." But it surely cannot be difficult to teach school personnel that the kind of attitude that Sean or Zack describes—the routine and self-confirming labeling of some students as bad apples and the extra monitoring and surveillance that help ensure that they continue to feel like outsiders—is both counterproductive and inhumane.

The schools are too little interested in teaching adolescents about the realities of social life and too much concerned with enforcing conformity to the constricting norms of an increasingly competitive and exclusive middle class. Here we can learn from the relative success of community colleges and universities in providing a context in which even deeply troubled young men and women could reach their potential and find their center. We've seen that community colleges were a crucial channel of escape from apathy and peril for many of the students in this book, and other studies show the same pattern. These institutions offered opportunity without extraneous judgment; they were there to facilitate learning, not to enforce compliance. We would do well to apply the same principles in the earlier school years. Too often, we take for granted that the schools exist in good part to instill conformity, but the result is to narrow the range of acceptable diversity among students and to turn the schools into arenas devoted as much to cultural judgment as to intellectual endeavor. This approach fosters a moral climate in which students are too easily defined as beyond the pale and breeds the self-perpetuating cycle of scrutiny and punishment that pushes many adolescents into real trouble.

High schools would be more positive places if they were less invidious and more supportive, and we can surely make more of them that way. But some adolescents would still find regular schools alien, even if they were better and more nurturing places. So there will always be a need for alternatives. Those alternatives, however, have to be very different from the typical continuation schools that are often the sole option for students in trouble at regular school. Conventional continuation schools fail troubled students in many ways. They are widely, if mostly unofficially, defined as third-class institutions, the places where the "dumb kids" and the "bad kids" get sent, which of course helps confirm the feeling among those kids that they are indeed dumb or bad or both. These schools rarely challenge their students intellectually and in fact are usually regarded by students as "too easy" and hence boring and estranging. This pattern is especially troublesome since the problem for many alienated students is not that they find regular school too hard but that they find it insufficiently absorbing. For many of the adolescents I spoke with, continuation school was little more than a part-time hangout where they "kicked back" and did drugs together but were never motivated or made excited; at worst, it was an administrative dumping ground, and they experienced it as such. But it need not be this way, and a few of the teenagers in this book—like Trey—went to alternative public schools that challenged and engaged them, often for the first time. It isn't that we do not know how to provide a more compelling setting for alternative education but that we too rarely attempt to do so.

Part of the problem is that, in yet another illustration of the inverted priorities of the culture of care-lessness, school districts typically put the *least* resources and the least dynamic or skilled teachers in these schools, since there is neither much expectation that the kids sent to them will succeed or much interest in helping them do so. These priorities reflect our increasing willingness to write off as superfluous those adolescents who perform poorly, but they are both unjust and self-defeating. What if we staffed the public alternative schools with the *most* enthusiastic teachers and the *most* skilled and dynamic counselors, developed a compelling curriculum (with student input), and saw what happened? An alternative school curriculum that engaged adolescents in social advocacy and community service might work especially well for some of those who find regular school boring and irrelevant to their lives; we might accordingly try linking alternative schooling with the community action programs I've described above. Such programs could provide productive outlets for young people who can't tolerate regular schools or who just need a break for a while. Let them take a leave for three months or six months or a year, be required to do something useful and potentially enriching in their community during that time, and come back to school with new accomplishments, new perspectives, and perhaps new confidence. Few things would do more to jog them out of the sense of meaninglessness, the feeling that nothing matters, than to do something that is undeniably important and be recognized for it. It could also mitigate the problem of what I've called contingent worth, by creating a wider array of sources of personal satisfaction and achievement, as well as more arenas, beyond school and family, to do well in and by refocusing adolescents on something beyond the relentless scramble to win in an individual competitive struggle.

4. A Community of "Shepherds"

Adolescents, then, need a richer set of educational options, both inside the schools and beyond them. Many also need intervention outside the orbit of the schools that is intensive but not necessarily "therapeutic." What the adolescents in this book felt they most lacked was someone outside the family or the various official treatment programs whose job it was to provide empathic and attentive assistance. And that isn't surprising, for we have never been comfortable giving this kind of assistance. The uncomplicated provision of help is not widely valued in our society, and we are inclined not to offer help at all unless it can be shown that something is demonstrably wrong with the people to whom we give it. So we have programs for youth who are already abusing drugs or throwing up their food or who have tried to kill themselves, but we do not have many that are designed to offer the sustained nurturance and attention that might keep these things from happening in the first place. One after another, the teenagers in this book said that there was virtually no one to talk to, apart from their friends, about the issues that troubled them or the dangers they faced. Whether there was ever really a time when adolescents got more of this sort of attention from empathic adults outside the family is hard to judge, although I suspect that the "stripping" of middle-class communities, the relentless cutbacks in public services, and the hectic movement from place to place that now characterizes the American middle have worsened the problem; but it is clear that they aren't getting it now.

This is a critical deficit because trusted and respected adults outside the family can play a crucial role in helping adolescents stay out of trouble and make the most of the opportunities before them. In looking at Hawaiian children who had been defined as learning disabled but who ended up doing well in midlife, Emmy Werner and Ruth Smith found that the availability of adults in the community who could "foster trust" was a crucial factor in their success. The presence of "caring adults outside the family" served as a common "protective factor" among these "vulnerable but invincible" children, who had overcome a variety of childhood adversities and achieved stability and fulfillment as adults. Werner and Smith speak of these caring adults as an example of the importance of "naturally occurring support systems in the community"; but the problem is that they no longer occur "naturally" to the extent they did in the past.

There are many ways we could provide youth with a steady

supply of capable and interested adults who could inspire trust and offer reliable guidance, attention, and advocacy. What's important is to get the principles right. The community-based counselor-advocates I have in mind must be empathic, nonjudgmental, and permanent; their job is to provide not therapy but what the noted youth researcher Joy Dryfoos calls "shepherding." We could establish a cadre of "shepherds" in every community—perhaps, again, enlisting older adults to do the job, or tapping the enthusiasm and savvy of recent college graduates or graduate students. We could set up independent programs with their own funding to provide these counselors, or we could make them part of broader programs for young people at the community level. As with the "civic action" programs I am proposing, I don't think it is a good idea to have them wholly based in, or answerable to, the schools, for although the schools have the advantage that many teenagers are already in them, many of those who need shepherding the most are not or, if they are, may be deeply alienated from school and disinclined to trust anything connected with it. And it would be difficult for someone whose paycheck came from the school district to feel free to act as an unabashed and forceful advocate for students who were being treated badly at school.

5. A New Kind of Treatment

I've said that the attention most adolescents need, most of the time, is not formal therapy or individual psychological intervention, because the problems that are most salient in their lives so often arise from restricted options and inadequate institutions. It is a reflection of our relentlessly individualistic culture that we tend to define most problems as stemming ultimately from personal deficiency and most help as individual "therapy." Among the teenagers in this book, that inversion of the public into the private was a constant source of frustration and alienation. This isn't to say that formal therapy has no place. Some adolescents surely need a level of sustained and intensive help beyond the shepherding I've proposed. But the experience of the teenagers in this book confirms that there are right ways and wrong ways of providing it. Formal intervention by a mental health professional helped save the lives of a few of them. Too often, however, it alienated and angered them, and sometimes it pushed them deeper into self-doubt, confusion, and isolation.

Several qualities distinguished the help that worked from the sort that made things worse. Above all, help that worked was supportive, pragmatic, and nonjudgmental. This does not mean that it was half-hearted or lenient. When adolescents speak positively about their experiences with "shrinks" or treatment programs, they often describe them as firm but empathic: they "didn't take any shit," but they didn't give any either. This kind of therapy held them to standards of morality, respect, and responsibility but did not treat them as if they were the problem or assume that their difficulties were simply due to their own choices. Indeed, it did just the opposite: it conveyed to them, perhaps for the first time in their lives, that they were probably being too hard on themselves, that they needed to recognize that other people's choices might have a lot to do with their own difficulties. That revelation allowed teenagers to get out from under the negative definitions imposed on them by others— especially their parents—and cleared the way for them to begin constructing a more positive sense of who they were and to take themselves seriously in a way that had not been possible before.

Many speak about how important it was to them, during their worst times, to have adults in positions of authority—counselors, therapists, program staff—who were willing to break the rules or at least bend them. Adolescents usually appreciated the structure these authoritative adults provided, especially since they had often grown up in chaotic families, but the structure was flexible and supportive, designed to facilitate the provision of assistance rather than to enforce compliance for its own sake.

The kind of help that they rejected—and that frequently aggravated the problems it was ostensibly designed to solve—stood these principles on their head. Above all, it was delivered in a pejorative style. Whether by design or unreflective habit, the agencies that offered this sort of help exhorted teenagers to locate the source of their problems in themselves and sought to convince them that the responsibility for change rested almost wholly on their own shoulders. They taught adolescents to internalize blame (as if they didn't already) and deflected attention from the forces in the world around them that made their lives difficult and that might need changing. They reprised the peculiarly exclusionary responses that many teenagers had already experienced in their schools and in their families. They were quick to punish and imposed elaborate or arcane rules that seemed designed to ensure that many kids failed. They often relied on harsh and demeaning "treatments" that made their clients feel angry or ashamed and that many experienced as simply silly. And they typically shut youth out altogether if they stumbled too badly. At its worst, such treatment felt like an effort to frighten them into submission, not to tackle the real issues in their lives. It often provoked their resistance; at the very least, it discouraged their engagement.

Stated so simply, the contrasts between these styles of help seem glaring, and it is difficult to comprehend why we continue to invest in strategies of adolescent treatment that seem so obviously fated to fail, if not to make things worse. The reason cannot be that these strategies are supported by evidence of their effectiveness, for such evidence doesn't exist—and indeed most agencies that employ these approaches have traditionally resisted any attempt to assess whether they actually work. These practices usually persist for less savory reasons, including the fact that most people, including most parents, simply do not realize how bad some of this help really is. Some of the parents in this book pulled their children out of questionable programs when they realized what was going on in them, and many parents across the country have done the same (especially those who sent children to the authoritarian for-profit treatment centers that sprang up during the 1990s). But without outside sources of honest information, it is difficult for parents to know what to expect; that problem is aggravated by the fact that many agencies that offer treatment to adolescents are remarkably closed and inaccessible institutions, wary of outside scrutiny, and their clients rarely have the power or even the language to make their own views heard. As a result, parents and others concerned about adolescents' welfare know much less than they need to about how these agencies operate. We tend to assume that the people who run them must know what they are doing, since most have some sort of credentials, but that is a very shaky assumption.

Another reason inadequate or even destructive programs stay in business is that there are so few alternatives; in many communities, there may literally be only one program for miles around—or only one that isn't already full. In that situation, even a program that seems worrisome may be seen, by parents or school authorities, as better than no program at all. That may not in fact be true, but it is natural to think it is if your child is in crisis and you are at the end of your rope. Part of the problem could be alleviated if there were agencies in every community whose job it was to link adolescents and their parents with sources of help and to provide reliable information about the programs that are available. As it stands now, adolescents and their families often have no idea where to go for help, even if there is help to be had, and they are even less likely to have any way of evaluating its quality in advance. Among other things, the presence of independent sources of evaluation might help raise standards and expectations within the helping agencies.

We also need to provide a broader range of treatment options. By stimulating a healthy competition among the agencies that purport to offer help to adolescents, that could improve quality and increase accountability. What's essential, however, is not just more treatment programs but better ones, and improving their quality may require a revolution within the professions that staff them.

Part of the reason ineffective and counterproductive approaches to treatment are so prevalent is that they still find considerable support in the mental health professions—in their conceptual approaches to adolescent problems, their routine training, and indeed their very language. If nothing else, there is a crying need for more attention to quality and to self-policing on the part of those professions. Too much now goes on in their name that is poorly conceived and at worst unconscionable.

I want to be absolutely clear: at their best, mental health professionals can and frequently do save the lives and spirits of troubled adolescents. But the best is rarely what adolescents get. There should be much more careful professional monitoring of what goes on in programs for teenagers—including the current drift toward addressing nearly every emotional problem as a pharmaceutical problem. As I've argued, the increasing reliance on pills as the option of first resort can be dangerous and ensures that the real issues in teenagers' lives remain mostly unaddressed. I am not suggesting that adolescents shouldn't get appropriate medication, carefully administered and monitored, if they really need it. But the overmedication of children and the increasing replacement of empathic engagement with chemical intervention is a blindingly clear example of our retreat from confronting the forces in our society that make life difficult for teenagers and, for that matter, everyone else. At the very least, this trend calls for a kind of serious debate that has been mostly missing in the mental health professions and is only now emerging amid growing concern about the misuse of certain antidepressant drugs for children and adolescents. But the issue is deeper. What needs challenging is not just the overuse of specific medications but the substitution of chemical shortcuts for more effective and more labor-intensive work with troubled young people. To paraphrase B.J., adolescents in serious trouble need more than just a guy who passes out pills; they need a personal doctor.

The mental health professions must also confront the cavalier use of some of the vaguer diagnostic categories that are routinely deployed to sift and sort troubled youth and that often determine what sort of treatment, if any, they will receive. I'm not suggesting that there is no use whatever for psychiatric classification, but what happens now is that we often use loose and often tautological concepts to turn young people's real-life problems with families, schools, and peers into quasi-medical "disorders." That practice can lead directly to abusive treatment; more subtly, it also serves, like the overuse of medication, to obscure the complex roots of those problems and to ensure that they remain unresolved. I'm not sure, for example, that I believe that there is such a thing as "oppositional defiant disorder" at all. I *am* sure that a concept so vague and transparently open to abuse needs rethinking.

On a still deeper level, there is need for the mental health professions to look hard at what we might call the meta-assumptions that, often in subterranean ways, guide their approach to the troubles of adolescents—in particular, what I've called the pejorative assumption, the reflexive tendency to locate the source of problems within the individual and to avoid (or reject) exploring the ways in which those problems are shaped by institutions and actions outside the individual's control. That assumption operates today as a semiofficial ideology among many helping professionals. As such, it profoundly influences their approach to a host of issues, not just the emotional troubles of teenagers but such deep-rooted social problems as poverty, homelessness, and domestic violence. It is the contemporary psychological and psychiatric rendering of the traditional Darwinian denial that individuals' lives are much affected by larger social forces. Its dominance in the mental health world virtually guarantees that we rarely reach the root of adolescents' troubles. Indeed, this worldview is often part of the problem for troubled adolescents because it exacerbates their self-blame and sense of personal failure. Part of the necessary revolution in mental health care, then, is to challenge those pervasive and naive meta-assumptions wherever they appear and to replace them with less undercutting and more sophisticated understandings of how individuals interact with their social worlds. Treatment grounded in a more generous and sophisticated social awareness would look very different from most of what is now offered to adolescents and would also be much more appealing to them—which means, in turn, that they would be more likely to seek it out and to stay with it once they started.

6. Family-Friendly Policies

I've said that I do not want to attempt a detailed blueprint for social policy here, but there are clearly some broader measures that, had they been in place, could have made the lives of the adolescents in this book less stressful, less lonely, and less dangerous. Some of the parents in this book might have treated their children harshly and carelessly even if they had had all the resources and all the time in the world (indeed, a few of them did). But, like many other middle-class Americans, most were sufficiently pinched for both resources and time that it would have been hard for them to "be there" for their children in any case. The structural obstacles to being consistently available for their children forced them to look to underfunded or questionable outside agencies for help or made them sufficiently desperate that taking a harsh and excluding stance with their children was about all they could think of doing. Those who ultimately descended to calling the police on their teenagers whenever trouble appeared were likely to be single parents with at least one full-time job and perhaps two and with no way of getting out from under the demands of work to put in serious time building a nurturing relationship with their children. Their own unavailability, combined with the widespread stripping of community support, worsened the isolation and drift of teenagers in trouble. If parents were away at work, there was rarely any other kind of stable adult supervision or support available in the community, and outside the public schools almost none. Thus, if part of the answer is to increase the variety of competent adult institutions in these communities, the other is to free hard-pressed parents from the overly rigid demands of the Darwinian workplace.

The lack of explicitly family-friendly social policies in the United States as opposed to many other countries—especially European countries—has been thoroughly documented. Suffice it to say that the same sociocultural reluctance to provide help that so profoundly affects the lives of American adolescents also helps explain why we have done so little, in comparison with those countries, to ease the strains between work and home for middle-class families. A package of policies that includes generous paid parental leaves, reduced work hours for parents, better pay and benefits for part-time workers, and much more investment in high-quality child care is an indispensable foundation for any enduring attack on the stress and social isolation of mainstream families, the critical public infrastructure on which everything else depends. Having these policies won't guarantee that middle-class parents will do a better job of attentive and engaged parenting. Their absence ensures that many will not.

Such explicitly family-oriented policies should be backed by a commitment to universal health care. The drift toward managed care has diminished the already meager sources of affordable help for adolescents struggling with drugs, violence, or depression. Among other things, universal health care could support the flowering of a wider range of alternatives in mental health and drug abuse treatment and might make it possible to provide the sustained help that, according to a growing body of research, is what adolescents need. Today, what troubled teenagers increasingly get, if they get any help at all, is short-term, time-limited intervention that few people believe can make much difference. Taking health care out of the profit-driven market—and providing real funding for public alternatives—is the first and essential step toward reversing that drift.

These policies are crucial not only because they provide concrete supports for children and families but for a less tangible reason as well: they embody a different way of ordering our social and personal lives. For there is a profound sense in which harsh social policies breed the worldview that perpetuates them. I've argued throughout this book that the process of growing up in America, even for the middle class, is made needlessly difficult by a peculiarly harsh and irresponsible culture. But that culture, of course, doesn't come from nowhere: whatever its ultimate historical origins, it is influenced by real-world conditions and especially by the eroding social supports and constricting opportunities that are now so much a part of ordinary life for Americans, including, increasingly, those relatively high on the social ladder. I do not think that much can change for the better in our treatment of adolescents until that culture itself changes. But changing cultures is a very hard thing to do, and it is virtually impossible without altering the structural conditions that underlie them. Exhorting middle-class parents to be more nurturing and less punitive might help, a little, if we did enough of it. But a real shift in their attitudes is much more likely to come if we begin to change the broader rules of the game. Insisting on more generous, flexible, and inclusive policies across a variety of American institutions can thus begin an upward cultural spiral. By establishing more humane policies for families, schools, and workplaces, we not only make life easier for Americans in ways that should reduce the stresses and fears that help breed a heedless "me first" ethic, we also model the outlines of a more supportive community. A society that begins to care better for its people, in short, both diminishes the conditions that lead to care-lessness and demonstrates that there are other, and better, ways to live.

NOTES

PAGE   INTRODUCTION: "A WHITE KIND OF MESSING UP"

2   "By some measures": The statistical evidence for these assertions is drawn from the University of Michigan's annual survey of drug and alcohol use among high school seniors, Jerrold Bachman et al., *Monitoring the Future, 2002*, Ann Arbor: University of Michigan Survey Research Center, 2003; the National Survey on Drug Use and Health from the U.S. Department of Health and Human Services (Substance Abuse and Mental Health Services Administration, *Overview of Findings from the 2002 National Survey on Drug Use and Health*, Rockville, Maryland, 2003); and the National Longitudinal Study of Adolescent Health (see, for example, Robert W. Blum et al., "The Effects of Race, Ethnicity, Income and Family Structure on Adolescent Risk Behaviors," *American Journal of Public Health*, December 2000, pp. 1879–1884. On cigarette smoking, see Phyllis L. Ellickson et al., "From Adolescence to Young Adulthood: Racial/Ethnic Disparities in Smoking," *American Journal of Public Health*, February 2004, pp. 293–299. Adolescent drug abuse took a sharp upward turn in the 1990s, and the rise was sharpest for some of the drugs white and middle-class youth were most likely to abuse. Between 1994 and 2001, emergency room admissions nearly doubled for amphetamines, almost quadrupled for the painkiller oxycodone, and rose twenty-fold for Ecstasy. Emergency room data from *Drug Abuse Warning Network (DAWN) Estimates, 2001*, Washington:

National Institute on Drug Abuse, 2002. On racial differences in suicide, see, for example, Toni Terling Watt and Susan F. Sharp, "Race Differences in Strains Associated with Suicidal Behavior among Adolescents," *Youth and Society*, December 2003, pp. 232–56. For useful journalistic accounts of drug use among white youth, see "Face of Heroin: It's Younger and More Suburban," *New York Times*, April 25, 2000; Aparna Kumar, "Prescription-Drug Abuse Soars: Youth at the Forefront," *Los Angles Times*, January 17, 2003.

2   "possible to debate": Survey studies like those on which these statistics are based have often been criticized as significantly underrepresenting more marginal people, thus skewing the picture of the social distribution of drug use, delinquency, and other problems. The annual survey of high school seniors from the University of Michigan, for example, by definition leaves out high school dropouts, who are more likely to use drugs heavily than students who remain in school and are also more likely to be low-income and/or minority youth. But the surveys do show credibly that these problems are indeed widespread among middle-class and white youth—much more so than we would think on the basis of official records such as arrest statistics.

3   " 'The Monsters Next Door' ": *Time*, May 3, 1999.

4   " 'moral panic' ": The term was coined by British sociologists in the 1970s to describe the tendency of the public (and the media) to overreact to relatively isolated acts of deviance. A classic discussion is Stanley Cohen, *Folk Devils and Moral Panics*, 3rd ed., New York: Routledge, 2002.

5   "recent textbook": Donald Shoemaker, *Theories of Delinquency*, 2nd ed., New York: Oxford University Press, 1990, p. 290.

6   "A popular book on parenting": James Dobson, *The New Dare to Discipline*, Wheaton: Tyndale House, 1992. The publisher claims that more than 3.5 million copies of the book have been sold.

6   "As the authority": Kay S. Hymowitz, "Tweens: Ten Going on Sixteen," *City Journal*, Autumn 1998, p. 3.

6   "An article asking": Kay S. Hymowitz, "Who Killed School Discipline?" *City Journal*, Spring 2000, p. 4.

7   "harder stance": See, for example, Vincent Schiraldi and Jason Ziedenberg, *School House Hype: Two Years Later*, Washington: Justice Policy Institute and the Children's Law Center, 2000; American Academy of Pediatrics, "Policy Statement: Out-of-School

Suspension and Expulsion," *Pediatrics*, vol. 112, no. 5, November 2003; U.S. Department of Education, National Center for Education Statistics, *Violence and Discipline Problems in U.S. Public Schools: 1996–97*, Washington: Government Printing Office, 1998.

7   corporal punishment: See generally Murray A. Straus and Denise A. Donnelly, *Beating the Devil Out of Them*, 2nd ed., New York: Transaction Publishers, 2001. See also Lonnie Harp and Laura Miller, "States Turn Up Heat in Debate over Paddlings," *Education Week*, September 6, 1995.

7   Juvenile death penalty: See Death Penalty Information Center, "Juveniles and the Death Penalty," 2003, at www.deathpenaltyinfo.org.

8   "weakest . . . social supports": See generally Sheila B. Kamerman and Alfred J. Kahn, *Starting Right: How America Neglects Its Youngest Children and What We Can Do About It*, New York: Oxford University Press, 1995.

8   " 'nonhelping hand' ": John Micklethwait and Adrian Wooldridge, *The Right Nation: Conservative Power in America*, New York: Penguin, 2004, p. 303.

12   Cohen quote: Albert K. Cohen, *Delinquent Boys: The Culture of the Gang*, Glencoe: Free Press, 1955, p. 173.

12   Mills: C. Wright Mills, *The Sociological Imagination*, New York: Oxford University Press, 1959, Ch. 1.

CHAPTER 1: "WHATEVER, DUDE":
THE ELEMENTS OF CARE-LESSNESS

30   Matza argument: David Matza, *Delinquency and Drift*, New York: Wiley, 1964, p. 64.

31   " 'initiative' ": Erik Erikson, *Childhood and Society*, New York: Norton, 1963, p. 255.

CHAPTER 2: THE SINK-OR-SWIM FAMILY

46   "bestselling book": Daniel J. Kindlon, *Too Much of a Good Thing: Raising Children of Character in an Indulgent Age*, New York: Hyperion, 2001, back cover.

46   tough love: Quoted from the Web site of Tough Love International, www.toughlove.org, accessed March 2004.

49   "place of 'help' and support in general": Compare the comment by Robert N. Bellah and his colleagues on the influence of individualism on American conceptions of family relations: "For highly individuated

Americans, there is something anomalous about the relation between parents and children, for the biologically normal dependence of children on parents is perceived as morally abnormal" (Robert N. Bellah et al., *Habits of the Heart: Individualism and Commitment in American Life*, New York: Harper and Row, 1986, p. 82).

69   Merton analysis: Robert K. Merton, "Social Structure and Anomie," *Social Theory and Social Structure*, Glencoe: Free Press, 1959.

69   "host of followers": See especially Richard A. Cloward and Lloyd Ohlin, *Delinquency and Opportunity*, New York: Free Press, 1960.

69   "Poor youth can point to discrimination": For a compelling analysis of expectations and achievement among poor white youth, see Jay Macleod, *Ain't No Makin' It*, Boulder, Colorado, Westview Press, revised edition, 1995.

71   "'concerted cultivation'": Annette Larreau, *Unequal Childhoods*, Berkeley and Los Angeles: University of California Press, 2003, ch. 3.

88   Drug policy: On this issue generally, see Elliott Currie, *Reckoning: Drugs, the Cities, and the American Future*, New York: Hill and Wang, 1994, ch. 4. On teen sexuality, see Jane E. Brody, "Abstinence-Only: Does It Work?" *New York Times*, June 1, 2004.

88   "demand abstinence": James Dobson's best-selling book on parenting blames "the safe-sex gurus and condom promoters" for the spread of HIV and other sexually transmitted diseases (*New Dare to Discipline*, p. 209). A Connecticut church recently produced a newspaper advertisement that captures the flavor of this attitude: "Safe sin is a flat contradiction. It would be like talking of a "healthy disease" or "harmless poison" or "clean dirt" or a "lively death." It would be like a mouse talking about a safe mousetrap or a fish speaking of a safe hook or a pig thinking of a safe slaughterhouse. SIN IS NEVER SAFE. It is always dangerous, destructive, damning and always brings with it disastrous consequences" (from the Middletown Bible Church, Middletown, Connecticut, published in *USA Today*, August 15, 2003).

89   Teenagers and religion: John M. Wallace et al., "Religion and U.S. Secondary School Students: Current Patterns, Recent Trends, and Sociodemographic Correlates," *Youth and Society*, September 2003, pp. 98–125. I am not suggesting that religious belief in general leads to higher rates of deviance. Indeed, research shows that adolescents with some kind of religious affiliation are less likely to

use drugs or to engage in most other illicit activities. (See, for example, Lisa Miller et al., "Religiosity and Substance Use and Abuse among Adolescents in the National Comorbidity Survey," *Journal of the American Academy of Child and Adolescent Psychiatry*, September 2000, p. 1190.) The point here is that the rigid approach to deviance that characterizes some religious beliefs can lead those who stray from the path to feel that they have little left to lose.

94   Tough Love quotation: www.toughlove.org, accessed March 2004.

94   Teens in Crisis: http://troubled-teenagers.org, accessed March 2004.

103   Straus and Field data: Murray A. Straus and Carolyn J. Field, "Psychological Aggression by American Parents: National Data on Prevalence, Chronicity, and Severity, *Journal of Marriage and the Family*, November 2003, pp. 795–808.

111   California case: Stuart Pfeifer, "Tough Love or Abuse?" *Los Angeles Times*, November 21, 2002.

CHAPTER 3: "THERE'S NO HELP OUT THERE":
THE WORLD OF THERAPEUTIC DARWINISM

126   "lack of resources to do much else": During the time I was interviewing these teenagers, the American Academy of Pediatrics concluded that the decreasing availability of mental health services for children and adolescents was "a serious and worsening problem," and blamed "attempts to restrain health costs," especially "benefits packages that provide limited mental health services or carve out plans, in which behavioral health care may be carved out (not included) or contracted for separately, making mental health services more difficult to obtain." American Academy of Pediatrics, "Insurance Coverage of Mental Health and Substance Abuse Services for Children and Adolescents: A Consensus Statement," *Pediatrics*, October 2000, pp. 860–862.

135   Rise in prescriptions: Christopher K. Varley, "Psychopharmacological Treatment of Major Depressive Disorder in Children and Adolescents, *JAMA*, August 27, 2003, p. 1092.

135   Abuse of Ritalin: A Massachusetts survey in 2001 found that 13 percent of high school students admitted using Ritalin illicitly (Carleton Kendrick, "Recreational Ritalin: A Disturbing Trend," *San Francisco Chronicle*, March 18, 2001).

136   Duke University study: Adrian Angold et al., "Stimulant Treat-
        ment for Children: A Community Perspective," *Journal of the
        American Academy of Child and Adolescent Psychiatry*, August 2000,
        pp. 978–83.

136   *Pediatrics* article: J. Guevara et al., "Psychotropic Medication Use in a
        Population of Children Who Have Attention-Deficit/Hyperactivity
        Disorder," *Pediatrics*, May 2002, pp. 733–39.

137   Rhode Island study: E. H. Harel and W. D. Brown, "Attention
        Deficit Hyperactivity Disorder in Elementary School Children in
        Rhode Island: Associated Psychosocial Factors and Medications
        Used," *Clinical Pediatrics*, July–August 2003, pp. 497–503.

137   Virginia study: G. B. LeFever, K. V. Dawson, and A. L. Morrow,
        "The Extent of Drug Therapy for Attention Deficit-Hyperactivity
        Disorder among Children in Public Schools," *American Journal of
        Public Health*, September 1999, pp. 1359–64.

138   SSRIs: See generally Benedetto Vitiello and Susan Swedo, "Antide-
        pressant Medications in Children," *New England Journal of Medi-
        cine*, April 8, 2004, pp. 1489–91; Paul Ramchandani, "Treatment of
        Major Depressive Disorder in Children and Adolescents: Most
        Selective Serotonin Reuptake Inhibitors Are No Longer Recom-
        mended," *British Medical Journal*, January 3, 2004, pp. 3–4. Australian
        study: John I. Jureidini et al., "Efficacy and Safety of Antidepres-
        sants for Children and Adolescents," *British Medical Journal*, April
        10, 2004, pp. 879–83. Figures on numbers of children taking SSRIs
        from Elizabeth Shogren, "Parents Blame Medicines for Suicides,"
        Los Angeles Times, February 3, 2004.

138   " 'All psychotropic medications' ": Mina R. Dulcan and D.
        Richard Martini, *Concise Guide to Child and Adolescent Psychiatry*,
        2nd ed., Washington: American Psychiatric Association, 1999,
        p. 244.

140   " 'before initiating anticonvulsants' ": *Concise Guide*, p. 284.

146   " 'It's Our Lives' ": Elliott Currie, " 'It's Our Lives They're Dealing
        with Here': Some Adolescent Perceptions of Residential Treat-
        ment," *Journal of Drug Issues*, Fall 2003, pp. 833–64.

148   Ryan quotation: William Ryan, *Blaming the Victim*, New York: Ran-
        dom House, 1971, p. 25.

148   "everyday individualism of the larger culture": A recent study finds
        that white parents are more likely than others to attribute their

children's problems to internal versus "sociological" causes (May Yeh et al., "Parental Beliefs about the Causes of Child Problems: Exploring Racial/Ethnic Patterns," *Journal of the American Academy of Child and Adolescent Psychiatry*, May 2004, pp. 605–10).

149 "'disruptive behavior disorders'": *Concise Guide*, pp. 23–24.

150 "'can include virtually any psychotropic drug'": *Concise Guide*, p. 55.

151 Conners scale: Reprinted in *Concise Guide*, p. 38.

151 "'society certainly does need'": Allen Frances and Michael B. First, *Am I Okay? A Layman's Guide to the Psychiatrist's Bible*, New York: Simon and Schuster, 2000, p. 378.

152 Diagnosis more common in the United States: See *Concise Guide*, p. 28.

154 "absence of sufficient resources": For a recent study of the effects of managed care, see Todd Olmstead, William D. White, and Jody Sindelar, "The Impact of Managed Care on Substance Abuse Treatment Services," *HSR: Health Services Research*, April 2004, pp. 319–43.

155 Growth of "specialty" schools: Tim Weiner, "Parents, Shopping for Discipline, Turn to Tough Schools Abroad," *New York Times*, May 9, 2003.

155 "'Today's teens are given'": Troubled Teen Advisor, http:// troubled-teen-advisor.com, accessed May 2004.

156 "'We run a tight ship'": Tim Weiner, "Charges of Cruelty at a Jamaica Discipline Academy," *New York Times*, June 17, 2003. Another "boarding school" required its "students" to "carry around, and sit on, a 'baby chair'" and sometimes to "wear a pacifier around their necks" ("My School Was All about Fear," *Your Magazine*, May 2003, p. 136).

156 "schools shut down": Weiner, "Charges of Cruelty"; Decca Aitkenhead, "The Last Resort," *Observer* (London), June 29, 2003.

156 "California congressman": John-Thor Dahlburg, "Lawmaker Urges Probe of Schools," *Los Angeles Times*, November 6, 2003.

161 "'Observation Placement'": Aitkenhead, "Last Resort."

162 Confrontation sessions: On this issue generally, see Currie, "'It's Our Lives They're Dealing with Here.'"

174 Becker: Howard S. Becker, *Outsiders: Studies in the Sociology of Deviance*, Glencoe: Free Press, 1963, esp. ch. 3.

177 "'secondary deviance'": See, for example, Becker, *Outsiders*, ch. 2.

CHAPTER 4: THE SCHOOL AS OPPONENT

198 Studies of expulsion and suspension: Richard E. Mattison, "School Consultation: A Review of Research on Issues Unique to the School Environment," *Journal of the American Academy of Child and Adolescent Psychiatry*, April 2000, pp. 404–11.

199 "even more severe problems": According to data from the U.S. Department of Education, whites were 63 percent of public school students in 1998–99 but 50 percent of those suspended (Robert C. Johnston, "Federal Data Highlight Disparities in Discipline," *Education Week*, June 21, 2000).

199 "zero-tolerance policies": American Academy of Pediatrics, "Policy Statement: Out-of-School Suspension and Expulsion," *Pediatrics*, November 2003, pp. 1206–09.

200 Suspension in smaller towns: Vincent Schiraldi and Jason Ziedenberg, *School House Hype: Two Years Later*, Washington: Justice Policy Institute and Children's Law Center, 2000.

201 "'Children who use'": American Academy of Pediatrics, "Policy Statement," p. 1207.

202 "'detected a problem'": Tustin Amole, "Slain Suspect 'Angry at the Whole World,'" *Rocky Mountain News*, September 9, 1998.

202 "opinion polls": American Academy of Pediatrics, "Policy Statement," p. 1206.

CHAPTER 5: TURNING IT AROUND

217 "growing body of research": For a good general discussion of this research, see Emmy S. Werner and Ruth S. Smith, *Journeys from Childhood to Midlife: Risk, Resilience, and Recovery*, Ithaca: Cornell University Press, 2001, ch. 1.

234 "'inner locus of control'": See studies noted in Werner and Smith, *Journeys from Childhood*, p. 12.

239 Emmy Werner: Werner and Smith, *Journeys from Childhood*, ch. 6.

246 Importance of public postsecondary education: Glen H. Elder Jr., *Children of the Great Depression*, Boulder: Westview Press, 1999; George Vaillant, *Adaptation to Life*, Boston: Little, Brown, 1977; Werner and Smith, *Journeys from Childhood*, ch. 7.

248 "'Fewer than 10 percent'": Werner and Smith, *Journeys from Childhood*, p. 111.

CHAPTER 6: TOWARD A CULTURE OF SUPPORT

256 " 'personal providence' ": Richard Hofstadter, *Social Darwinism in American Thought*, Boston: Beacon Press, 1955, p. 11.

258 "shift from an economy based on production": A classic statement of this shift is David Riesman, Nathan Glazer, and Reuel Denney, *The Lonely Crowd*, New Haven: Yale University Press, 1955.

260 " 'The most tangible sign' ": Richard Sennett, *The Corrosion of Character: The Personal Consequences of Work in the New Capitalism*, New York: Norton, 1998, pp. 22–24.

261 "unprecedented influence": On this transformation of postwar society and culture generally, see Micklethwait and Wooldridge, *Right Nation*, and Jock Young, *The Exclusive Society*, London: Sage, 1999.

267 "need to think more systematically": There are now many programs offering some sort of community service experience to high school students, but many do not engage them in the kind of meaningful engagement with social issues that I am calling for here. For an interesting analysis of why some community service efforts are more effective than others, see Edward Metz, Jeffrey McLellan, and James Youniss, "Types of Voluntary Service and Adolescents' Civic Development," *Journal of Adolescent Research*, March 2003, pp. 188–203. See also Jim Myers, "Service Learning Sits in School," *Youth Today*, November 2002.

267 " 'civic action' projects": "Is Civic Activism the Answer?" *Youth Today*, March 2004.

268 "moral equivalent of the military experience": See Werner and Smith, *Journeys from Childhood*, pp. 126–28.

269 Early critiques of schools: Edgar Z. Friedenberg, *Coming of Age in America*, New York: Vintage Books, 1965; Charles E. Silberman, *Crisis in the Classroom*, New York: Vintage Books, 1971.

271 Quantum Opportunity Program: *Blueprints for Violence Prevention: The Quantum Opportunity Program*, Boulder: Institute for Social Research, University of Colorado, 1999, p. 24. For a general discussion of the evidence on the effectiveness of community-based programs along these lines, see National Academies, *Community Programs to Promote Youth Development*, Washington: National Academy Press, 2001.

271 "community of learning": On the frequently alienating character of American high schools and some suggestions for improvement, see

National Research Council, *Engaging Schools: Fostering High School Students' Motivation to Learn*, Washington: National Academy Press, 2003.

275   " 'foster trust' ": Werner and Smith, *Journeys from Childhood*, p. 139.

276   " 'shepherding' ": Joy Dryfoos, *Safe Passage: Making It through Adolescence in a Risky Society*, New York: Oxford University Press, 1998, p. 139.

279   "no idea where to go for help": Recognizing this problem, the American Academy of Pediatrics calls for "mechanisms to provide user-friendly information to families and purchasers regarding the availability, adequacy, and quality of mental and behavioral health and substance abuse services. . . ," American Academy of Pediatrics, "Insurance Coverage of Mental Health and Substance Abuse Services for Children and Adolescents: A Consensus Statement," *Pediatrics*, October 2000, p. 862.

ACKNOWLEDGMENTS

My deepest thanks go to the young people who graciously offered to talk with me about their lives. I can't mention them by name, but their frankness and courage have been a constant inspiration, and without them there would, of course, be no book. I've learned a great deal from all of them.

Thanks also to Sara Bershtel, Riva Hocherman, and Shara Kay at Metropolitan Books for all their work on this book. John Brockman and Katinka Matson, as always, helped greatly to bring this project into being. Marcy McGaugh, Ambreen Chowdhry, and Emily Wohl did the difficult and indispensable work of transcribing interviews with skill and good cheer, and Linda Coco worked hard and long to help arrange them.

Some of the research that informs this book was done under a grant from the Center for Substance Abuse Treatment of the Substance Abuse and Mental Health Services Administration (SAMHSA), U.S. Department of Health and Human Services. Special thanks to Randy Muck of CSAT for his commitment to the project and to my colleagues in the ethnography group of the Adolescent Treatment Models Project for stimulating discussions and helpful feedback on that work. That research was conducted while

I was Senior Research Scientist at the Public Health Institute, and I thank the many colleagues and staff at the institute who offered support and assistance—especially Richard Spieglman, who encouraged the project from the start. Some early thoughts on the study appeared in a lecture sponsored by the Addiction Research Centre at Trinity College, Dublin, and I thank the staff there, especially Barry Cullen, for the invitation. A more detailed discussion of adolescents' response to drug treatment appeared in the *Journal of Drug Issues* for Fall 2003; thanks to Bruce Bullington and Jeanne Meliori.

A considerable part of the writing was done while I was Visiting Professor at the School of Criminology and Criminal Justice at Florida State University, and I thank Dean Daniel Maier-Katkin for providing a welcoming environment. Thanks, too, to my colleagues at the Legal Studies Program at the University of California, Berkeley, and at the Department of Criminology, Law, and Society at the University of California at Irvine: it would be difficult to imagine a more creative and stimulating group. As always, I've benefited enormously from conversations with good friends, notably Alan Curtis, Bob Dunn, Dave Fogarty, and Terry Kandal. Rachael Peltz and Sonia Peltz-Currie weathered the book's intrusion into our household with grace and patience.

Finally, I am once again amazed by how much the work of a splendid group of social scientists, many of them my own teachers, has continued to shape my own. For this, special thanks to Howard S. Becker, David Matza, Jerome Skolnick, and the late Sheldon Messinger.

INDEX

adolescence. *See also* youth
  achievement and, 86–87, 88
  care-lessness of, 21–22
  competition and, 68–69
  emergence from, 15
  inversion of responsibility in,
    48–51
  "normal deviance" of, 96–97
  sink or swim mentality and, 48
  trauma in, 56, 59
  turning around in, 217
adolescents. *See also* teenagers
  "all or nothing" mentality of,
    82–83, 84, 93, 95
  assistance for, 274–75
  care-lessness of, 17–19, 20–21, 23,
    25–26, 70, 109, 212
  CD, ODD, and, 149
  community and, 265–66
  community college and, 245–48
  contingent worth and, 68–71
  counseling for, 141
  crisis of, 19, 28
  disengagement of, 196–97
  downward spiral of, 262, 268
  drug exposure of, 22–23

drug use by, 2
drugs' appeal for, 58
early intervention for, 270–71
educational options for, 274
estrangement of, 209–10
expectations of, 74, 186
help for, 123–24, 248, 275
helping institutions and, 245
high demand, low support
  environment for, 47
housing for, 263–65
idea exchange among, 174–75
independence of, 225, 234–35
individual responsibility and, 146,
  183–84, 191
"inner locus of control" of,
  233–34
institutional indifference to,
  126–27, 165
intrinsic worth of, 231
learning disability and, 187
marginalization of, 106
medications and, 138–40, 150,
  280
"multiproblem" of, 31–32, 33–35
new treatment for, 276–82

ABOUT THE AUTHOR

ELLIOTT CURRIE is the author of *Confronting Crime; Reckoning: Drugs, the Cities, and the American Future;* and *Crime and Punishment in America,* a finalist for the Pulitzer Prize in General Nonfiction. An internationally recognized authority on crime, juvenile delinquency, and drug abuse, Currie has taught at Yale and the University of California, Berkeley, and is currently a professor of Criminology, Law, and Society at the University of California, Irvine.